Mothe

On The Edge

A critical examination of mothering within
child protection systems

Edited by
Brooke Richardson

DEMETER

Mothering On The Edge

A critical examination of mothering within child protection systems

Edited by Brooke Richardson

Copyright © 2022 Demeter Press

Individual copyright to their work is retained by the authors. All rights reserved. No part of this book may be reproduced or transmitted in any form by any means without permission in writing from the publisher.

Demeter Press
PO Box 197
Coe Hill, Ontario
Canada
K0L 1P0
Tel: 289-383-0134
Email: info@demeterpress.org
Website: www.demeterpress.org

Demeter Press logo based on the sculpture "Demeter" by Maria-Luise Bodirsky www.keramik-atelier.bodirsky.de

Printed and Bound in Canada

Cover image: Brooke Richardson
Cover design and typesetting: Michelle Pirovich
Proof reading: Jena Woodhouse

Library and Archives Canada Cataloguing in Publication
Title: Mothering on the edge: a critical examination of mothering within child protection systems / edited by Brooke Richardson.
Names: Richardson, Brooke, editor.
Description: Includes bibliographical references.
Identifiers: Canadiana 20220285853 | ISBN 9781772584066 (softcover)
Subjects: LCSH: Welfare recipients. | LCSH: Child welfare. | LCSH: Mothers. | LCSH: Motherhood.
Classification: LCC HV697 .M68 2022 | DDC 362.82—dc23

Land Acknowledgment

I would like to acknowledge that the land I am living and working on is the traditional territory of many nations, including the Mississaugas of the Credit, the Anishnabeg, the Chippewa, the Haudenosaunee, and the Wendat peoples, and is now home to many diverse First Nations, Inuit, and Métis peoples. These lands, colonially known as the City of Toronto in Ontario, Canada, are covered by Treaty 13, which was signed with the Mississaugas of the Credit, and the Williams Treaties, which was signed with multiple Mississaugas and Chippewa bands. I recognize this acknowledgment is only one symbolic step towards recognizing the ongoing colonization of Indigenous people in Canada. As a colonizer, I am committed to doing better at honouring the truth and acting with Indigenous peoples Canada in a way that leads to both healing from past traumas and preventing further trauma.

Miigwech.

Acknowledgments
and Dedication

I am grateful to so many people for their ongoing practical, emotional and intellectual support while writing and editing this anthology. First and foremost, I wish to thank my family; Ava, Holly, Kai, Arlie and Steve. You are what keep me going. To the core safety team that I am forever indebted to for keeping my family together: my sister Danielle, my Mom and Dad, Aunt Nancy, Megan, and the many neighbours and friends who stepped in to ensure all 168 hours were covered every week. I'd also like to thank all those colleagues who continued to believe *in* me and believe *me* through some of the darkest days: Rachel L., Kate B., Monica L., Andrea O., Irwin E. and every-one at the AECEO. I know you have my back. And finally, to the professionals who provided invaluable guidance and support: Sarah C., Richard S., Diane M., Julie H.

I am dedicating this book to Megan: the absolute best friend a person could ever ask for. You didn't hesitate for a moment to restructure your and your family's life to keep mine from falling apart. You have been and continue to be my rock, always pushing me in the gentlest of ways to do what is right. My thinking shared in this book reflects our hours of conversations and tears over the past four years, trying to make sense and find meaning in it all. I am eternally grateful and truly honoured to call you my friend.

Contents

Why This Book?

Brooke Richardson

The purpose of this book is to bring critical, scholarly attention to the systematic positioning and subjective experiences of mothers involved in child protection processes in risk-based child protection systems (Parton, Thorpe, and Wattam; Connolley; Swift and Callahan). Although mothers are typically the primary focus of child protection prevention and investigations (Azzopardi et al.; Fallon et al.; Swift and Callahan), their gendered experiences, challenges, and triumphs are seldom given space in the academic literature and/or public spaces to be seen or heard. And even though some literature does theoretically and practically explore the phenomena of service users within child protection (e.g., Buckley; Buckley et al.; Boer and Coady; Gaffer, Manby, and Racel; Slettebø), much less literature specifically takes up the gendered phenomena of mothering within child protection (notable exceptions include Camaeron and Hoy; Clarke; Featherstone; Freymond; Krane and Davies). Chapters in this volume build on existing literature to illustrate the structural positioning and/or lived experiences of mothers who encounter child protection for a variety of reasons, including the following: substance (ab)use, positive HIV status, a medical diagnosis of nonaccidental injury, fetal alcohol syndrome, colonial assessment methodologies, young age, incarceration, childbirth, and intimate partner violence.

This book offers three unique contributions to existing literature on mothering in child protection. First, it creates space for mothers involved in child protection to have their voices heard. Second, it acknowledges the centrality of mothers' subjective experience in keeping children safe. Finally, it challenges dominant, often dehumanizing narratives of mothers involved in child protection through providing a more nuanced understanding of their lives.

Coming to This Topic

The idea for this book was born out of my own pain and passion as a woman, mother, researcher, scholar, and human being doing what I can so we may all may live in the world as well as possible. I am a Canadian childcare policy researcher, activist, and educator, who is fuelled by my commitment to ensuring all Canadian children and families have access to high-quality, affordable childcare services. I share this simply to say that my area of professional expertise has been primarily Canadian childcare policy rather than mothering or child protection. Although I have worked alongside these bodies of literature for some time, I had no awareness or expectation that the topic would become a core area of my personal and professional life.

In the fall of 2018, that changed. While teaching in a School of Early Childhood Studies at a Canadian university, my family unexpectedly and erroneously became the subject of a child protection investigation. Medical error, combined with poor communication within and between medical and social service professionals, nearly led to the apprehension of our seven-month-old daughter. The experience was life changing. I came to realize that systems meant to support and protect children and families—systems I have devoted significant personal and professional energy advocating for—may function in a way that causes overt harm. Even though I never faltered in my belief that state supported systems—childcare and child protection—are necessary, I came to see that there is much work to be done to ensure existing and/ or future systems are able to provide good, ethical care experiences for mothers, fathers, children, other caregivers, and families as a whole.

Bridging the Gap between Research, Policy, and Practice

I come to my academic and community-based work from a critical perspective and am thus always interested in identifying how power relations play out between children, educators, and families. As a policy scholar, I am troubled by the gap between what we think and write about in academia and the realities of what children and families experience in the real world (Langford and Richardson; Mahon; Richardson, "Government"). Acting on this, I have been in the role of President of the Association of Early Childhood Educators of Ontario (AECEO) since 2017. In this role, I have had the honour of learning from and working with early childhood educators (ECEs) across the province to build our collective voice and meaningfully participate in public policy debates and development related to childcare policy.

When encountering the child protection system, I saw similar theoretical and practical gaps between policy rhetoric, scholarly research, and the lived realities of those involved in child protection. There has been a lot of important writing and theorizing connecting ethics with practice in social work and child protection (e.g., Featherstone and Morris; Lonne et al., "Emergent"; Orme; Swift and Parada). Yet my experience, as well as the plethora of data revealing the systematic bias within the system (Ontario Human Rights Commission; Turner), suggests there is much work to be done to connect ethical guidelines to policy and practice. Of particular concern is how socially constructed categories—such as race, gender, and class—intersect within a futuristic, forensic, risk-based approach to child protection (Clarke; Middela et al.; Parton; Swift and Callahan). Thinking with intersectionality (Collins; Crenshaw) is therefore a foundational element of this work, which always has political implications. Whereas the chapters in this volume provide a starting point for such analysis, much work remains to be done to illustrate how policy (or lack thereof) constructs and maintains intersections of oppressions in relation to mothers involved in child protection.

Along these lines, I understand my experience with one child protection system is not representative of most mothers' experiences with these systems. I interacted with the system as the prototype of the so-called good mother: white, middle class, educated, financially secure, breastfeeding, professional, and devoted to my children. Yet the experience nearly broke me. I was constantly asking myself, if this was my experience, what was happening to others less privileged than me? Conversations with lawyers, social workers, and other professionals (many of them friends and/or colleagues) revealed that my experience paled into comparison to the horrors other mothers, children, and families face within child protection proceedings. Once I became aware of the deep and troubling inequities between mothers and systems responsible for keeping children safe, I could not unsee it. I continue my community and academic work in relation to childcare policy while also extending my thinking and activism to child protection. Working on and publishing this book is my first step into this world. I recognize I have much to learn from others who have worked for their entire careers to study and actively resist the ongoing oppressions of mothers, children, and families within child protection spaces. I humbly hope that this anthology provokes further thinking about the subjective experiences of and possibilities for mothers intersecting with risk-based child protection systems.

A Note on Terminology and Language

There are several terms used throughout this anthology. The first is "mothers." The call for proposals explicitly defined mothers to include all who identify as mothers beyond biological ties (e.g., foster, step, and adoptive). The submissions focused primarily on the experience of biological mothers in relation to child protection systems. I enthusiastically encourage further research that engages with broader conceptualizations of mothering within child protection while recognizing that the contributions made here provide a starting place for the discussion.

The book also uses the term "child protection systems" both in the title and throughout. This is the term used internationally to refer to systems put in place to protect children from abuse and neglect. "Child welfare" is also sometimes used to refer to these systems. I would argue that the current systems we have in place are not designed to ensure children or families are well but rather that children are protected from abuse and or neglect. In Canada, where I and most of my coauthors are located, publicly funded but privately managed Children's Aid Societies are the agency that carry out much of the work related to identifying, investigating, and/or intervening when there are concerns about child abuse or neglect.

Similarly, the term "child protection worker" is also used throughout. Although the term "worker" may in some contexts be understood as the antithesis to "professional," I see the terms as interchangeable in a context where "social worker" is the formal, professional designation.

I understand child protection workers to be professionals of the highest calibre, constantly grappling with incredibly complex, high-stakes situations and often without adequate time, support, and resources. Furthermore, I appreciate that child protection workers exist within a system that may be at odds with their own ethical guidelines: For example, assigning a risk assessment score to a family (often a primary task in this work) does not reflect anti-oppressive critical theories that are central to professional training.

"Risk" is also a term that is central to the child protection discussion internationally (Connolley; Parton, Thorpe and Wattam; Parton; Swift and Callahan). Where possible, I have encouraged authors to explicitly define their understanding and use of the word as well as to think about how conceptualizations of risk situate mothers involved in child protection systems. Consistent with the scholars referenced above, I feel the risk orientation to child protection is highly problematic for children, families, and child protection workers. It reflects the broader neoliberal agenda whereby limited resources are allocated to surveillance and control rather than meeting the inevitable needs of human beings struggling to get by in the world (Swift and Callahan). Furthermore, the notion of risk is deeply embedded within a culture of blame and liability, whereby professionals prioritize defensible decisions over more ethical decisions (Parton 5). Indeed, I would suggest that the risk paradigm in child protection is dangerous when presented as objective, scientifically reliable, and valid tools to measure risk. It becomes a mechanism of systemic discrimination, whereby families experiencing poverty, often racialized or otherwise marginalized communities, are much more likely to be flagged as high risk and be subjected to invasive child protection proceedings. In this way, risk-based child protection processes may compound stress and trauma rather than meaningfully address human subjectivities and practical needs. This is a theme that weaves throughout all chapters in this anthology.

Geographical Context

Five of the nine chapters in this book refer to research conducted in Ontario, Canada. Three other chapters focus on research from Alberta, whereas one chapter addresses the United Kingdom (UK) context. Given that only two Canadian provinces and one other country are represented here, the implications of our findings have contextual limitations. Although risk-oriented child protection systems share many similarities in wealthy, English-speaking liberal welfare states, such as Canada, the United States, Australia and the UK, there are also important jurisdictional differences, such as culture, social policy, and the political environment. In this way, this book is a first step towards systematically identifying and addressing the unique challenges faced by mothers in child protection systems. More research is needed across contexts, particularly outside of Canada.

Why Mothers?

This book embraces a gendered lens, avoiding terms such as "parents," "caregivers," or "service users." Almost twenty years ago, Brid Featherstone warned that using the gender-neutral term "parent" in child protection work may have the "effect of trapping women further" (49). Carol-Ann Hooper and Catherine Humphreys similarly flagged the term "nonabusing parents," noting this language "obscures the different roles of and potential for conflict between men and women within families and has limitations for all forms of abuse" (299). In this way, gender-neutral language, such as "parents," makes invisible the complex power relations between mothers and fathers, particularly those involved in child protection proceedings. In cases where either domestic violence or sexual abuse has occurred—typically to women and/or their children (Fallon et al.)—deep power inequities exist. Lumping "parents" into one entity can easily lead to further trauma and harm for mothers who are then held responsible for the abuse (Azzopardi et al.).

Within and outside of child protection, I feel mothering is unique from fathering and parenting in four important ways: 1) traditional attitudes about gender roles; 2) deeply entrenched dominant discourses of the "good" (and therefore "bad") mother; 3) physiological connections between mothers and their children in the case of biological mothers; and 4) the externally and internally imposed connections between mothering and a woman's identity.

First and foremost, traditional attitudes about gender situate mothers as the primary caregivers in most English-speaking nations. Even when fathers are more involved caring for children than they have been in the past, mothers continue to carry out the bulk of care labour (Johnston et al.; Richardson, "Shifting"). In contemporary liberal welfare states, such as those featured in this anthology, the socio-economic circumstances further demand that mothers engage in full-time paid labour in order to achieve a decent standard of living. Balancing (paid or unpaid) work and caring well for themselves and others has become the mythological goal of the contemporary mother, whereby failing to achieve this goal is seen as individual inadequacy rather than systemic failure (Caitlyn Collins). That she is working against the odds at the micro, meso, and macro levels becomes increasingly invisible in the context of neoliberal state policies (e.g., privatized, unaffordable childcare services, and increasingly precarious employment arrangements).

Second, alongside the default mother-as-primary caretaker enforced by traditional gendered discourses, expectations of mothers have never been higher. Neuroscientific evidence has clearly demarcated childhood (especially early childhood) as critical for later success in all aspects of life (Heckman and Masterov; McCain et al.). In an attempt to optimize children's development, there are increasing expectations for mothers not only to be the primary caregiver and to prioritize mothering over paid work but to also spend "copious amounts of time, energy and material resources on the child" (O'Reilly, "Maternal Theory" 24). Mothers are expected to be ever giving, selfless and to expend (perhaps excessive) time, resources, attention as well as emotional, psychological, cognitive, and physical energy on their children (Rock). Furthermore, contemporary mothers are constantly inundated by information from social media feeds, doctors, friends, colleagues, and even strangers telling them how to mother best. These parenting expectations do not appear to apply to fathers in the same way. Much less appears to be required for fathers to meet the "good" threshold.

Third, when it comes to biological mothers (the focus in this book), there is a unique physiological connection between mother and child. This connection begins prior to the birth of the child, in the complex, grey period of pregnancy. Twenty years ago, Susan Bordo asked a critical question in relation to pregnant women: "Are mothers persons?" In asking this question, Bordo contrasted women as "mere bodies" (i.e., vessels of reproduction) with women as embodied persons. Reviewing legal cases in which pregnant women were forced to undergo medical testing or procedures, she noted how women's bodies are positioned as *"res extensa,"* or "bodies stripped of their animating, dignifying and humanizing subjectivity" (Bordo 73). Similar themes emerge in this anthology in relation to HIV-positive mothers, birth alerts, as well in relation to my own subjective experience throughout the child protection investigation related to my daughter.

Finally, I think it is important to recognize that for women with children, being a mother is almost always a central aspect of her/their identity (O'Reilly, "Matricentric Feminism"). In doing my research for this book, I have been struck by the strength and determination of so many mothers involved in child protection. They often find themselves in extremely complex situations and make significant sacrifices to fulfill what they feel are their responsibilities to be a good mother. For some, being a good mother and protecting their maternal identity may mean allowing or even encouraging others to temporarily or permanently care for her children (Kennedy). For others without access to the material and emotional resources to be able to keep themselves and/or their children safe, it means reluctantly (or forcefully) permitting their children to be taken into state care and then, to the best of their ability, doing what is required to remain involved in their child's life. In a Canadian research study in which mothers of children in state care were interviewed, Nancy Freymond concludes these mothers are not only survivors but also "heroines"—that is, a "woman admired for her courage" (59). Regardless of whether children remain in or are removed from mothers' care, this anthology reveals that the identities of mothers are deeply shaken by the child protection investigation process. Again, this is not to say that public officials should not play a role in engaging mothers where there is a concern about a child's safety but rather that there is a great deal of space to think about and talk about how this could be done in a way that meaningfully considers the subjective experiences of mothers.

Theoretical Influences: Feminist Ethics of Care

Though not always explicitly stated or required, many of the chapters in this anthology reflect a feminist ethics of care (FEC) theoretical orientation. FEC is helpful in studying mothering within child protection because it provides the framework to identify and analyze power relations between people: mother and child, child and family, family and community, worker and mother, mother and father, family and state, etc. At the same time, FEC takes up the "different voice" Carol Gilligan first identified in her work on moral development of girls and women. This "different voice" challenges the previously accepted (masculine) idea that decontextualized universal truths should guide moral behaviour. Instead, FEC situates human beings as "inevitably dependent and inextricably interdependent" (Kittay 51) and care as relational and embedded within power relations; it also embraces emotions as informative moral tools (Engster and Hamington, "Introduction").

FEC fundamentally problematizes the insatiable pursuit of independence in all aspects of life as a key marker of success. All chapters in this anthology problematize contemporary neoliberal ideals that perpetuate dependence and/or need as a sign of weakness—particularly in relation to mothers involved in child protection proceedings. Understanding the world through an ethics of care perspective reframes care from being a burden to positioning it not only as an inevitability but also as a key opportunity to find meaning in our lives. Instead of constantly striving to exist independently of others, FEC insists that this pursuit is both futile and counterproductive; it further removes humans from the very thing that provides our lives with purpose: responsive, empathetic relationships with others.

FEC is not new to social work and/or child protection theorizing and practice. Scholars, particularly in the UK and Australia, have written extensively on the topic (Featherstone and Morris; Featherstone et al. *Re-Imagining Child Protection*; Lonne et al. *Working Ethically*; Meagher and Parton; Orme; Pease et al.). Back in 2004, Meagher and Parton argued: "Unless care is relocated at the centre of debates, policies and practices, the elements which can be seen to make social work and social care more generally distinctive will be lost" (4).

Not only do contemporary social work scholars appear to agree that the care-justice binary problematized in FEC is not helpful in social work, but they also assert that ethics of care is necessary to promote social justice (Featherstone and Morris; Pease et al.). I agree, although I still feel this leaves unresolved the ongoing tension between justice and care at the micro level—particularly for mothers involved in child protection systems that are fundamentally rooted in forensic evidence.

Until this changes, social justice will remain an ideal rather than a reality.

Criticism of FEC

FEC is not without its critics. As pointed out by Bob Pease et al., it can be equated with essentialist, maternal discourses that depoliticize care and make way for paternalistic care practices at a micro, meso, and macro level (Pease et al.). This critique appears to have emerged out of the disability studies literature, which has long critiqued oppressive and patriarchal caring relations (Featherstone and Morris). As I understand FEC, particularly the writings of contemporary scholars (Engster and Hamington, *Care Ethics and Political Theory;* Langford; Orme; Tronto, "Can Caring Democracy"; Tronto, *Caring Democracy),* it explicitly challenges the caregiver-care receiver, public-private, and male-female binaries, which essentialize and systematically devalue gendered caring relations within the context of inequitable power relations.

FEC has also been criticized for centring white, middle-class women's experience and/or taking an additive approach to other categories of difference (e.g., race, class, and Indigeneity) (Hankivsky). I recognize that the intersection of race, culture, gender, sexual orientation, and a plethora of other axes position humans in what Patricia Hill Collins has referred to as the "matrix of domination" (239). I am inspired and humbled by the care ethics research consortium conference (Spring 2021), where the title was "Decentering Ethics: Challenging Privileges, Building Solidarities." Attending (virtual) sessions and engaging in conversations related to this topic were helpful in furthering my own thinking around the limitations and possibilities of FEC in relation to intersectionality. I agree that "contemporary individualizing, mother blaming and risk averse service responses to women as mothers conceal the complexities of mothering associated with unequal power relations" (Zuffery and Buchanan 3). I am committed to doing better at holding, acknowledging, and honouring the intersectional experiences of women, mothers, and others in my work and life.

Matricentric Feminism

This book is also deeply influenced by Andrea O'Reilly's theory of matricentric feminism. In many ways, matricentric feminism has grown out of the interdisciplinary FEC literature, albeit with a specific focus on mothering as care practice. In contrast to maternalism, which continues to embrace a child-centred approach, matricentric feminism considers a mother's value, experiences, needs, wants, and desires in her/their own right (O'Reilly, "Matricentric Feminism"). Although matricentric feminism explicitly rejects the idea that a woman's life is incomplete without being a mother, it does suggest that any under-standing of the lives of those who are mothers is incomplete without an appreciation of their experiences as a mother. Matricentric feminism brings attention to the real and significant gaps between mothers and "others" in terms of equitable participation in paid labour (the "maternal wall" and/or being "mommy tracked") and social life (O'Reilly, "Matricentric Feminism").

Central to this anthology, matricentric feminism provides a space to critically analyze assumptions about the good mother. Like other caregivers, mothers have been rendered invisible at the macro level while being subjected to intense scrutiny at the micro level. The "good mother" construct externally and internally imposed on mothers within the context of a neoliberal, patriarchal society permeates every aspect of her life. It has significant consequences *for* mothers but has been largely immune to input *from* mothers (much like the child protection system). As a result, mothers carry tremendous amounts of guilt and shame for not being good enough. Furthermore, there are few things more shameful in society than feeling like (or being flagged as) a bad mother. For mothers who have already faced tremendous suffering and grief, becoming involved in child protection may be yet another blow rather than the support it claims to be (Cameron and Hoy; Freymond).

Problematizing the Forensic Approach to Child Protection: Key Literature

There are four key books that have influenced my thinking in relation to forensic, risk-based approaches to child protection: *At Risk: Social Justice in Child Welfare and Other Human Services* (Karen Swift and

Marilyn Callahan); 2) *Beyond the Risk Paradigm in Child Protection* (edited by Marie Connolly, series editor Nigel Parton); 3) *Re-imagining Child Protection: Towards Humane Social Work with Families* (Brid Featherstone, Sue White, and Kate Morris); and 4) *Protecting Children: A Social Model* (Brid Featherstone et al.). In this section, I highlight key ideas from these books that are relevant to this anthology.

Writing in the Canadian context, Swift and Callahan situate the emergence of the risk paradigm in child protection within broader neoliberal ideals and state structures. They illustrate how the hyper-individualized risk associated with neoliberalism facilitated the allocation of limited state resources to surveillance, standardization, and control rather than children's and family's needs and/or support. They also clearly articulate how an increasing audit culture in child protection has decreased space for meaningful relationship building between child protection workers and children and/or families. Although their book does not focus specifically on mothers, these authors include the voices of mothers alongside the voices of child protection workers, centring gender in their analysis of risk-based child protection systems.

Like Swift and Callahan, Buckley problematizes a highly individualized approach to child maltreatment, whereby risk is associated with individual parents, and social risks are no longer a part of the equation. Buckley articulates that this was not always the case. She argues that there was a tendency in the 1970s and 1980s for child protection workers "to think the best of parents ... applying tolerance if parents passed the test of loving their children" (79). Similarly, Featherstone notes that "in the 1960s and 1970s their [parents] own needs were interrogated more explicitly in the sense that it was assumed that unmet needs on the part of parents contributed to child abuse" (49). However, the pendulum swung back the other way with a vengeance in the late 1980s and 1990s, as highly mediatized child deaths put political pressures to reform child protection systems in many English-speaking countries. The solution to the child abuse problem was instituting risk assessments that would (theoretically) prevent child abuse and/or child deaths from occurring.

Around the same time, child abuse was gaining prominence as a medical phenomenon (i.e., a nonaccidental injury), which could be predicted by objective questionnaires (e.g., given to mothers in the hospital) (Swift and Callahan). In this way, child protection increasingly became a forensic rather than social issue, rooted in objective evidence rather than relationships. Featherstone et al. refer to this as "rewriting social deprivation in bodies and brains: the great leap backwards" (Featherstone et al., *Protecting Children* 46).

Alongside this shift, funding to community-based programs to support children, mothers, and families were cut. For example, in Canada, the elimination of the fifty/fifty federal-provincial cost-sharing Canada Assistance Plan in 1996 saw federal funds to provinces for community-based programs, such as childcare and family support programs, cut dramatically (Friendly and Prentice). Families—particularly mothers—were left with fewer resources alongside greater responsibility for themselves and their children.

At the same time, referrals and funding to child protection agencies have grown significantly since the 1980s (Parton, Thorpe, and Whittam). Kate Morris and Gale Burford argue that the "increasingly structured and forensic approach to [child protection] practice, means the messy, shapeshifting nature of concepts such as care are pushed to one side" (101). Several scholars (i.e., Cameron et al; Featherstone; Featherstone et al., *Re-Imagining Child Protection*; Morris and Burford; Swift and Callahan) make the case that when this occurs, the wellbeing of children, parents, and families is undermined rather than strengthened. An increasing audit culture coupled with "deliverology" has made the work "bureaucratically complicated while failing to take into account human complexity" (Featherstone et al., *Protecting Children* 40).

Human Capital as a Path to Resistance? The Discourse of the 1990s

In the 1990s, a neoliberally compatible "human capital" discourse began to drive social policies relating to children and families (Featherstone et al., *Protecting Children*; Featherstone et al., *Re-Imagining Child Protection*; Prentice; Richardson, and Langford). In contrast to risk thinking, which seeks to minimize future harm, the human capital discourse aims to maximize children's development. The thinking here is that as a society, we have a responsiblity to ensure children— the drivers of economic productivity of individuals and societies—are performing optimally in all developmental domains. The human capital discourse has been taken up by economists with the rationale that spending on children offers the greatest "bang for your buck". Several economic analyses suggest that investment in social services accessed early in a child's life yields significant economic returns throughout the life course (Fortin et al.; Heckman and Masterov).

Although this discourse continues to be widely taken up and has sometimes positively informed policy direction—for example, the establishment of full-day kindergarten in most Canadian provinces— it is problematic in that it denies children and families' subjective experiences in the here and now. In many ways, the human capital discourse reinforces the body-as-a-vessel metaphor put forth by Bordo: instead of objectifying women's bodies however, children are objectified through seeing them as containers of their brains. And, of course, this has major implications for mothers, as there is now increased pressure, particularly on marginalized mothers, to make up for any material disadvantages through offering enriching cognitive stimulation (Featherstone et al., *Protecting Children*).

Resisting the Forensic Model of Child Protection: A Social Model

The forensic approach to child protection has not gone unchallenged. Inspired by decades of work by disability scholars and activists resisting a medical model of disability, a social model of child protection brings attention to the systemic causes of child abuse (Featherstone et al., *Protecting Children*). A social model of child protection situates relative deprivation and/or systematic oppression of children, mothers, and families as the focal point. More specifically, a lack of financial resources (lack of decent and full-time stable work)—alongside limited access to necessary social programs (e.g., counselling, regulated childcare, and respite care) and time to engage proactively with identified issues (e.g., attending appointments and parents spending time with their children)—leads to the "othering" and vilification of mothers as well as individual families (Featherstone et al., *Protecting Children*). Without addressing these material and experiential realities at the systems level, it is no wonder that racialized and/or otherwise marginalized groups are overrepresented in child protection systems. For example, in Ontario, Indigenous children represent approximately

30 per cent of foster children despite being only 4.1 per cent of the population in Ontario under age fifteen (Ontario Human Rights Commission). In Manitoba, these numbers are even more concerning: 90 per cent of children in care are Indigenous, even though only 30 per cent of the child population identify as Indigenous (Legislative Review Committee).

There is some hope, however. At the same time the forensic model has taken hold, social workers and allies have fought to bring families into the child protection process. Family-led practices, such as the Australian-based "Signs of Safety Program" (now widely taken up in many jurisdictions) explicitly attempt to bring families into the decision-making process with the goal of emphasizing strengths as well as potential risks families face (Turnell et al. 135). Family case conferencing has become standard in many child protection systems in Canada and abroad.

However, meaningful participation is very different from structural participation (Turnell et al.). For myself, the family case conference was one of the most traumatizing experiences of the whole process. My husband, my family, my best friend, and I sat there while doctors communicated misconstrued information (i.e., my child had "two broken legs"), social workers crafted elaborate "safety plans," and lawyers documented the process. It was in the case conference where I ultimately realized that what I said or did in this situation did not matter. I was completely powerless. Nevertheless, that I was in the room and could bear witness to the conversations between professionals involved in my case was illuminating. I could observe how power relations were playing out. Other researchers have similarly characterized case conferences as "daunting" and "intimidating" from the perspective of parents (Gaffer, Manby, and Race).

At a paradigmatic level, Featherstone et al. discuss the use of the poverty aware paradigm (PAP) as a fruitful approach to enacting a social model of child protection. Key to PAP is an awareness of not only material and social capital, to which families have access, but also *symbolic* capital. Symbolic capital refers to the degree to which individual children and their families have a voice within and beyond the child protection process (Featherstone et al., *Protecting Children*). The PAP model points out that it is not the only the material deprivation itself that causes suffering for those living in poverty but also that they are shamed, stigmatized, and denied human dignity through being "othered" and blamed for their suffering (Featherstone et al. *Protecting Children*).

What about Child Protection Workers?

As I have made clear, I am not a child protection worker or even a social worker. I cannot, and do not claim to, speak from this perspective. I am a mother, an early childhood educator, and a social policy scholar who has thought extensively about and empirically examined how social structures (or lack thereof) position the complex, time-intensive process of caring for children, mothers, and families. In my role as a university course instructor in early childhood studies, sociology, and child and youth studies, as well as my community leadership role with the Association of Early Childhood Educators of Ontario (AECEO), I have thought deeply about the devalued, gendered nature of caring for children within contemporary social, economic, and political systems. I do believe that the work of child protection workers shares many similarities.

But, of course, there are many important differences. The high-stakes, state-sanctioned nature of child protection work, the starkly imbalanced power relations between children, mothers, fathers, and workers are unique. What I have come to appreciate through my own experiences and reading the child protection literature is that these workers are often stuck in the crossfire of their professional and ethical obligations (e.g., pursuing equitable, supportive relationships with children and families) and standardized, routinized procedures (e.g., risk assessments). New managerialism's obsession with accountability and mitigating risk denies not only the voices of mothers, children, and families, but also those of gendered child protection workers. She may be powerful in relation to the families with whom she assesses, but she is powerless in relation to the broader system in which she works. This can lead to what Merlinda Weinberg calls "moral distress": "the psychological and emotional effects experienced by professionals when they feel blocked by institutional constraints from pursuing a course they perceive is right" (139). Furthermore, her own and her family's material wellbeing (i.e., her paycheque and career trajectory) is tied to her adherence to institutionalized practices.

Just as this anthology resists "othering" mothers involved in child protection, individual workers must also not be blamed for paradigmatic and structural inadequacies of child protection systems. Featherstone et al. ask: "What is the role of the social worker and the viability, indeed fairness, of asking the profession to drive the change that is needed?" (Featherstone et al., *Protecting Children* 102). As Nel Noddings argues, structures and systems create the conditions in which good care can occur (or not). In this way, practice cannot be decontextualized from the broader hegemonic sociopolitical order. Changing this order, through policy reform, must be developed with children, youth, mothers, fathers, families, and child protection workers at the table. To *not* do this is politically and ethically irresponsible.

What Is the Role of the State in Ensuring Children Are Protected?

I wish to make it abundantly clear that I fully support a state role in caring about, for and with children, women, and families. What I question is the sweeping legal authority (power) of child protection systems amid increasingly skeletal community supports for families. I believe the state's responsibilities are not limited to intervening in the most extreme cases of abuse and neglect; indeed, a state should provide the necessary social, educational, and health resources for all families to be well.

As it currently stands, child protection systems are largely reactive. When there are concerns about the physical, emotional, or social safety of a child, the stakes are high for all involved. One of the key mechanisms of becoming involved in child protection in liberal welfare states is through the duty to report. In Canada, every province has some form of "duty to report" legislation, although it is different in every jurisdiction. This "duty" requires professionals, volunteers, and sometimes lay citizens to report suspicions of child abuse or neglect to child protection authorities. For professionals such as doctors, social workers, nurses, teachers, and early childhood educators, this duty is a key professional obligation with implications for their ongoing registration with their professional college. To fail to report a suspicion of child abuse, no matter what the circumstances, could lead to significant, deleterious professional consequences, including losing one's license to practice.

In Canada, Children's Aid Societies (CAS) are tasked with investigating reports of suspected abuse. Social workers within these agencies make decisions regarding the course of action (supported by legal counsel). If CAS determines the child needs protection from abuse, they have significant legal power to intervene. Intervention may take many forms (e.g., mandatory parenting classes and weekly check-ins with social workers), with the most extreme form (typically the last resort) being the removal of the child from parental care. Though not common, it is possible that parents may lose custody and/or access to their child entirely. These arrangements may be temporary (weeks or months) or permanent (until the child becomes a legal adult or the child is adopted into another family). What has become apparent in this anthology is that even if the actual occurrence of the state apprehending a child is rare, the possibility of this happening instantiates a threat and therefore significant anxiety for many mothers involved in child protection investigations. It is in this way that they are on the edge. The threshold of how close to the edge and how far the fall is different for each mother, child, and family.

My fellow authors and I understand, appreciate, and fully support having a system in place to ensure children and families do not experience abuse, neglect, or exploitation. We are all personally and professionally committed to ensuring all children, mothers, and families have the opportunity to live a life of integrity free from unnecessary suffering. This book humbly attempts to provide insight into the experience of mothering to inform policy and practice that productively engages with the needs of families in context. Whereas dominant societal discourses enforce the idea that mothers involved in child protection cases must be bad and therefore deserve to suffer (causing harm in and of itself), we take a more nuanced look at the realities, struggles, and triumphs of these heroines.

Chapter Outlines

In Chapter 1, I juxtapose an ethics of justice with an ethics of care through reflecting on my own experiences as a mother of four navigating a forensic child protection investigation rooted in medical error. In Chapter 2, Allyson Ion provides insight into the experience of mothers who are HIV positive throughout the prenatal and perinatal period, problematizing the deficit positioning of these mothers in both medical and child protection spaces. In Chapter 3, Meredith Berrouard and I name and explore the high-stakes help-harm paradox that child protection workers experience when working with mothers in the perinatal period. Chapters 4 and 5 explore the narratives of mothers experiencing intimate partner violence (IPV) and their intersection with child protection systems. In Chapter 4, Angela Hovey, Susan Scott, and Lori Chambers draw on qualitative interviews with mothers residing in shelters who are already involved, or worried about becoming involved, with child protection systems. The authors advocate for a harm-reduction approach to substance use in shelters for mothers who have experienced IPV. In Chapter 5, Angelique Jenney challenges readers to critically deconstruct the maternal, mother-blaming discourse that mothers experiencing IPV frequently encounter.

Chapters 6, 7, 8 and 9 problematize the positioning of particular groups of mothers: Indigenous, young, those affected by fetal alcohol syndrome disorders, and incarcerated. In Chapter 6, Peter W. Choate and Gabriel Lindstrom propose a lens of humility to address the ongoing, systemic discrimination Indigenous mothers and their children face in their overrepresentation in the Canadian child welfare system. These authors assert that the current, standardized, and top-down assessment approaches of child-protection systems must give way to Indigenous ways of knowing in order for a genuine process of reconciliation to begin. In Chapter 7, Sarah Bekaert and I analyze serious case reviews (SRCs) involving young mothers in the UK. We conclude that focusing on young mothers and their children's needs rather than risk may be a more fruitful way of preventing the death or injury of their children. In Chapter 8, Dorothy Badry et al. explore the complexities of mothers affected by fetal alcohol syndrome disorders who come into contact with child protection systems. By reflecting on the Parent-Child Assistance Program (PCAP) embraced in Alberta, Badry et al. highlight the importance of a trauma-informed approach to practice that seeks to understand and support these mothers. Finally, in Chapter 9, Lauren Hawthorne and I reflect on the heart-wrenching stories of two formerly incarcerated mothers who identify the major barriers the carceral system, in combination with the child protection system, has posed in maintaining and/or reestablishing relationships with their children during and following incarceration.

Works Cited

Azzopardi, Corry, et al. "From Freud to Feminism: Gendered Constructions of Blame across Theories of Child Sexual Abuse." *Journal of Child Sexual Abuse*, vol. 27, no. 3, 2018, pp. 245-75.

Blackstock, Sarah, et al. "Poverty Fight Must Continue." *Toronto Star*, 17 Mar 2009, www.thestar.com/opinion/2009/03/17/poverty_fight_must_continue.html. Accessed 1 June 2022.

Bordo, Susan. *Unbearable Weight*. University of California Press, 2003.

Braedley, Susan, and Meg Luxton. *Neoliberalism and Everyday Life*. McGill-Queens University Press, 2010.

Brittain, Melissa, and Cindy Blackstock. "First Nations Child Poverty: A Literature Review and Analysis." *First Nations Child and Caring Society of Canada*, First Nations Children's Action Research and Education Service, 2015.

Buckley, Helen. "Services Users as Receivers of Risk-Dominated Practice." *Beyond the Risk Paradigm in Child Protection*, edited by Nigel Parton, Palgrave, 2017, pp. 77-90.

Buckley, Helen, et al. "'Like Walking on Eggshells': Service User Views and Expectations of the Child Protection System." *Child and Family Social Work*, vol. 16, 2011, pp. 101-10.

Cameron, Gary. "Introduction." *Creating Positive Systems of Child and Family Welfare: Congruence with the Everyday Lives of Children and Parent*, edited by Gary Cameron et al., University of Toronto Press, 2013, pp. 3-20.

Clarke, Jennifer. "Beyond Child Protection: Afro-Caribbean Service Users of Child Welfare." *Journal of Progressive Human Services*, vol. 23, no. 3, 2012, pp. 223-57.

Collins, Caitlyn. *Making Motherhood Work*. Princeton University Press, 2019.

Collins, Patricia Hill. *Intersectionality as Critical Social Theory*. Duke University Press, 2019.

Connolley, Marie, editor. *Beyond the Risk Paradigm in Child Protection*. Palgrave, 2017.

Crenshaw, Kimberle. "Mapping the Margins: Intersectionality, Identity Politics, Violence against Women of Colour." *Stanford Law*

Review, vol. 43, no. 6, 1991, pp. 1241-99.

De Boer, C., and N. Coady. "Good Helping Relationships in Child Welfare: Learning from Stories of Success." *Child and Family Social Work*, vol. 12, no. 1, 2007, pp. 32-42.

Engster, Daniel, and Maurice Hamington, editors. *Care Ethics and Political Theory*. Oxford University Press, 2015.

Engster, Daniel, and Maurice Hamington. "Introduction." *Care Ethics and Political Theory*, edited by Daniel Engster and Maurice Hamington, Oxford, 2015, pp. 1-18.

Fallon, Barbara, et al. "Ontario Incidence Study of Reported Child Abuse and Neglect—2018 Major Findings." *Child Welfare Research Portal*, 2018, cwrp.ca/sites/default/files/publications/Ontario%20 Incidence%20Study%20of%20Reported%20Child%20Abuse%20 and%20Neglect%202018.pdf. Accessed 1 June 2022.

Featherstone, Brid. "Taking Mothering Seriously: The Implications for Child Protection." *Child and Family Social Work*, vol. 4, no. 1, 1999, pp. 43-53.

Featherstone, Brid, et al. *Protecting Children: A Social Model*. Policy Press, 2018.

Featherstone, Brid, and Kate Morris. "The Feminist Ethics of Care." *The Sage Handbook of Social Work*, edited by Mel Gray et al. Sage, 2012, pp. 341-54.

Featherstone, Brid, et al. *Re-Imagining Child Protection: Towards Humane Social Work with Families*. Policy Press, 2014.

Fortin, Pierre, et al. "Economic Consequences of Quebec's Educational Childcare Policy." *OISE: Early Years Economics Forum*. 2011, www. oise.utoronto.ca/atkinson/UserFiles/File/Events/2011-06-22%20 -%20Economic%20Forum/EarlyLearningEconomicForum_Fortin. pdf. Accessed 1 June 2022.

Freymond, Nancy. "Home Truths: What Mothers of Children in Placement Say about Their Lives." *Creating Positive Systems of Child and Family Welfare: Congruence with the Everyday Lives of Children and Parents*, edited by Gary Cameron et al., University of Toronto Press, 2013, pp. 68-93.

Friendly, Martha, and Susan Prentice. *About Canada: Childcare*. Fernwood Publishing, 2009.

Hankivsky, Olena. "Rethinking Care Ethics: On the Promise and Potential of an Intersectional Analysis." *American Political Science Association*, vol. 108, no. 2, 2014, pp. 252-64.

Heckman, James, and D. Masterov. "The Productivity Argument for Investing in Young Children." *Review of Agricultural Economics*, vol. 29, no. 3, 2007, pp. 446-93.

Hooper, Carol-Ann, and Catherine Humphreys. "What's in a Name? Reflection on the Term 'Non-Abusing Parent.'" *Child Abuse Review*, vol. 6, 1997, pp. 298-303.

Johnston, Regan, et al. "Evidence of Exacerbated Gender Inequality in Child Care Obligations in Canada and Australia During the Covid-19 Pandemic." *Policy and Gender*, vol. 16, no. 4, 2020, pp. 1-16.

Kennedy, Sue. *Seeing the Child in Child Protection Social Work*. Red Globe Press, 2020.

Kittay, Eva. "A Theory of Justice as Fair Terms of Social Life Given Our Inevitable Dependency and Our Inextricable Interdependency." *Care Ethics and Political Theory*, edited by Daniel Engster and Maurice Hamington, Oxford, 2015, pp. 51-71.

Krane, Julia, and Linda Davies. "Mothering and Child Protection Practice: Rethinking Risk Assessment." *Child and Family Social Work*, vol. 5, 2001, pp. 35-45.

Langford, Rachel, editor. *Theorizing Feminist Ethics of Care in Early Childhood*. Bloomsbury, 2019.

Langford, Rachel, and Brooke Richardson. "Ethics of Care in Practice: An Observational Study of Interactions and Power Relations between Children and Educators in Urban Ontario Early Childhood Settings." *Journal of Childhood Studies*, vol. 45, no. 1, 2020, pp. 33-47.

Legislative Review Committee. "Transforming Child Welfare Legislation in Manitoba: Opportunities to Improve Outcomes for Children and Youth." *Government of Manitoba*, September 2018, www.gov.mb.ca/fs/child_welfare_reform/pubs/final_report.pdf. Accessed 1 June 2022.

Lonne, Bob, et al. "Emergent Ethical Theories." *Working Ethically in Child Protection*. Routledge, 2015.

Lonne, Bob, et al. *Working Ethically in Child Protection*. Routledge, 2016.

Mahon, Rianne. "Canada's Early Childhood Education and Care Policy: Still a Laggard?" *International Journal of Child Care and Education Policy*, vol. 3, no. 1, 2011, pp. 27-42.

McCain, Margaret, et al. "Early Years Study 3: Making Decisions, Taking Action." *Margaret & Wallace McCain Family Foundation*, 2011, ecereport.ca/media/uploads/pdfs/early-years-study3-2011.pdf. Accessed 1 June 2022.

Middela, Floor, et al. "The Effects of Migrant Background and Parent Gender on Child Protection Decision-Making: An Intersectional Analysis." *Child Abuse and Neglect*, vol. 104, 2020, research.rug.nl/files/122020332/1_s2.0_S0145213420301344_main.pdf. Accessed 1 June 2022.

Morris, Kate, and Gale Burford. "Engaging Families and Managing Risk in Practice." *Beyond the Risk Paradigm in Child Protection*, edited by Marie Connolley, Palgrave, 2017, pp. 91-108.

Noddings, Nel. "Care Ethics and 'Caring' Organizations." *Care Ethics and Political Theory*, edited by Daniel Engster and Maurice Hamington, Oxford University Press, 2015, pp. 72-84.

O'Reilly, Andrea. "Maternal Theory." *The Routledge Companion to Motherhood*, edited by Lynn O'Brien Hallstein et al. Routledge, 2020, pp. 19-35.

O'Reilly, Andrea. "Matricentric Feminism: A Feminism for Mothers." *Journal of the Motherhood Initiative*, vol. 10, no. 1-2, 2020, pp. 13-26.

Ontario Human Rights Commission. "Interrupted Childhoods: Over-Representation of Indigenous and Black Children in Ontario Child Welfare." *Ontario Human Rights Commission*, 18 April 2021, www.ohrc.on.ca/en/interrupted-childhoods. Accessed 1 June 2022.

Orme, Joan. "Social Work: Gender, Care and Justice." *British Journal of Social Work*, vol. 32, no. 6, 2002, pp. 799-814.

Parton, Nigel, et al. *Child Protection: Risk and the Moral Order.* Palgrave Macmillan, 1997.

Pease, Bob, et al., editors. *Critical Ethics of Care in Social Work: Transforming the Politics and Practices of Caring.* Routledge, 2018.

Prentice, Susan. "High Stakes: The 'Investable' Child and the Economic Reframing of Childcare." *Signs*, vol. 34, no. 3, 2009, pp. 687-710.

Richardson, Brooke. "Government, Policy, and the Role of the State." *Bloomsbury Education and Childhood Studies*, edited by Rachel Heydon and Manjula Waniganayake, Bloomsbury, 2019, www.becs-bloomsbury.com/article?docid=b-9781350996519&tocid=b-9781350996519-019. Accessed 8 June 2022.

Richardson, Brooke. "Shifting Gender Norms and Childcare in Canada." *The Routledge Motherhood Companion*, edited by Lynn O'Brien Hallstein et al., Routledge, 2020, pp. 353-61.

Richardson, Brooke, and Rachel Langford. "Citizen Engagement in Child Care Policy: Examining Child Care Policy Problematisations in Canadian Newspaper Articles from 2008 to 2015." *Policification of Early Childhood Education and Care: Early Childhood Education in the 21st Century*, vol. 3, edited by Susanne Garvis and Sivanes Phillipson. Routledge, 2020, pp. 23-36.

Rock, Lindsay. "The 'Good Mother' Vs. the 'Other' Mother the Girl-Mom." *Journal of the Motherhood Initiative for Research and Community Involvement*, vol. 9, no. 1, 2007, pp. 20-28.

Slettebø, Tor. "Parnership with Parents of Children in Care." *British Journal of Social Work*, vol. 43, 2013, pp. 579-95.

Swift, Karen, and Marilyn Callahan. *At Risk: Social Justice in Child Welfare and Other Human Services.* University of Toronto Press, 2009.

Swift, Karen, and Henry Parada. "Child Welfare Reform: Protecting Children or Policing the Poor." *Journal of Law and Social Policy*, vol. 19, 2004, pp. 1-17.

Tronto, Joan. "Can Caring Democracy Be a Political Concept for Transformation?" *Arguments*, vol. 58, no. 6, 2016, pp. 839-48.

Tronto, Joan. *Caring Democracy: Markets, Equality, and Justice.* New York University Press, 2013.

Turnell, Andrea, et al. "Signs of Safety: Reorientaing Work with Children, Families and Communities." *Beyond the Risk Paradigm in Child Protection*, edited by Marie Connolley, Palgrave, 2017, pp. 130-146.

Turner, Tana. "One Vision One Voice: Changing the Ontario Child Welfare System to Better Serve African Canadians." *Ontario Association of Children's Aid Societies*, 2016, www.oacas.org/wp-content/uploads/2016/09/One-Vision-One-Voice-Part-2_digital_english-

May-2019.pdf. Accessed 1 June 2022.

Weinberg, Merlinda. "Moral Distress: A Missing but Relevant Concept for Ethics in Social Work." *Canadian Social Work Review*, vol. 26, no. 2, 2009, pp. 139-51.

Zuffery, Carole, and Fiona Buchanan, editors. *Intersections of Mothering: Feminist Accounts*. Routledge, 2020.

Chapter 1

At the Intersection of Care and Justice in Child Protection: A Reflective Account

Brooke Richardson

Introduction

"Care" and "justice" are practical, political, and moral concepts. A great deal of philosophical debate has been devoted to how these two concepts guide moral and political decisions at the personal, local, national, and international levels. Part of the complexity of these concepts is that they operate on fundamentally different ontological assumptions about the world—assumptions that perpetually come into conflict with one another. Philosophies of care promote supportive structures (e.g., childcare, respite, and counselling), whereas philosophies of justice focus on identifying crimes, assigning guilt, and determining consequences.

By sharing my story, I add to existing literature that problematizes the increasingly standardized child protection systems rooted in justice frameworks without adequate recognition of families, particularly mothers and their children (Buckley; Cameron and Hoy; Connolly; Freymond and Cameron). I understand that "the standardization of child welfare practices has been the political response to public criticism that children have suffered fatal maltreatment because of the negligence of the child welfare system" (Freymond and Cameron 108). However, I remain fundamentally concerned that this approach is compounding family trauma rather than providing a space for healing, recovery, and good care experiences. Mothers and children who become involved in child protection—many of whom have experienced and continue to experience abuse, discrimination, and poverty— struggle to be good mothers within a system that fails to recognize the complexities of their lives and their remarkable strength and courage (Cameron and Hoy; Freymond; Freymond and Cameron).

My Story

In the fall of 2018, while working on a research project on care ethics and childcare policy, I became the subject of a Children's Aid Society (CAS) investigation related to my seven-month-old daughter. (My older children were ten, eight, and four.) A combination of medical error and miscommunication between doctors and other professionals led to a five-month-long CAS investigation of our family. Although I had never done anything wrong, and there were never any actual injuries to my daughter, we came close to having our daughter apprehended. When I initially wrote this chapter and submitted the book for peer review, I did not go into the details of my story as I did not think it was necessary. Now—a year and a half after first writing the chapter—I realize it is. Sharing the details of my story is owning my story and acknowledging my subjective experiences, which is necessary for reforming child protection. It is also the basis for my thinking and motivation to edit this book. I realize that my analysis does not work in an abstract sense: It has to be embedded within the details of my lived experiences. Sharing my story in its entirety is the only way I can be authentic in my personal and professional life.

My story began when I sought medical advice relating to what appeared to be a bruise on my daughter's forearm. (This was later diagnosed as a benign skin condition identified as benign telan-giectasias.). My paediatrician referred me to a suspected child abuse clinic at a local hospital. She said she did not suspect me of child abuse, only assuring me "that we could get important blood work done immediately if we went this route." I did not think I had any reason to be worried because I knew that no abuse had occurred, and I trusted this paediatrician who had cared for my children for six years. I was much more terrified that my daughter might have leukemia, as I knew that unexplained bruising is a key symptom of the disease (and knew another family who went through this). Reflecting back now, I can clearly see how my naivety was rooted in my privilege. I fully trusted doctors and social systems as they had always served me—a white, middle/upper-class professional in a traditional heterosexual marriage —well.

I drove to the hospital in a panic with my daughter screaming all the way. Whereas I would normally stop and nurse her when she cried like this, I kept driving as I was scared. When I opened the car door to get her out, she had dots on one side of her face just like she had on her arm. This made me more scared. Once I arrived at the child abuse clinic, my fate was sealed. She went through several examinations and blood draws as well as a full skeletal survey, which required my daughter to be strapped to the x-ray table with her head in a clamp for a total of forty-two x-rays. I cried along with her and tried to comfort her, all the while being terrified that something was seriously wrong with my baby. What was more, because of her intense crying on the x-ray table, the speckled red dots on her face became worse.

At first, I was told they found an abnormality in one of her knees in one of the x-rays, but that it was likely benign. But because it could also indicate a fracture, they called CAS. At this point, the hospital sent me home, and CAS followed up with a brief phone call. I was required to go back to the hospital two weeks later to have another x-ray of my daughter's legs. I was told that this could confirm whether or not it was a fracture or a benign abnormality, as whenever there is a fracture, bone regrowth (know as "periosteal reaction") will occur. I was also told that if the irregularity was present in both of her knees and con-sistent over time, it was likely indicative of a congenital abnormality rather than an injury.

So we went home and waited. Two weeks later, my husband and I trudged back to the hospital. I thought this would be the end of the ordeal, as Arlie's "bruise" was gone, and she did not have any new ones. She was by every indication a happy, healthy baby. But I was wrong. After going through the tedious x-ray process again, we were brought back up to the child abuse clinic. After the x-rays and extreme crying, Arlie again had the red dots on her face and on her arm where the original "bruise" had been. Again I pointed this out to doctors. My husband and I went as far as to have a resident stay in the room during this round of x-rays in case the red dots appeared again—which they did. But as we would later find out, this resident could not be contacted to confirm the marks appeared *during* the x-ray process.

The child abuse specialist then came in and delivered the most shocking news of my life: Arlie was diagnosed with metaphyseal fractures in both knees. I almost threw up. The blood drained from my head, and I thought I might also pass out. I was beyond shocked. She seemed perfectly fine, and now they were telling me she has two broken legs? And not only were they broken legs, but they were also metaphyseal fractures, which are considered pathogenic to child abuse in the medical literature. As the doctor repeatedly told me, CAS, and the police, these fractures are caused by extreme "yanking or pulling" on an infant's legs. I did not have the presence of mind to ask if bone regrowth had occurred or remember to ask about the possibility of congenital abnormality. I assumed that these possibilities had been systematically ruled out.[1]

I was dumbfounded and absolutely terrified on so many levels. I knew this meant the possibility of apprehension of my daughter, and I also knew that something must be seriously wrong with her if nothing had happened, and both her legs were broken. I had never been away from her for more than an hour or two, and even then, she was with people I fully trusted: my mother, my best friend, and my husband. Because my husband was ill at the time, he had not even been alone with her for several weeks preceding this. I had no suspicions that he could have done this. It was practically impossible. I was always there.

From there, the police and CAS came to the hospital. I was distraught, crying uncontrollably while nursing Arlie in the child abuse clinic. I called my sister and my best friend, who came immediately to the hospital. (My husband was already with me at this point.) We sat there going through every possible scenario in our minds. Had one of the other kids grabbed her legs when we were not looking? Perhaps it was when her legs got stuck in the highchair, and I pulled her out? But on no occasion did Arlie ever scream or cry in a way that would indicate acute pain. When the police and CAS arrived, they interviewed me, my husband, my sister, and best friend (separately), on camera, for over three hours. Because the doctors said the injury would have occurred within the two weeks prior, each of us went over every minute detail of our lives leading up to that day. Yes, it had been a stressful time. My husband was ill, and I had broken my arm playing soccer a few months prior. (My cast was removed a week before the first x-ray.) We had three other young children. Life was not a cakewalk. But it also was not a story of child abuse or domestic violence. Although I cannot confirm it, I felt throughout the investigation that the doctors suspected my husband of breaking my arm and then abusing our daughter. He felt the same way. But I knew this was not the case. I was asked leading questions along these narrative lines in the interview with CAS and police and firmly indicated that was not what happened. What my husband and I did not know was that our voices did not matter.

The police and CAS came to the (correct) conclusion that day that we "did not do this" (we did not yet know there were no actual injuries). They sent us home with a follow-up visit scheduled with the CAS social worker assigned to my case. I had hope at this point that people would see the light, and the child abuse accusations would be dropped. I wanted to focus on what mattered: What was with wrong my daughter that had resulted in both her legs being "broken"? Furthermore, how was she in absolutely no pain? During the interview with the police officer, she was bouncing and smiling on my legs. I was baffled.

The officer gave me his card in case I thought of anything over the weekend. And I did. This happened on a Friday. That Saturday I thought I figured it out: I must have broken her legs on the x-ray table when pulling her legs down to try and get the required images. That was the only thing that made sense. I was pulling on her legs, and she was screaming and resisting me. In fact, my husband had to come take over because my left arm was too weak from my own fracture to hold her foot down. I called the police officer first thing Monday morning. I was distraught, of course, thinking that this was my fault. I told him point blank: I did this. He took note, but he did not seem to think this made sense. For the next several weeks, until I got the medical records and realized there were no fractures, I relived those x-rays and the horror of thinking I broke my own baby's legs.

That week a CAS worker came to our home, talked to me, talked to our children, and called others involved in our lives. No concerns of child maltreatment or neglect emerged. My parents were required to check in on us daily, but other than that, life continued. A week later, at the case conference with CAS supervisors, their lawyer, the child abuse specialist, and my (hired-the-night-before) lawyer was when I became aware of how things were going to play out. Sitting in this room, I listened to the doctor tell everyone that Arlie had "two broken legs and unexplained bruising" (the "bruises" being spotting on her arm or face that is more accurately described as petechiae). That the "bruises" had showed up at the hospital, on the x-ray table, and in front of a doctor did not matter. The doctor's narrative was that the petechiae was a manifestation of a previous injury that was reappearing when she cried. My thought that the fractures had occurred during the x-rays was quickly dismissed. When I asked about the resident who witnessed the petechiae appear, they were unable to get in touch with him.

The outcome of this meeting was a 24/7 safety plan, whereby neither my husband nor I could be alone with Arlie. This required friends and family to be screened as supervisors and provide 168 hours of care a week. My sister was in charge of scheduling shifts for friends and family. My best friend and her son moved in part time. My sister, my parents, and my husband's aunt all put their own lives on hold to be able to be with us all hours of every day. I slept with Arlie in my oldest daughter's bed, and she moved into Arlie's room while our supervisor slept beside us in the same room. We were clearly told that if we did not adhere to the safety plan, Arlie would be taken to "a place of safety". When we specifically inquired what that meant in the case conference, we were told she would be apprehended. At no point did we feel safe to admit that 168 hours a week of supervision was taxing our social capital and gruelling. Admitting this risked apprehension. It was also made clear to us that if we did not carry out the MRI that was being recommended by the hospital, which I was terrified of, she would also be apprehended.

Having lost all trust and faith in the hospital and doctors, my husband and I were understandably fearful of the MRI. At this point, we felt they were looking for anything to reinforce the child abuse narrative. Furthermore, there is a real risk of harm to put a seven-month-old baby under an anesthetic. Although this might have been routine procedure for the doctors, it was not for me. I did consent to a biopsy of her arm to check for a vascular condition. I watched them and cried, as they cut a chunk out of her arm and stitched it up. A few days later, the nurse called to tell me the biopsy was normal. The dermatologist (who we later found out was not a licensed dermatologist) did not know that the nurse had called me and continued to suggest that there could be a vascular condition and therefore used this as the reason to insist on the MRI. My CAS worker asked me: "Don't you want to know if there's bleeding in your baby's brain?" What could I say? Of course, I did, but there was not any evidence to suggest that this was a legitimate concern at that point. Having gone through the medical literature myself, I could tell the way the marks on Arlie were presenting was not at all consistent with vasculitis. And her biopsy was normal.

Because of my privilege, I was able to get another lawyer, who got me in to see an internationally esteemed dermatologist. I took Arlie to this doctor. He brought out a special light, took one look at her, and said, "She's got benign telangiectasia," He scribbled down on a notepad, "no MRI needed." I passed that to CAS, and they dropped it. That was the first victory in my story.

It was shortly after this that I received the medical records, which I had been trying to secure for weeks. I pulled up the radiology report. To my disbelief, the fractures had never been definitively diagnosed by radiologists. The report noted that the image was "suggestive of metaphyseal fractures" but explicitly noted there was "no periosteal reaction" and the area of concern was consistent over time. These were the very elements the doctors told me were needed to conclusively diagnose a fracture. I thought this was the ticket out of this nightmare. I was ready to say, "See?! It was all a mistake!" Furthermore, I did not have to feel terrible that I did it or that something else was wrong with her. This was a clear case of misdiagnoses and miscommunication. As became evident then and even more clear years later, the radiologists did not reach the same conclusion that the child abuse specialist communicated to us, the police and CAS.

I immediately called my CAS worker and brought this to the attention of the child-abuse specialist. But, of course, everything was too far gone by that point. No one was willing to admit there might have been an error, or at the very least, that the diagnosis of meta-physeal fractures was not 100% certain. I had already been cast as the bad mother and felt my words were being interpreted as yet another sign that I was being deceitful.

Throughout the five months of the investigation, I experienced firsthand how care must go on without justice. I had to continue to provide responsive care to all of my children despite feeling intense desperation and hopelessness. It took a significant amount of strength to take basic care of myself—such as eating, sleeping, smiling, and engaging with my children—amid the bombardment of messaging positioning me as a bad mother and overall terrible person. What was particularly shocking to me was how terrified, powerless, and alone I felt despite having an extensive network of friends and family going to extreme lengths to keep our family intact. Unlike many mothers going through a child protection investigation, I did not have to cope with the stressors of systemic racism, poverty, intergenerational trauma, or inter-partner violence. I was not working three part-time, minimum-wage jobs struggling to feed my children and pay rent. Instead, I was living a very comfortable life in a safe home in a nice neighbourhood. And still, I could barely function. I lived in perpetual fear that my baby—who I had never been away from for more than an hour or two at a time—could be taken from me.

Throughout our ordeal, I felt invisible in a system that operated all around me with no recognition of me, my husband, our supervisors, or any of our other children, including Arlie. Decision-makers working within the medical and child protection system literally had trouble looking at me and repeatedly ignored or dismissed everything I said. As a professional in the field, I was used to having a voice and a venue to speak. But that was instantly taken away from me as an ethos of justice took over the child protection process. The space for care evaporated within the medical system, particularly a children's hospital with a unit specializing in child abuse. A hyper-individualized conceptualization of justice prioritized the needs of those already with power: the doctors, lawyers and state officials. One poorly interpreted medical test of my seven-month-old daughter coupled with poor communication between doctors landed me square in the middle of the impossible care-justice dilemma I was studying. I clung to the idea, and strength of many women before me, that I could (and had to) care for myself and my children amidst overt abuse/oppression by the system meant to "support" families. In a situation that felt completely and utterly hopeless, I had no choice but to keep going.

The only thing that got me through this incredibly difficult time was promising myself to find meaning in it. I promised that when this ended (I had to believe the truth would be known and it would end), I would act to address the terrible injustice and assault on care that I and my family experienced. My child protection involvement came to an underwhelming and dissatisfying ending just before my daughter's first birthday in January 2019 when our CAS file was finally closed. In June of 2019 (six months after the case closed), I received a formal report that I had sought out from an internationally esteemed radiologist confirming what we already knew. Not only had there never been any fractures in her knees, but the radiologist was able to name the precise irregularity—a benign, normal variant in bone growth—my daughter had in both her knees. To date, there have never been any apologies or admission of poor communication or wrongdoing by any medical professionals or the child protection system, despite there being legislation in Ontario (Canada) allowing doctors to make apologies without any negative repercussions to themselves. The experience rattled me on a personal, political, and professional level while opening my eyes to the harsh reality that necessary institutional systems have much work to do to address how care and justice are experienced by citizens, particularly mothers involved in child protection investigations.

Care and Justice: Opposite Epistemological and Ontological Orientations?

Before diving into analysis of my story and experiences, it is helpful to review the concepts I am thinking with: ethics of justice and ethics of care. An ethics of justice is rooted in the idea that people function, or should function, as autonomous, rational individuals guided by universal truths applied to all aspects of social, economic, and political life. In contrast, an ethics of care embraces human beings as "inevitably dependent and inextricably interdependent" (Kittay 50) and as always existing in particular sociopolitical contexts and relationships with others. Whereas a ethics of justice understands caregivers and care receivers as distinct groups, a feminist ethics of care embraces all human beings as both. An ethics of care acknowledges that we are all both givers and receivers of care at different points in our lives as well as in different relationships. Care is not a weakness or a deficit but an inevitability through which one can find meaning (or not) in their lives.

Finally, an ethics of care prioritizes relationships and emotion as the centre of all decision making and meaning in life, whereas an ethics of justice asserts that emotion and feeling interfere with rather than inform decision making. Justice seeks to distill the inevitably muddy waters of decision making, taking out the "mud" (e.g., emotions and relationships) from the process. The "mud" is what makes the water what it is—a particular mix of everything that has coalesced at a particular moment in time and space. To decontextualize and distill families to objective events or injuries is dehumanizing for each member of the family.

Virginia Held argues that it is both possible and advisable to keep the concepts of care and justice distinct. She advises drawing on either justice or care to guide moral decisions in different domains of social, economic, and political life: "There can be care without justice: There has historically been little justice in the family, but care and life have gone on without it. There can be no justice without care, however, for without care no child would survive and there would be no persons to respect" (Held, *The Ethics of Care* 17). In making this statement, she acknowledges that responsive and consistent emotional and physical relationships have been provided by women for centuries despite systemic conditions of abuse and oppression. Simply put, she considers it possible to have care without justice, but theoretically impossible to have justice without care.

Care and Justice? A Dialogical Approach

Other ethics of care theorists, myself included, argue for a more dialogical approach to thinking about and understanding care and justice. In conceptualizing human beings as "inevitably dependent and inextricably interdependent" (Kittay 50) and positioning care as the most fundamental aspect of social and political life, I cannot theoretically or practically conceptualize justice without care (Engster and Hamington). Noddings makes the argument that one cannot have rights (a justice approach) without their fundamental needs being met (Noddings). An ethics of care asserts that it is only through attending to difference in social and relational contexts (notably gender but also race, class, trauma, indigeneity, and a host of other variables) that equitable and just relations can be pursued.

Joan Orme concludes that a dialogical approach to justice is needed, whereby a plurality of voices, existing in relation to each, are heard in the deliberative process. Embracing a dialogical, nonbinary approach to care and justice, however, fundamentally destabilizes the objective, knowable, and universal understanding of justice that forensic approaches to child welfare currently prioritize. The status quo cannot continue if an ethics of care were to be fundamentally embraced at a structural level in child protection. One Ontario-based organization comprised of youth and former youth in care suggests an "ethical systems reset" is needed (Ontario Children's Advancement Coalition), and I could not agree more.

Shifting an Ethics of Care to the Public Sphere

Historically, care ethics has and continues to be more widely accepted as a moral theory to guide private, domestic, life rather than public-political life. This divide highlights the gendered dimension of care, as the private sphere has traditionally been, and continues to be, the realm of women (Bezanson and Luxton).

In accepting an ethics of justice in public life as the status quo, the important power imbalances between caregivers (usually mothers) and receivers, both in daily interactions and at the broader sociopolitical level, are occluded. The idea that everybody is equal before the law fails to recognize the unique contextualized positioning of individuals and groups in society. Those providing care are powerful in their interactions with care receivers but powerless in sociopolitical contexts that systematically devalue their work and ignore the context of their lives. This trend translates into concerning practices in systems where care and justice come into conflict, particularly state-sanctioned child protection systems. It is not shocking that marginalized groups that face systematic barriers to achieving the marker of the "good mother" are wildly overrepresented in apprehension cases.

My Experience of Care and Justice in Relation to Child Protection

As I learned firsthand, this largely theoretical discussion comes to a head for mothers involved in child protection systems. The sudden shift from being a respected, professional, and good mother to feeling invisible and demonized was devastating and terrifying. My voice was either ignored or, when heard, treated as suspect. Because of my background as a care scholar, I was also keenly aware of my privilege in the situation: Not only am I white, middle/upper class and in a heterosexual relationship, I had extensive practical, social, emotional, and financial support to help navigate the incredibly intimidating system in which I found myself. A system that claims to support families was systematically tearing us apart through making wildly outlandish demands (i.e., requiring 168 hours of care a week from family and friends who were acting as "supervisors", coercing us into invasive, painful medical testing). Even with all my very real privileges, the level of distress for myself and our family was overwhelming. I was terrified every moment of every day. I lost faith and trust in the medical and social systems I had reached out to for support. My suffering was meaningless and irrelevant to a justice-oriented process seemingly more concerned with assigning blame (and managing liability for those who had power—doctors, social workers, and administrators) than critically examining the myriad of social, emotional, and physiological factors at play. Ironically, and surprisingly, care was nowhere to be found in a system whose purpose is to ensure adequate (if not good) care is provided to children. Instead, extreme demands were placed on us as parents as well as on our baby, our other children, and our family and friends.

The guiding vision of the CAS agency that managed my family's case purports to advance a "city where children are safe, families are strong, and communities are supported". Yet I had never felt as scared, vulnerable, and alone in my life. The pursuit of justice in accordance with very narrow conceptualizations of the child's "best interest" without recognizing the foundational relationships in which the child is embedded felt incredibly backwards. For the professionals involved in this system daily (e.g., doctors, lawyers, and agency supervisors), this was widely accepted as the only safe way for the agency (backed by the state) to engage with me and my family. At the case conference, the lawyer representing the child protection agency refused to make eye contact with me and at one point referred to me as "the poor woman." In hearing her say that, though, I felt at least somewhat seen, even if it was through an entirely deficit framework.

I consistently felt belittled and had my subjectivity denied in my interactions with medical professionals as well. Administrative assistants at doctor's offices sighed heavily when I called trying to get medical records—the records that eventually revealed there was no conclusive evidence of fractures. My family doctor who referred me to the child abuse clinic would not call me back or book an appointment with me (even to remove the stitches from the biopsy of her arm). She literally refused to care for me and my child, only offering for a colleague to take out Arlie's stitches. Doctors at the hospital limited my agency and failed to share with me key pieces of information, such as the results of her blood tests (all normal) or medical records, in a timely fashion.

Perhaps most upsetting was the apparent collusion between the dermatologist and child abuse specialist who continued to advise the CAS that an MRI was required to check for vasculitis. The reality, which has been confirmed in my follow up communications with the hospital, was that they wanted the MRI to check for signs of abuse. Again, all this harm, indeed abuse, was justified through the "child's best interest" discourse with absolutely no apparent regard for any contextual considerations. It was such a clear example of an ethics of justice negating the possibility of good care.

Are Mothers Involved in Child Protection Persons? A Return to Bordo

I did not feel like a person throughout this ordeal. Particularly in relation to the medical system, I felt like a monster—a lying, deceitful monster. I suffered from daily nightmares and intrusive thoughts of the moment they would come and pry my daughter from my arms. I had three other children with whom I could not be honest, as they had to continue living their lives. My other children would have been completely distraught had they been aware there was a possibility that Arlie, or any of them, could have been taken away. There were days when I woke up at 4:00 a.m. worried I was going to jail. Furthermore, until I received the medical records where I discovered her legs were not fractured, I believed the doctors that her legs were broken and that I had caused it. Because it was inconceivable to me that such a major error could be made by medical professionals working within such an esteemed hospital, I also continued to worry that my daughter may have some other rare, serious medical condition that I had no way of identifying.

I was clearly nothing more than a vessel of care for my daughter—an extremely deficient one at that. And after months of living like this, I began to believe that I was a terrible mother and a terrible human. While I intellectually knew better, I began to feel like the monster the medical and child protection system constructed me to be. I no longer felt safe to share any of the pain or suffering with friends and family. My lawyer advised me to never cry around CAS, as it might make me look unstable. And, of course, if I had been unstable, I would have had a mental illness box ticked and that could have been the ticked box that took Arlie away.

While going through this, I could not help but think of all the mothers before me for whom the fear of losing a child is simply a part of their daily lives; mothers already dealing with complex health, financial, relational, and social challenges. I could not help but wonder how my situation would have played out differently if I had been marginalized in any way—racialized, of low socioeconomic status, Indigenous, or uneducated. I had no visible or official markers of marginalization. And, even here, I was flagged as an "at-risk mother" due to having received treatment for postpartum depression in the period immediately after my daughter's birth. What I thought was a demonstration of strength and resilience—ensuring I had professional support post-partum—was now a formal liability.

Perhaps most importantly, I thought of the mothers and children who were experiencing or had experienced domestic violence. I was terrified and I had a very safe, loving family, and friend network. If I had experienced domestic violence, which from what I could see was the narrative the doctors constructed, I would have lost my baby and likely my other children. Professionals—particularly medical, legal, and supervisors in the child protection system—never expressed empathy or concern or even took the time to hear my voice. As I noted above, most of them could not even look at me. At one point, when Arlie was having yet another x-ray and I was standing in the waiting area sobbing listening to her screams, I was offered a private space to cry—in a broom closet. And I was genuinely grateful. It might have been a broom closet, but at least someone (the hospital social worker) saw my pain and tried to give me a space be with it.

A Moment of Care in the Chaos

As a care scholar, I sought comfort and moral guidance in feminist ethics of care literature throughout this ordeal. I read and reread Held, who reminded me that care can and must go on amidst overt and ongoing abuses of power by those in positions of privilege (ironically in the name of "justice"). My friends and family demonstrated a level of care and support I could never have expected but truly could not have functioned without. Interestingly, I did feel some indirect care from our initial CAS intake worker, although this care was demonstrated in contradiction to the formal systems of which she was a part. She indirectly communicated the constraints of the systems within which she had to function while recognizing my suffering and providing as much comfort as she could. She recognized she was in a position of power over me, and I saw that she was powerless within the system, as no important decisions could be made without her supervisor's approval. Although she did her justice-oriented job (standardized risk assessments, interviews with any professionals who had worked with me, random home visits to ensure I was complying with the safety plan, etc.), she cautiously and carefully communicated her discomfort with the process and genuine concern for me and our family.

This one social worker's approach, often in opposition to the institutional duties she was expected to fulfill, is what provides me with some hope that care is possible within systems of child protection. In her interactions with me and our family, she took a risk to care, though of course in a strategic way. This social worker, a Black woman and mother with over 25 years of experience in the system, was the only professional that took the time to look at the situation beyond one (erroneous) medical test. By the time of the case conference, she had come into our home, spoken to all my children, interviewed me and my husband, spoken to our health professionals, and interacted with our extended family. She knew the context. After our case conference, once everyone except my friends and family had left, she came back into the room and said: "I am a parent. I have a son. I know this is hard. But you are going to be okay. This is going to be okay." She gave me a hug, and I hugged her back. I do not tell this part of the story to elicit warm feelings. I tell it because the significance of one simple moment of caring (and sharing power) cannot be overstated. In a million moments of being villainized and suffering deeply, that one moment of recognition, openness, and vulnerability on her part made a world of difference for me.

The Impact of Being "Othered"

The bulk of my experience was feeling deficient, lacking, and pathologized. My experiences revealed that this unchecked "othering" of mothers appears to lead to a level of comfort on the part of professionals with the incredibly invasive and painful process of investigating child abuse. I felt my case was a hot potato repeatedly passed along to the next professional (social worker, doctor, lawyer, supervisor etc.) to figure out what to do next. It became clear in the case conference that the professional wielding the most power was the medical child abuse specialist: If she continued to stand by the "broken legs and unexplained bruises" narrative, I and my family were not safe. Although her perspective was that she was simply presenting the medical facts and that any child protection action was beyond her control, she failed to recognize her significant power in this situation, which would almost inevitably lead to apprehension. My lawyer frequently reminded me that 99 per cent of people in my situation would have most likely had their child apprehended. The medical specialists' extreme lack of reflexivity and/or humility (see Choate and Lindstrom this volume) could easily have led to trauma, pain, and suffering that could never have been undone for each member of our family for generations.

Because I work with an ethics of care orientation, I do wonder if she did not feel safe enough to admit her error when I pointed out the radiology report never concluded there were metaphyseal fractures. I recognize that she is a human too and is also working within powerful systems and structures. In this case, the clinic where she worked had already been through a number of scandals relating to misdiagnoses of child abuse and hundreds of children being removed from their families, in some cases permanently. In fact, at the time when my case occurred, a highly mediatized judicial inquiry was finishing its investigation and providing recommendations on how to prevent such errors from occurring in the future. I recently had the opportunity to meet with representatives from the hospital who apologized for my experience and listened as I provided practical recommendations for how to prevent such errors from occurring again (e.g., a blind peer review process of medical imaging, the provision of all written medical records to families and professionals as soon as possible in the process, transparency in medial rationales for invasive testing, as well as the availability of a hard copy of medical records at case conference meetings). But the key thing I was looking for, but knew I would not get, was an admission of wrongdoing and taking responsibility for the harm caused—a decision that continues to tear me apart.

Where to Go from Here? Reimagining Child Protection through a Social Model

As a first step in reimagining child protection, Featherstone et al. insist that "we [citizens and the state] ... design them [child protection systems] for the right species" (Featherstone et al., *Re-Imagining Child Protection* 89). In a follow-up publication, Featherstone et al. further develop a social model of child protection in theory and practice (Featherstone et al. *Protecting Children*). In this model, the starting point for action must meaningfully acknowledge everyone's most basic human need to be seen and heard, to care, and be cared for while grappling with the messy complexities of oppressive social systems and structures. Selma Sevenhuijsen centres the subjectivity of the care receiver: "The recipient of care, is, for her, not an 'object to be known', but someone to whom she listens, whom she tries to understand and with whom she communicates" (61). It is messy work that is fundamentally at odds with existing forensic, justice approaches to protecting children. But this work is absolutely necessary if we as a society are serious about caring well about, for and with children, mothers, and their families. It is the responsibility of all of us to provide the conditions whereby meaningful caring relations are not a privilege for a few but a reality for all.

Conclusion

In this chapter, I have attempted to use my lived experience as a mother involved in child protection to illustrate the tensions between two competing moral frameworks in child protection work: an ethic of care and an ethic of justice. Identifying as a feminist ethics of care (FEC) scholar going into this experience, it is difficult to capture my confusion and shock at how uncaring a system meant to support families could be. Indeed, I do not hesitate to use the word "abuse" in relation to how I, Arlie, and my family were treated. But it is indeed my FEC roots that have pushed me to share my story and pull together this anthology. This is what I, in a position of extreme privilege, can do to address the oppressive realities faced by children, mothers, and families involved in child protection proceedings. What I put on the line in sharing my story is, again, my subjectivity. I risk not being believed and being discredited and/or disproved—most likely by medical professionals who have made it clear there is no space for admission of error. And as a professional and scholar working with and studying children, families, and social policy, this is a real risk. But to not tell my story feels inauthentic. I can only hope it provides some insight and hope for those who take the time to read it: mothers, social workers, doctors, lawyers, children, youth, and others. I am eager to work with anyone and everyone interested in not only reimagining child protection but dismantling and rebuilding it.

Epilogue

Much has happened since I first wrote, and then revised, this chapter. Over the past year, while the book has been in line for publishing, I have had the opportunity to share my story in academic and child protection spaces that are actively working towards a more caring child protection system. I have shared it with colleagues and friends who have no idea that this ever happened to me. I have felt what it is like to be seen and heard and taken seriously as a person in my own right and as a mother doing my best to ensure my children live in the world as well as possible. My tears are no longer tears of desperation but of hope and of feeling connected to others who also want to build something better. I have been humbled and inspired by so many other mothers and former youth in care who have survived the system. They keep me going.

My fear is not gone, however. Pushing back against the oppressive structures in society and working towards something better is not comfortable work. I recently spoke to a child abuse specialist who told me that metaphyseal fractures may heal without periosteal reaction—or bone regrowth. It stopped me in my tracks as maybe my story and my experience will no longer believed. I do not have the required evidence to be taken seriously as a human being. But then I realized, this is fear again. This is what keeps us immobilized. I know my story. I know my daughter was never hurt. She never exhibited any pain (outside of the brutal medical testing process). And my experience matters. Files obtained through a review of my College of Physican and Surgeons complaint have futher revealed that the there was never consensus among the original radiology team that the areas of concern were fractures as the child abuse specialist indicated to us, the police and CAS. I am currently considering next steps.

Nothing worth doing is easy. Resisting oppressive social structures is messy, exhausting, and terrifying work. We do it despite the fear. I do it because I recognize I have the privilege to be able to speak and that maybe people will listen. I leave you with a poem I wrote the night before doing an invited keynote panel presentation at a child welfare reform conference (hosted by the Kempe Centre) this past year. Inspired by my copanellists who I had gotten to know briefly in a few Zoom meetings, I threw away my speaking notes, and wrote this poem. It felt real. It felt important. And even though the presentation was online in webinar mode, I felt heard. Comments of support and inspiration poured in through the Q and A function. I am still doing my best to hold this pencil alongside the amazing mothers, social workers, children, and families who dare to imagine something better.

The Heaviest Pencil in the World

Why am I here?

Good question.

Why am I here?

I guess I'm here because I desperately want to hang onto hope that things can be different

I'm here to shatter the shame of silence I've been trapped in for too long

I'm here to listen, share, and understand how we have ended up in
a place where vulnerability has become equated with liability rather
than courage

I'm here because the only way I can bear the pain of what I went
through, and continue to go through, is to find meaning through
journeying alongside others

I wish I never had to be here

In so many ways, I wish this had never happened to me

It's left me feeling broken even though it has revealed strength and
resilience I never knew I had

It's left a path of devastation for me and my family who will never,
and can never, trust the very institutions that claim to care

I wish I never had to be here, but I am here. And so are you

So since we are here, let's imagine something different

Imagine a system where it's not me vs. you but me and you

No. Systems can't care. It's beyond their capability

But humans can

And systems are made of humans

And that gets lost amid piles of paperwork, checklists, and
assessments that further divide us

I am a mother

I am a mother who will never be the same after living with the terror
and the real possibility of having my baby, and my other children,
taken away from me

I am the lucky one

I am the privileged one

My case was closed, and my children are with me

But the terror remains and always will

I am deeply humbled by my co-panelists—incredibly bright, strong, and empathetic women who dare to care deeply

I am humbled by the academic and practice leaders who come to this space with an openness child protection systems are rigidly structured to shut down

There is an overwhelming amount of work to do

It's daunting and feels impossible most days

But we can't give up. We can't remain silent

And being here I feel less alone

Less frightened

Less shamed

And ultimately more hopeful

The only way things will change is together

The system seeks to separate us all through pathologizing our inevitable human needs

But we are the humans of the system: parents, children, social workers, researchers, doctors, psychiatrists, etc.

It's on us to write a new narrative

I'm scared... terrified in fact

But I am picking up that pencil—the heaviest pencil in the world

And with you, I am hopeful we can draw a different picture

Endnotes

1. The full medical records, received weeks before this book went to print (June 2022), indicate the doctors realized their error in late October 2018. A radiology conference at this time lead the doctors to change her language from a definitive diagnosis of "metaphyseal fractures" to "suggestive of metaphyseal fractures". This subtle change in language remains the only validation from doctors that I have ever, and likely will ever, receive. Looking at the same images (several months after our CAS case had closed), another practicing radiologist (who is also an assistant professor of radiology at an American university) concluded: "There is irregularity of the growing end of the bone which shows no change over time (no healing response). The location is in an area of rapidly growing bone

and irregularity has been described in this location as a normal variant. In this case, the radiographic findings are consistent with normal variation, not fracture."

Works Cited

Barnes, Marion. *Care in Everyday Life: An Ethic of Care in Practice.* Policy Press, University of Bristol, 2012.

Bezanson, Kate, and Meg Luxton. "Introduction: Social Reproduction and Feminist Political Economy." *Social Reproduction Feminist Political Economy Challenges Neo-Liberalism,* edited by Kate Bezanson and Meg Luxton, McGill-Queens University Press, 2006, pp. 3-10.

Buckley, Helen. "Services Users as Receivers of Risk-Dominated Practice." *Beyond the Risk Paradigm in Child Protection,* edited by Nigel Parton, Palgrave, 2017.

Cameron, Gary, and Sandy Hoy. "Mothers and Child Welfare." *Creating Positive Systems of Child and Family Welfare: Congruence with the Everyday Lives of Children and Parents,* edited by Gary Cameron et al., University of Toronto Press, 2013, pp. 44-66.

Connolly, Marie, editor. *Beyond the Risk Paradigm in Child Protection.* Palgrave, 2017.

Engster, Daniel and Maurice Hamington, editors. *Care Ethics and Political Theory.* Oxford University Press, 2015.

Featherstone, Brid, et al. *Protecting Children: A Social Model.* Policy Press, 2018.

Featherstone, Brid, et al. *Re-Imagining Child Protection: Towards Humane Social Work with Families.* Policy Press, 2014.

Freymond, Nancy. "Home Truths: What Mothers of Children in Placement Say about Their Lives." *Creating Positive Systems of Child and Family Welfare: Congruence with the Everyday Lives of Children and Parents,* edited by Gary Cameron et al., University of Toronto Press. 2013, pp.94-114.

Freymond, Nancy, and Gary Cameron. "Mothers and Child Welfare Child Placements." *Moving toward Positive Systems of Child and Family Welfare: Current Issues and Future Directions,* edited by Gary Cameron et al., Wilfred Laurier University Press, 2007, pp. 79-109.

Held, Virginia. *The Ethics of Care: Personal, Political and Global.* Oxford University Press, 2006.

Held, Virginia. "A Theory of Justice as Fair Terms of Social Life Given Our Inevitable Dependence and Our Inextricable Interdependency." *Care Ethics and Political Theory* edited by Daniel Engster and Maurice Hamington, Oxford University Press, 2015, pp. 50-71.

Kittay, Eva. "A Theory of Justice as Fair Terms of Social Life Given Our Inevitable Dependency and Our Inextricable Interdependency." *Care Ethics and Political Theory*, edited by Daniel Engster and Maurice Hamington, Oxford, 2015, pp. 51-71.

Noddings, Nel. "Care Ethics and 'Caring' Organizations." *Care Ethics and Political Theory*, edited by Daniel Engster and Maurice Hamington, Oxford University Press, 2015, pp. 72-84.

Ontario Children's Advancement Coalition. "Ethical Systems Reset Presentation: Making the Case for Implementing First-Voice-Led Readiness-Based System." August 6, 2020. https://www.facebook.com/ChildCoalition/videos/611905516415582/

Orme, Joan. "Social Work: Gender, Care and Justice." *British Journal of Social Work*, vol. 32, no. 6, 2002, pp. 799-814.

Sevenhuijsen, Selma. *Citizenship and the Ethics of Care: Feminist Considerations on Justice, Morality, and Politics.* Routledge, 1998.

Slote, Michael. "Care Ethics and Liberalism." *Care Ethics and Political Theory*, edited by Daniel Engster and Maurice Hamington, Oxford University Press, 2015, pp. 37-50.

Tronto, Joan. "Can Caring Democracy Be a Political Concept for Transformation?" *Arguments*, vol. 58, no. 6, 2016, pp. 839-48.

Chapter 2

Grounds for Protection? Examining the Intersection of HIV Infection, Risk, and Motherhood

Allyson Ion

Introduction

Framing pregnancy and motherhood in language of risk has become commonplace in neoliberal sociocultural contexts (Parton). This is reflected in Barbara Katz Rothman's provocation: "Is it even possible to talk about pregnancy and childbirth in language other than that of risk?" (1). Dominant risk discourses are visible in legislation, institutional policies, and routinized practice standards within health and social care settings. Conditions have been created in which it is expected that both lay people and professionals scrutinize women's pregnant bodies and doings as mothers. This is pronounced in contexts where people with authoritative positions (e.g., doctors and social workers) have a professional responsibility (e.g., a duty to report) to intervene once a normative risk threshold has been identified. This chapter explores the realities of pregnant women and mothers living with HIV, whose bodies are often categorized according to risk. It empirically investigates the relationship between the experiences of pregnancy and motherhood for women living with HIV, the practices of health and social care providers who enact discourses of risk, and the ruling relations that organize the actions of people operating within institutional settings where mothers living with HIV receive services. It is through an examination of experiences that we can see how risk discourses collide with beliefs about motherhood, living with HIV, and grounds for protecting children within a child welfare context.

The chapter begins with a review of risk literature as a dominant frame for understanding pregnancy and childbirth followed by implications of these ideas for mothers living with HIV. The institutional ethnographic approach employed in this research is described along with recommendations for health and social care practice with families affected by HIV.

Literature Review

Risk and Perinatal Care

Over the last century, "risk" has been a central theme in the perinatal care that women receive during pregnancy, childbirth, and early postpartum. In a medicalized approach to maternity care, a woman's risk status is assessed on the basis of possible "adverse pregnancy outcomes" (Gupton et al. 192), and "risk" is understood as quantifiable and objectivist (Carolan). Women are labelled as having complicated or high-risk pregnancies when they have certain medical conditions, and/ or there is an increased chance of complications developing in the pregnant woman and/or fetus (e.g., preeclampsia, preterm labour, and gestational diabetes) (Vanier Institute; Teijlingen). The risk of medical complications is often assessed from a biomedical and statistical perspective, whereby women's past obstetric and medical history is considered alongside population-level data (Gupton et al.). Risk, therefore, is a fundamental orientation within obstetrical care that guides assessments and pregnancy management (MacKinnon and McIntyre). Furthermore, classification of women's pregnancies as low risk, high risk, and/or at risk can determine how women become connected to health and social care, and the kinds of maternity care providers they will interact with. Importantly, scholars assert a shared understanding among a variety of obstetrical providers that there is always some risk that is present in pregnancy that needs to be considered and mitigated and, in the context of pregnancy no level of risk is acceptable (Hausman; MacKinnon and MacIntyre).

The Historical Context of Risk-Based Perinatal Care

The current organization of perinatal care, which is the care that women receive during pregnancy and up to twenty-eight days post-partum, stems from the increasing medicalization of pregnancy and childbirth as well as the emphasis on reducing perinatal mortality (Weir). Obstetrical practices evolved significantly from 1890 to 1945 as part of early industrial capitalism. Obstetricians cemented control as the dominant maternity care providers, and the hospital became the primary setting in which perinatal care was provided (Benoit et al.; Weir). These changes shifted how childbirth was defined and perceived, and what technological interventions were used on women's bodies (Declercq et al.). For example, twentieth-century maternity care re-defined pregnancy from a normal and natural occurrence to a "dangerous malady requiring specialized care that could only be provided in the now 'safe' hospital" (Declercq et al. 9).

The proportion of women receiving perinatal care also significantly increased throughout the early to mid-twentieth-century because of mounting clinical evidence that infant mortality could be prevented through improved prenatal care (Weir). After 1945, monitoring any aspect of pregnancy became the norm, and the "patient's body became a site for continuous data collection" (Weir 58). For healthcare providers, data collection related to risk assessment quickly sidelined the deeply emotive, gendered, and human experience that is pregnancy and childbirth. Prior to the 1960s, care provided during pregnancy was mainly to benefit maternal health. With the adoption of technologies to reduce perinatal mortality, pregnancy became connected to a "comprehensive regime of clinical assessment" focused on conserving fetal and neonatal health (Weir 34). The needs and experiences of mothers became positioned as secondary to the fetus/infant in contemporary medical practices.

The Intersection of Medical and Social Risks during the Perinatal Period

Early, risk-based epidemiological research also began to make connections between pregnancy outcomes and sociodemographic factors. Peller concludes that women who left paid labour earlier in pregnancy had reduced rates of infant mortality compared to those who worked until they went into labour (qtd. in Weir). This bolstered the idea that neonatal mortality depended on social factors or modifiable life conditions, including nutrition, work responsibilities, and marital status (Weir). Such research contributed to demographic and lifestyle factors being accounted for when assessing perinatal risk (Gupton et al.; Teijlingen), which fuelled the idea that women who did not govern themselves to limit risk exposures during pregnancy were selfish, irresponsible, or morally deficient.

This risk thinking has penetrated medical and social practices so deeply that the high-risk mother has been constituted as the primary source of perinatal mortality and the central target for health and social intervention (Haan and Connolly; Weir). Structural determinants of risk—such as poverty, trauma, and discrimination—are occluded in favour of holding the individual mother solely responsible for her own and her baby's outcomes (Hausman, *Viral Mothers*; Parton). The acceptable solution is increasing surveillance of women's bodies to identify risk and intervene to minimize risk to her baby (Browner and Press; Carolan). As Bernice L. Hausman states: "Fetuses and infants are seen as the innocent victims of modernity's side effects.... They become exemplars of humanity in its most pristine form, and women's bodies are the vehicles for their contamination" (*Viral Mothers* 58). This surveillance occurs beyond the perinatal period, whereby health and social care providers focus their efforts on at-risk mothers and engage in the surveillance of parents and their parenting skills in the name of child protection (Zadoroznyi et al.).

HIV, Pregnancy, and Motherhood

The intersection of pregnancy, motherhood, and HIV is an important microcosm wherein health and social care practices focused on risk come to a head. In Canada, the pregnancies of women living with HIV are classified as high risk because of the maternal HIV diagnosis, which is framed as a significant complication that requires medical intervention to facilitate HIV prevention to the fetus and infant (Money et al.; Vanier Institute; Teijlingen). Because HIV can be transmitted through blood and breastmilk, there are specific procedures that women living with HIV are expected to follow to reduce the likelihood of perinatal HIV transmission. These include maternal antiretroviral therapy (ART) throughout pregnancy, infant ART for six weeks postpartum, and exclusive formula feeding (Money et al.; WHO).

With the effective use of ART, the chance of HIV transmission during pregnancy, childbirth, and early postpartum is less than 1 per cent (Cooper et al.; Forbes et al.)

Many mothers living with HIV may also be contending with circumstances that not only contributed to their HIV acquisition but also complicate their experiences of living with the virus, including domestic violence; addictions and mental health challenges; precarious housing; precarious immigration status; poverty; histories of trauma related to colonization, residential schools, and the sixties scoop; racism; and HIV-related stigma and discrimination (Parker and Aggleton; Raphael). Saara Greene et al. argue that these determinants of health not only influence women's access to and engagement with health and social care but also increase the chances of coming under the gaze of health and social care providers vis-à-vis risk-based perinatal care.

It is critical to note, however, that despite the circumstances that women living with HIV may be facing, they are typically engaged in mechanisms to prevent perinatal HIV transmission. Most pregnant women living with HIV in Canada are aware of their HIV-positive status, have initiated HIV treatment, and are actively receiving care from an HIV specialist when they become pregnant (Bitnun et al.). The complication for these women is not necessarily HIV itself, but the oppressive, socially constructed norms and attitudes about HIV that construct them as a bad, immoral, or irresponsible mother, who is actively harming not only her child but public health (Greene et al.; Ion et al.)

There is a clear disjuncture between how HIV is known and experienced among women living with HIV and how health and social care providers engage with these women. The fears, hopes, goals, and actions of women living with HIV are often at odds with the standardized and routine medical practices they interact with. It is, therefore, important to critically examine the conditions that shape how women living with HIV experience motherhood, how discourses of risk and surveillance organize the work of health and social care providers, and how health and social care practices can be strengthened to acknowledge women's realities.

Methodological Approach: Institutional Ethnography (IE)

Dorothy Smith's sociology for people and IE are helpful when examining the social relations that produce women's experiences (Smith, *Everyday World*; Smith, *Institutional Ethnography*). Smith asserts that women do not inhabit imaginary spaces that are constituted by sociological modes of inquiry (*Everyday World*); rather, they must return to their embodied experiences, and the doings of actual people situated in particular sites at particular times, to discover the "ways in which [women] actually exist" (Smith, *Conceptual Practices* 200).

The goal of IE is to uncover the "ruling relations" or the discursive, managerial, and professional forms of governance that organize our lives (Smith, *Everyday World*; Smith, *Conceptual Practices of Power*; Smith, *Writing the Social*). Smith argues that we all participate in ruling relations through our work as individuals, as employees within institutional settings, and as actors who engage with texts that organize our ways of knowing and practicing (*Writing the Social*). We all take up ruling discourses and ideologies in our daily activities because we live in a society that relies on authorized knowledges, including knowledge routinely generated by sociologists, psychologists, and others who operate within institutional settings and hold positions of power (Smith, "K Is Mentally Ill").

IE studies make explicit the connection between people's everyday worlds and how their lives are coordinated by social relations that extend beyond them as individuals (Campbell and Gregor; McCoy; Smith, *Everyday World*). The inquiry is organized around a property of the everyday world, as it arises for those who live it in their local contexts (Smith, *Everyday World*).

Work is an orienting concept in IE; people are actively involved in and cannot be detached from actualities including their work, and it is through IE that these actualities can be made visible (Smith, *A Sociology for People*). IE is applied to uncover textually mediated social organization (DeVault and McCoy; Smith, *Everyday World*). Texts are an important "primary medium of power" (Smith, *Everyday World* 17), as they guide organizational processes inherent within ruling relations and uncover how work is coordinated and why people do the things they do within particular settings (Sinding; Smith, *Writing the Social*).

Through IE, researchers can begin from any local setting or event and arrive at a descriptive matrix of the generalizable text-mediated social relations that everyone is caught within (G. Smith).

The inquiry that is outlined in this chapter begins from the standpoint of four women living with HIV (given pseudonyms), who were interviewed once during pregnancy and again at three months postpartum. These women were recruited through a regional HIV clinic in Ontario, Canada. Participants were asked about the types, frequency, and nature of HIV and maternity care appointments they attended during the perinatal period and if they encountered any challenges or concerns along the way. In addition, twelve people working in HIV and maternity care were also interviewed. This group of participants included five physicians, three social workers, three nurses, and one pharmacist. These healthcare care providers were asked about their work caring for pregnant women living with HIV; their education and training related to pregnancy, motherhood, and HIV; and texts that inform their work (e.g., practice guidelines). An analytic process outlined by Susan Turner to trace the connections between institutionalized texts and daily-work practices. The ultimate goal was to empirically determine how the regimes of ruling these women encountered in healthcare interactions produced their experiences (G. Smith).

Findings

Women's Ways of Knowing and Mitigating Risk

Women discussed their actions to engage in healthcare and reduce the chance of perinatal HIV transmission. All women spoke about the importance of taking their HIV medications and how their medication adherence was a critical factor in reducing HIV risk. As Odette shared: "My [HIV specialist] advised me.... Take this medicine; never miss it. I was doing what my doctor was telling me always.... You're a good mom because you did what we're always telling you.... The medicine is going to save the baby.... It is not easy to take the medicine.... I'm taking for life. And why I'm doing that.... I want to make my kids safe." All participants shared this perspective and expressed a deep desire to protect their babies from acquiring HIV. Women had learned from their healthcare providers that the most effective way to reduce this risk was by adhering to their HIV treatment.

Beyond HIV medications, risk crept into women's maternity care experiences in other ways. Women acknowledged the importance of attending prenatal appointments to stay informed about their progress. Although prenatal appointments occur at the same frequency for mothers living with HIV as other mothers, the women interviewed expressed feeling intense pressure from their prenatal care team regarding appointment attendance. In some cases, the practical barriers these women faced getting to appointments was dismissed by healthcare providers. Joelle, a mother who relied on others to drive her an hour each way for every appointment, shared her interpretation of an interaction with a nurse who insisted that she comply with a specific prenatal schedule:

> My assumption and how I felt she was talking to me was "You're HIV positive. You're irresponsible. You're an ex-drug addict. You're not taking care."... It was like she was looking for something wrong ... because I'm HIV.... This is my third pregnancy [as a woman living with HIV].... I'm their lowest high-risk patient.... I'm on my meds. I don't use drugs and alcohol. I'm perfectly healthy.... I'm not going to breastfeed.... I'm not doing anything that would put my baby at risk.

Since this was her third pregnancy, Joelle had extensive knowledge about the actions she could take to reduce perinatal HIV transmission. With a history of injection drug and alcohol use, Joelle expressed the importance of sobriety to maintain her physical and mental health. She believed she did not pose any risks to her baby because of the proactive measures she was taking. At the same time, Joelle found it difficult to attend her prenatal appointments due to her need to travel to the hospital, to care for her older children, and to attend school. She expressed these difficulties with her healthcare providers and asked if allowances could be made, including delegating tasks to her local primary care provider, but her specialist team insisted that she attend regular appointments at the regional hospital. Joelle strongly believed that her HIV-positive status and history of drug use fuelled her healthcare team's resistance to afford her flexibility in her prenatal care and that they equated these identities with irresponsibility, risk, and suspicion. In the end, her healthcare team's standardized, risk-averse approach undermined her autonomy to care for herself, her unborn baby, and her other children. She was judged and shamed rather than empowered when questioning the standardized treatment approach.

Health and Social Care Providers' Ways of Knowing and Mitigating Risk

I asked healthcare providers about prenatal appointments, which were framed as important moments to assess and act upon medical complications and perinatal risk factors. I asked about the rationale for women to maintain a rigid appointment schedule, and while discussing women's compliance with prenatal appointments, healthcare providers blurred the lines between monitoring medical complications and responding to social risks. For example, if women did not attend appointments or did not adequately account for their nonattendance, some providers questioned their parenting capacity. As one obstetrician noted:

> We understand when the patients say... I lost my keys, or my car broke down ... and they miss a couple of appointments.... We don't harass them with...social work is going to be seeing you because...people are going to think that you're not looking after your baby.... Other patients however who are less compliant with visits, there's not really any obvious reason why they're not coming, or at least nothing that they're sharing with us... Sometimes you do actually have a concern...are they actually taking their medications regularly? ... Do they actually have the stuff at home to look after themselves and this baby because they don't seem to be able to have the means to come to appointments that they need to come to? Are they going to be able to do the care for the baby after delivery that needs to happen?

Hearing from healthcare providers about their view of appointment attendance helped to contextualize the resistance Joelle encountered. As the quote above indicates, women's appointment compliance appeared to serve as a proxy for their parenting capacity. Lack of compliance with appointments became another layer of risk that providers responded to as part of their work to deliver perinatal care. If women did not adequately meet narrow institutional expectations, their risk assessment was amplified by their healthcare team. As one provider explained: "People will come up with all sorts of explanations for not coming. And we don't know who's the one that's trying to stay under the radar and not get seen because of whatever else is going on versus who has legitimate reasons.... So some of those people, we do actually want to be seen [in the clinic] to make a point." The healthcare providers I spoke with connected women's prenatal care engagement to ensuring a healthy pregnancy and delivery because of the likelihood of reducing all possible risks through prenatal procedures and women's compliance with such procedures.

Prenatal healthcare providers' assessment of risk extended beyond prenatal practices. Maternity care providers sometimes had concerns about the baby following hospital discharge. It is at this point that prenatal risk intersects with child welfare risk for mothers living with HIV. One social worker explained:

> One's antenna has to be up for child welfare issues.... It has to be there for every patient. No matter how well or poorly dressed you are, no matter what your life situation.... Just being aware.... Are there risk factors here? You know, we had an HIV patient who went and delivered at another hospital and did not disclose. Like went in labour and did not disclose her status.... Everyone should be using universal precautions. So it shouldn't be a big thing. But it is a big thing for the baby because there are again time-sensitive requirements in caring for that infant.... She had a significant viral load. That's a children's aid referral.... That's a slam dunk because she put that baby at risk.

When asked about her philosophy of maternity care practice, and in particular with pregnant women and mothers living with HIV, this social worker described applying a similar biomedical-technocratic risk orientation to her child protection work. She equated a woman arriving at a different hospital in labour where she did not receive prenatal care and not disclosing her HIV status at the time of delivery (i.e., a mother's attempt to have a normal birth experience) as grounds to involve child welfare because of the assumed risk to the baby. The social worker also referenced the mother having a "significant viral load," which refers to the amount of HIV copies in the woman's blood.

What is not clear from this complex scenario is why this woman went to a different hospital if she was on HIV treatment during her pregnancy and why her HIV status was not known by the healthcare team who cared for her or why it was not disclosed by her at the time of delivery. Despite not having these key pieces of information, this social worker was firm in her belief that this scenario necessitated a referral to child welfare. It is through this social worker's interpretation of risk that we can begin to see how a woman's HIV status can be framed as grounds to enact one's professional duty to report to child welfare and to hook women living with HIV into another system of surveillance. The question becomes how and why the go-to response for this social worker was one of authoritarian-technocratic intervention and suspicion rather than empathy and compassion.

The Ruling Relations of Risk in Child Protection Work

In Ontario, the Child, Youth and Family Services Act (CYFSA; Government of Ontario) governs the work of child welfare professionals and organizations to promote the best interests, protection, and wellbeing of children. The legislation outlines parameters in which a child is "in need of protection" if suffering from physical, sexual, and/ or emotional abuse and/or the risk of such harms. The legislation includes grounds for protection if children are not adequately cared for, are physically or emotionally neglected, and/or do not receive treatments that they require for medical conditions or because of the harms to which they have been subjected. The Act also specifies that if someone who performs professional duties with respect to children has reasonable grounds to suspect that a child is "in need of protection" based on the Act's definitions, they are responsible to report their suspicions to Children's Aid Society. The CYFSA legislates actions regarding the protection of children but does not specify actions in the context of pregnancy. Moreover, HIV and other health conditions (e.g., mental illness and addictions) are not explicitly mentioned in the Act as grounds for protection; rather, the grounds for protection are stated as general concerns about abuse, neglect, and harms, which are left to be interpreted by child welfare officials. Pregnant women, including women living with HIV, however, often find themselves being referred to child welfare during pregnancy. The question becomes why? If these women are doing the right things (e.g., taking medications, expressing knowledge of how HIV is transmitted and avoiding these practices, and attending appointments to the best of their ability), then why are they reported to child welfare?

The Ontario Child Welfare Eligibility Spectrum (OACAS) is an assessment tool that was developed by the child welfare sector to assist staff in determining if child welfare involvement should be initiated. The Spectrum is the guideline through which the field has operationalized provincial legislation, research, practice, and child death inquest recommendations; it contains two provisions that allow child welfare officials and those working with children in a professional capacity to intervene before the baby's arrival. The first provision is noted as "Scale 3: Caregiver with Problem." This provision behooves professionals to act when "it is alleged/verified that caregiver of newborn used alcohol or drugs in significant amounts during later stages of pregnancy and traces of drugs or alcohol are found in child's urine or blood at birth" (OACAS 91). The second provision is noted as "Section 6: Request for Counselling," which enables professionals to implement birth planning services (essentially the "green light" for child intervention) and request a postbirth plan for the "caregiver regarding options for the unborn child (where adoption is not the primary plan)" (OACAS 97). The vague and unspecified wording of this provision allows for a child welfare referral to be made during pregnancy by any health or social care provider who believes it is warranted, which sets into motion child welfare involvement for a family.

If a call is made to a child welfare agency, staff apply the criteria outlined in the Eligibility Spectrum to initiate an assessment. If the worker determines the mother's medical and social circumstances position the child in need of protection, an investigation may commence. The level of risk must cross the threshold outlined in the Eligibility Spectrum, but the interpretation of risk is subjective and left to the judgment of the intervening child welfare officials. In the case of women living with HIV, her medical diagnoses, engagement in care, treatment adherence, and social circumstances (housing, income, access to resources, intimate partner relationships, histories of drug use, etc.) may all be factored in when determining grounds for protection because of concerns of possible neglect and harms. Furthermore, it is at this juncture that social risks intersect with medical conditions, which is typically accentuating risk. For women living with HIV who must actively demonstrate her adherence to biomedical interventions preventing HIV transmission, the intersection of medical and social risks may be particularly damning.

Once a child welfare investigation begins, a mother's HIV-positive status could be emphasized in her case when considering the child's best interests, and the resulting decisions can have lasting effects on families. One such case occurred in Alberta in 2017 (Alberta Provincial Court) when a permanent guardianship order was granted, and a child (pseudonym Alice) was to have no further access to their mother apart from a one-hour farewell visit. In the judgment, a parenting capacity assessor noted the following: "There were other troubling circumstances that came to the Director's attention which placed Alice at risk of contracting the mother's HIV infection. The mother allowed the baby to suck on her fingers, or would put the baby's soother in her own mouth before placing it into Alice's. These two behaviours are contrary to universal HIV health precautions but the mother continued to do them, although advised of the dangers this created for the child" (Alberta Provincial Court). It is impossible to transmit HIV in the scenarios mentioned above because HIV cannot be passed through saliva; however, in this judgment, these activities were framed as dangers. Although this case involved a number of factors that contributed to Alice's removal, referencing HIV in this way perpetuates incorrect and misleading information and HIV-related stigma. By equating specific mothering practices (e.g., sucking on fingers and the soother) with danger because of the mother's HIV-positive status and then writing these dangers into a guardianship order provides child protection officials with a legal precedent that can be used in other cases involving families affected by HIV. What is particularly disturbing is how incorrect information about HIV transmission can be written into a legal decision and can have permanent effects not only on this family but also on other families in similar circumstances.

Discussion

HIV treatment advancements have contributed to the evolution of HIV into a chronic health condition albeit with significant stigma attached (Samji et al.). Pregnancy is increasingly common for women living with HIV and need not directly translate into poor outcomes for mother and child (Loutfy et al.). As argued by Greene and colleagues, women living with HIV continue to experience surveillance, shame, and stigma when navigating perinatal care and unwanted intrusion in motherhood because of their HIV-positive status. It is not surprising that there is a strong emphasis on identifying and mitigating risks by health and social care providers, given the sociohistorical context of risk-based prenatal care and the increasing focus on monitoring women's pregnant bodies and parenting activities (Cahill; Hall, Tomkinson, and Klein; Weir; Zadoroznyi, Benoit and Berry). HIV is one complication that is considered across a broad continuum throughout the perinatal period. The issue of categorizing HIV as a source of risk during the perinatal period becomes problematic when it is framed as risk beyond the biomedical and measurable criteria of a woman's HIV viral load. When HIV is viewed as risk in a child welfare context simply because a woman is living with HIV, it can lead to practices and consequences that have significantly negative implications for women's and children's lives.

Perhaps because risk-based prenatal care is grounded in biomedical models seemingly rooted in objective evidence probabilities, the fact that subjective interpretation of potential risk or neglect guides practice becomes overlooked. In practice, maternity care providers "make subjective assessments based on their own available heuristics or 'rule of thumb'" (Gupton 194). Physicians, nurses, and pregnant women have different understandings of pregnancy-related risk, including how risk is defined, understood, and communicated (Carolan). This is problematic when a woman's HIV-positive status is linked to potential parenting capacity and when healthcare providers make assumptions that all mothers living with HIV are a threat to their unborn babies or that noncompliance with narrowly defined medical protocols con-stitutes an indicator of poor parenting behaviour. In fact, mothers who actively resist dogmatic, inflexible social and/or medical practices (for whatever complex reasons) are considered to be more of a risk to their fetus (MacKinnon and McIntyre). By questioning the authoritative knowledge of their healthcare providers, women living with HIV, such as Joelle, are viewed negatively and find themselves being held solely responsible for their pregnancy and childbirth outcomes (Hall, Tomkinson, and Klein).

If women's pregnancies are more complicated because of medical risks that have been identified, they are more likely to comply with perinatal interventions because they are "especially motivated to believe that technological mediations are necessary for reproductive success" (Hausman, "Risky Business" 30). This is certainly the case for women living with HIV, who are motivated to maintain perfect adherence to their treatments and heed the advice of their HIV specialists to ensure HIV prevention. Yet if women like Joelle assert their experiential knowledge related to childbirth, treatment, and mothering as women living with HIV—and their experience is in friction with the knowledges, routinized practices, and dominant discourse of risk that organize the work of their health and social care providers—then these women will also be viewed as difficult and may find themselves the focus of additional scrutiny and surveillance. The dominance and authority of healthcare providers and child welfare professionals' voices effectively silences the voices and experiences of mothers living with HIV.

Implications for Practice and Policy

This research highlights a number of possibilities to strengthen health and social care practice when working with families affected by HIV. First, it must be recognized that an HIV diagnosis is not in itself a child protection concern (Milton Keynes Safeguarding Children Board). Moreover, being pregnant and parenting with HIV does not constitute abuse or neglect and should not enact child protection legislation and/ or a duty to report. As was highlighted in the Alberta Provincial Court case, the perception of HIV as a child protection concern may be based on incorrect or outdated information about HIV and HIV-related stigma. In fact, because this mother would have been recommended to not breastfeed, comforting her baby by letting the child suck on her finger was an important way to bond with her child.

Second, health and social care providers should keep in mind that there are numerous procedures that women living with HIV are recommended to follow during the perinatal period to reduce the chance of HIV transmission (Money et al.). Women are typically already connected to HIV care when they discover that they are pregnant and know what steps they can take to reduce perinatal HIV transmission (Bitnun et al.). Most women have initiated their HIV treatment by the time they are seen in maternity care and, as a result, will have similar pregnancies to women who do not have HIV. Thus, it is not the HIV diagnosis itself that should be regarded as a social risk factor. It is vital that she at least be given the opportunity to engage meaningfully and sustainably with health and social care providers, including having her voice heard and taken seriously throughout the perinatal period.

Third, by normalizing the experiences of pregnancy and motherhood for women living with HIV, we can all work to disrupt the dominant discourse of risk and amplify the voices and expertise of mothers living with HIV who have known and enacted measures to reduce risks since the advent of HIV medications in the early days of the HIV epidemic. The experiences of mothers living with HIV could be very different, and much more positive, if health and social care providers, including child welfare professionals, contest the deficit, risk paradigm in child protection. Instead of positioning themselves as enforcers of compliance-based measures, they can position themselves as agents of change that contest the oppressive practices that are the norm in child welfare (Chaplin et al.; Haan and Connolly; Ion et al., 3Voices; Parton; Shlonsky and Mildon). In doing so, such providers can be a source of support and can disrupt social control practices that normalize surveillance and discrimination. Care that embraces agency and collaboration in a bidirectional way can replace forms of monitoring that leave women feeling like they are being checked to see if they are "doing the right thing" (Hall, Tomkinson, and Klein 580). It is critical to be clear and specific about why these risks are viewed as a concern, how support can be provided through health and social care channels, and how to make an explicit effort not to compound the medical and social risks.

At the same time, just as we have problematized situating mothers solely responsible for good enough care for their children, we must also not situate good care at the individual level of the professional. Professionals, particularly the gendered profession of social work, function within systems that are deeply risk averse. However, this chapter has clearly illustrated that risk aversive practices can be overtly harmful in their overly cautious attempts to prevent harm. And in most of these cases, it is the mother and child who suffer most. The suffering of the mother living with HIV who lost custody and access to her baby because she allowed her baby to suck on her finger was preventable and therefore unfathomably tragic. When the only tools child protection workers have at their disposal are coercive, the magnified power imbalances between caregiver and receiver negate the possibility of good, responsive, and meaningful caring relations. Mothers living with HIV are in particularly challenging and complex situations given the intersection of medical and social risk factors, alongside deep social stigma and widespread misunderstandings of their condition.

Instead of the coercive approach of child welfare practices (ultimately rooted in biotechnical and objective indicators of risk), it is entirely possible that systemically supported and adequately resourced professionals could provide mothers with both reparative relational experiences and/or viable and sustainable resources (e.g., access to respite care to attend appointments or other practical resources). In other cases, for example the mother who was denied the opportunity to transfer her care to her primary care provider closer to home, more flexibility on the part of medical professionals could have gone a long way towards meeting this mother's needs.

Perhaps the main take away of this chapter is that contrary to existing measures of risk within child protection, living with HIV is not an indicator of being an immoral or irresponsible mother. In fact, these mothers typically go to extreme lengths to protect their babies from harm. It should not be necessary for them to prove their worthiness as mothers in a way that mothers who do not have HIV by default enjoy. If we all critically reflect on these issues as part of our practices and interactions with mothers living with HIV and beyond, we can all do our part to ensure appropriate, sensitive, and antioppressive care.

Works Cited

Alberta Provincial Court. AN (Re), 2017 ABPC 300 (Alberta Provincial Court).

Benoit, Cecilia, M. Zadoroznyj, H. Hallgrimsdottir, A. Treloar, and K. Taylor. "Medical Dominance and Neoliberalisation in Maternal Care Provision: The Evidence from Canada and Australia." *Social Science Medicine*, vol. 71, no. 3, 2010, pp. 475-81.

Bitnun, Ari, et al. "Missed Opportunities for Prevention of Vertical HIV Transmission in Canada, 1997–2016: A Surveillance Study."

CMAJ Open, vol. 6, no. 2, 2018, pp. E202-E210.

Browner, C. H., and N. Press. "The Production of Authoritative Knowledge in American Prenatal Care." *Childbirth and Authoritative Knowledge: Cross-Cultural Perspectives*, edited by R. E. Davis-Floyd and C. F. Sargent, University of California Press, 1997, pp. 113-31.

Cahill, Heather A. "Male Appropriation and Medicalization of Childbirth: An Historical Analysis." *Journal of Advanced Nursing*, vol. 33, no. 3, 2001, pp. 334-342.

Campbell, Marie, and Frances Gregor. *Mapping Social Relations: A Primer in Doing Institutional Ethnography*. University of Toronto Press, 2002.

Carolan, M. C. "Towards Understanding the Concept of Risk for Pregnant Women: Some Nursing and Midwifery Implications." *Journal of Clinical Nursing*, vol. 18, no. 5, 2009, pp. 652-58.

Cartwright, E., and J. Thomas. "Constructing Risk: Maternity Care, Law, and Malpractice." *Birth by Design: Pregnancy, Maternity Care, and Midwifery in North America and Europe*, edited by R. Devries et al., Routledge, 2001, pp. 218-28.

Chaplin, Janice, et al. "Preparing for Critical Practice in Child Welfare: A Collaborative Justice-Focused Educational Program towards Transformation in Child Welfare." Oral Presentation given by Allyson Ion on behalf of authors at the Canadian Association of Social Work Education Conference, Vancouver, British Columbia, 6 June 2019.

Government of Ontario. Child, Youth, and Family Services Act. 2017, S.O. 2017, c. 14, Sched. 1, www.ontario.ca/laws/statute/17c14. Accessed 3 June 2022.

Cooper, Ellen R., et al. "Combination Antiretroviral Strategies for the Treatment of Pregnant HIV-1-Infected Women and Prevention of Perinatal HIV-1 Transmission." *Journal of Acquired Immune Deficiency Syndromes*, vol. 29, no. 5, 2002, pp. 484-94.

Declercq, Eugene, R., et al. "Where to Give Birth? Politics and the Place of Birth." Birth By Design: Pregnancy, Maternity Care and Midwifery in North America and Europe, edited by R. DeVries et al., Routledge, 2001, pp. 7-27.

DeVault, M. L., and Liza McCoy. "Institutional Ethnography: Using

Interviews to Investigate Ruling Relations." Institutional Ethnography as Practice, edited by Dorothy E. Smith, Rowman & Littlefield Publishers, 2006, pp. 15-44.

Edwards, Kyle. "Fighting Foster Care." *Macleans*, 1 Feb. 2018, archive. macleans.ca/article/2018/2/1/fighting-foster-care. Accessed 3 June 2022.

Forbes, John C., et al. "A National Review of Vertical HIV Transmission." *AIDS*, vol. 26, no. 6, 2012, pp. 757-63.

Greene, Saara, et al. "It's Better Late than Never: A Community-Based HIV Research and Training Response to Supporting Mothers Living with HIV Who Have Child Welfare Involvement." *Journal of Law and Social Policy*, vol. 28, 2018, pp. 61-81.

Greene, Saara, et al. "(M)othering with HIV: Resisting and Reconstructing Experiences of Health and Social Surveillance." *Criminalized Mothers, Criminalizing Motherhood*, edited by B. Hogeveen and J. Minaker, Demeter Press, 2015, pp. 231-263.

Greene, Saara, et al. "Surviving Surveillance: How Pregnant Women and Mothers Living with HIV Respond to Medical and Social Surveillance." *Qualitative Health Research*, vol. 27, no. 14, 2017, pp. 2088-99.

Greene, Saara, et al. "'Why Are You Pregnant? What Were You Thinking?': How Women Navigate Experiences of HIV-related Stigma in Medical Settings during Pregnancy and Birth." *Social Work in Health Care*, vol. 55, no. 2, 2016, pp. 161-79.

Gupton, A., M. Heaman, and L. W. K. Cheung. "Complicated and Uncomplicated Pregnancies: Women's Perception of Risk." *Journal of Obstetric, Gynecologic, & Neonatal Nursing*, vol. 30, no. 2, 2001, pp. 192-201.

Hall, Wendy A., Jocelyn Tomkinson, and Michael C. Klein. "Canadian Care Providers' and Pregnant Women's Approaches to Managing Birth: Minimizing Risk While Maximizing Integrity." *Qualitative Health Research*, vol. 22, no. 5, 2012, pp. 575-86.

Haan, Irene de, and Marie Connolly. "Anticipating Risk: Predictive Risk Modelling as a Signal of Adversity." *Beyond the Risk Paradigm in Child Protection*, edited by Marie Connolly, Palgrave MacMillan, 2017, pp. 29-45.

Hausman, Bernice. "Risky Business: Framing Childbirth in Hospital Settings." *Journal of Medical Humanities*, vol. 26, no. 1, 2005, pp. 23-38.

Hausman, Bernice. *Viral Mothers: Breastfeeding in the Age of HIV/AIDS.* The University of Michigan Press, 2011.

Ion, Allyson, et al. "Perinatal Care Experiences of Mothers Living with HIV in Ontario, Canada." *Journal of HIV/AIDS & Social Services*, vol. 15, no. 2, 2016, pp. 180-201.

Ion, Allyson, et al. "The Principle of 3Voices in Child Welfare: Bringing Service Users, Service Providers, and Academics Together." Oral Presentation at the Canadian Association of Social Work Education Conference, Vancouver, British Columbia, 6 June 2019.

Rothman, Barbara Katz. "Pregnancy, Birth, and Risk: An Introduction." *Health, Risk, & Society*, vol. 16, no. 1, 2014, pp. 1-6.

Loutfy, Mona R., et al. "Fertility Desires and Intentions of HIV-positive Women of Reproductive Age in Ontario, Canada: A Cross-Sectional Study." *PLoS One*, vol. 4, no. 12, 2009, p. e7925.

MacKinnon, Karen, and Marjorie McIntyre. "From Braxton Hicks to Preterm Labour: The Constitution of Risk in Pregnancy." *Canadian Journal of Nursing Research Archive*, vol. 38, no. 2, 2006, pp. 56-72.

McCoy, Liza. "Keeping the Institution in View: Working with Interview Accounts of Everyday Experience." *Institutional Ethnography as Practice*, edited by Dorothy E. Smith, Rowman & Littlefield, 2006, pp. 109-126.

Milton Keynes Safeguarding Children Board. "1.4.12 HIV and Blood Borne Viruses." *Milton Keynes Safeguarding Children Board Procedures Manual*, 2020, mkscb.procedures.org.uk/ykyyqz/assessing-need-and-providing-help/hiv-and-blood-borne-viruses. Accessed 3 June 2022.

Money, Deborah, et al. "Guidelines for the Care of Pregnant Women Living with HIV and Interventions to Reduce Perinatal Transmission: Executive Summary." *Journal of Obstetrics and Gynaecology Canada*, vol. 36, no. 8, 2014, pp. 721-34.

Ontario Association of Children's Aid Societies (OACAS). *Ontario Child Welfare Eligibility Spectrum*, 2016, www.oacas.org/publications-and-newsroom/professional-resources/eligibility-spectrum/. Accessed 3

June 2022.

Parker, Richard, and Peter Aggleton. "HIV and AIDS-Related Stigma and Discrimination: A Conceptual Framework and Implications for Action." *Social Science & Medicine*, vol. 57, no. 1, 2003, pp. 13-24.

Parton, Nigel. "Concerns about Risk as a Major Driver of Professional Knowledge." *Beyond the Risk Paradigm in Child Protection*, edited by Marie Connolly, Palgrave MacMillan, 2017, pp. 3-14.

Raphael, Dennis. "Social Determinants of Health: Present Status, Unanswered Questions, and Future Directions." *International Journal of Health Services*, vol. 36, no. 4, 2006, pp. 651-77.

Samji, Hasina, et al. "Closing the Gap: Increases in Life Expectancy among Treated HIV-Positive individuals in the United States and Canada." *PLoS One*, vol. 8, no. 12, 2013, p. e81355.

Shlonsky, Aron, and Robyn Mildon. "Assessment and Decision Making to Improve Outcomes in Child Protection." *Beyond the Risk Paradigm in Child Protection*, edited by Marie Connolly, Palgrave MacMillan, 2017, pp. 111-29.

Sinding, Christina. "Using Institutional Ethnography to Understand the Production of Health Care Disparities." *Qualitative Health Research*, vol. 20, no. 12, 2010, pp. 1656-63.

Smith, Dorothy. "'K Is Mentally Ill': The Anatomy of a Factual Account." *Sociology*, vol. 12, no. 1, 1978, pp. 23-53.

Smith, Dorothy. *Institutional Ethnography: A Sociology for People*. Lanham, Altamira, 2005.

Smith, Dorothy. *The Conceptual Practices of Power: A Feminist Sociology of Knowledge*. University of Toronto Press, 1990.

Smith, Dorothy. *The Everyday World as Problematic: A Feminist Sociology*. Northeastern University Press, 1987.

Smith, Dorothy. *Writing the Social: Critique, Theory, and Investigations*. Toronto, University of Toronto Press, 1999.

Smith, George W. "Political Activist as Ethnographer." *Social Problems*, vol. 37, no. 4, 1990, pp. 629-48.

Teijlingen, Edwin van. "A Critical Analysis of the Medical Model as Used in the Study of Pregnancy and Childbirth." *Sociological Research Online*, vol. 10, no. 2, 2005, pp. 63-77.

Turner, S. M. "Mapping Institutions as Work and Texts." *Institutional Ethnography as Practice*, edited by Dorothy E. Smith, Rowman & Littlefield Publishers Inc., 2006, pp. 139-62.

Vanier Institute of the Family (Vanier). "In Context: Understanding Maternity Care in Canada." *Vanier Institute*, 2017, vanierinstitute. ca/context-understanding-maternity-care-canada/. Accessed on 21 Oct. 2018.

UNAIDS. "The Gap Report 2014: Children and Pregnant Women Living with HIV." *UNAIDS*, 2014, www.unaids.org/sites/default/ files/media_asset/09_ChildrenandpregnantwomenlivingwithHIV. pdf. Accessed 3 June 2022.

Warick, Jason. "Sask First Nations Call for End to Practice of 'Birth Alerts.'" *CBC*, 4 Feb. 2020, www.cbc.ca/news/canada/saskatoon/ first-nations-call-for-end-birth-alerts-1.5451236. 3 June 2022.

Weir, Lorna. *Pregnancy, Risk, and Biopolitics: On the Threshold of the Living Subject*. Routledge, 2006.

World Health Organization (WHO). "Guideline: Updates on HIV and Infant Feeding: The Duration of Breastfeeding, and Support from Health Services to Improve Feeding Practices among Mothers Living with HIV." *World Health Organization and the United Nations Children's Fund*, 2016, www.who.int/maternal_child_adolescent/ documents/hiv-infant-feeding-2016/en/. Accessed 3 June 2022.

World Health Organization (WHO). "WHO Recommendations on Antenatal Care for a Positive Pregnancy Experience." *World Health Organization*, www.who.int/reproductivehealth/publications/ maternal_perinatal_health/anc-positive-pregnancy-experience/ en/. Accessed 3 June 2022.

Zadoroznyj, Maria, Cecilia Benoit, and Sarah Berry. "Motherhood, Medicine, & Markets: The Changing Cultural Politics of Postnatal Care Provision." *Sociological Research Online*, vol. 17, no. 3, 2012, pp. 134-44.

Chapter 3

Helping or Hurting? Exploring the Help-Harm Paradox Experienced by Mothers at the Intersection of Child Protection and Healthcare Systems in Ontario

Meredith Berrouard and Brooke Richardson

Introduction

Despite efforts towards antioppressive, strengths-based practice in the field of child protection in recent years, assessing and managing risk remain cornerstones of this work (Brown; Scourfield and Welsh; Wrennall). The outcome of a risk orientation is often punitive surveillance—that is, focused interventions for families that undermine rather than support individuals entangled in complex social, economic, and political contexts (Connolly).

The general risk orientation in child protection practice is made more complex when this system intersects with other powerful structures. Drawing on Foucault's concept of "governmentality," some scholars have highlighted the need to examine the overlap of neoliberal regulatory practices across institutional boundaries (McCorkel; Pollack; Rose). Even though medical and child protection structures frequently overlap, there has been limited research and discussion about how these systems jointly perpetuate risk thinking as well as stigma and harm in the lives of mothers.

This chapter critically explores how existing medical and child protection institutions in Southwestern Ontario position new mothers—particularly those whom medical professionals believe present a risk to their child. The data include interviews conducted with four child protection workers. We begin this chapter by reviewing the theoretical orientation of the project, with particular attention to neoliberalism and risk thinking in child protection practice. We use a feminist lens to gain insight into how risk thinking affects the lived experiences of mothers involved with the child protection and health-care systems. A brief overview of the study's qualitative methodological approach is then provided. The findings reveal several concerning trends from the perspective of child protection workers in relation to mothers whose experiences intersect child protection and health-care systems. These include the emergence of a surveillance/invisibility paradox for mothers, pressure on child protection workers to prioritize professional partnerships over genuinely supporting mothers, child protection workers' concerns about the practice of birth alerts, and age and Indigeneity as default markers of so-called bad mothering by healthcare professionals. Taken together, we discuss these phenomena in relation to an overall help-harm paradox, whereby the greater the need for support ("help") on the part of mothers, the more mothers have to lose ("harm") in relation to the involvement of child protection and medical systems in their lives. We problematize this paradox, which mothers habitually face in their interactions with child protection and medical systems, and conclude with recommendations on how to address the systemic "othering" of mothers in this space.

Theoretical Framework

Neoliberalism and the Erosion of the Social

Neoliberalism can be understood as a governing ideology that prioritizes hyperindividualized responsibility for wellbeing and unfettered markets within the context of unlimited economic growth and globalization (Braedley and Luxton; Dean 63; Rice and Prince). In Canada, neoliberalism took hold in the 1980s when the government began "treating the state like a business" (McKenna 43). Fundamentally, neoliberalism is characterized by a shrinking of the welfare state and an "enfolding of the social realm into the economic" (Pollack and Rossiter 158; Webb).

Neoliberal values and ideals rooted in rugged individualism reinforce Victorian-era discourses related to the "cultural pathology of the poor, and the "valourization" of participation in the labour market (Gillies 81). Related to neoliberalism's pathologizing of the poor is a preoccupation with risk thinking at a hyperindividual level. Neoliberal values perpetuate the surveillance and regulation of individuals, particularly those in more marginalized groups, who are seen as being unable to effectively manage their own lives (Gillies; Rose). Under neoliberalism, need has been reconstructed as "risk", as "a diverse cast of people and issues [have become] known only through the language of risk" (Featherstone, Morris, and White 22). Expert state actors are tasked with assessing the burden or risk these individuals allegedly pose to society (Pollack; Rose). Echoing Foucault's thinking around governmentality, Rianne Mahon describes this feature of neoliberal governance as a "disciplinary apparatus [used] to contain the marginalized and dispossessed" (344). Such an approach dismisses systemic barriers and harms and essentially holds individuals solely and personally responsible for their marginalization.

Unsurprisingly, neoliberal ideals have deeply affected the human and social service realm. As Steve Rogowski states, the "functional objectives" of many human and social service organizations under neoliberalism are to "ration resources, manage risk and police the socially marginalized ... the move [within organizations] has essentially been from therapy to surveillance and control" (102). This is also true of child protection and healthcare systems. Within these systems, notions and worries related to risk, liability, and regulation dictate practice and policy decisions.

Risk and Motherhood

Working in the United Kingdom (UK), Nigel Parton outlines the central tenets of risk thinking. He suggests that risk is: 1) future oriented; 2) focused on negative consequences and outcomes; 3) presented as predictable and calculable and, therefore, a direct result of human (in)action; and 4) deeply connected to the forensic, objective trend in knowledge acquisition (Parton 6). In relation to child protection practice, the first three features of risk place a primary emphasis on situating risk within individuals, often mothers, who are viewed as solely responsible for their own and their children's outcomes in life. The last feature, the entrenchment of risk thinking in objective ways of knowing, also has gendered implications in practice.

In her groundbreaking work *Of Woman Born*, Adrienne Rich speaks to the oppressive and patriarchal nature of the expectations placed upon mothers. She emphasizes two main features of patriarchal motherhood. The first is the notion, emerging in dominant maternal discourse (see Jenney this volume), that mothering is natural to all women and therefore the sole responsibility of biological mothers (Rich). The second is the fact that mothers are assigned the sole responsibility of parenting but are afforded no power to choose the conditions under which they mother (Rich; O'Reilly).

By virtue of being cast as the primary caregiver under this maternal narrative, the lives of women as mothers are more likely to be subjected to and constructed by the views of various social bodies and state institutions whose assessments of mothers centre around their potential risks to children. Such frameworks have little regard for the complex social, political, and economic contexts in which women mother (Krane and Davies; Minaker and Hogeveen; Ruddick). As Debra Jackson and Judy Mannix argue: "As mothers, the behaviour and actions of women are subject to scrutiny in ways that men as fathers are not and these behaviours and actions are often linked to family and child protection in ways that male activities are not" (150). The authors go on to state that concepts "of blame and liability [are] directed at women as mothers from the moment of their infant's conception and continue through the pregnancy and child's life" (Jackson and Mannix 151).

Literature Review

Mothering and the Child Protection System

As several chapters in this volume (see Jenney; Richardson; Badry et al.; Ion; Bakeart) have asserted, existing child protection systems continually hold mothers primarily accountable for the actions, behaviours, health, and wellbeing of their children (McDonald-Harker). Maternal responsibility remains the primary focus of investigation and intervention in many instances (Hooper; Jackson and Mannix; Mc Donald-Harker), which is referred to as "mother-blaming" (Croghan and Miell; Jackson and Mannix).

Cases of domestic violence and child sexual abuse are recurring examples of mother-blaming and the "soft" criminalization that mothers experience within child protection practice (Hooper; Savarese). Child protection discourses and assessments rooted in risk thinking are often less concerned with the causality of the abuse and more with maternal responsibility during and following the abuse (Hooper; McDonald-Harker). This deeply gendered failure to protect discourse shifts crucial attention away from the inappropriate behaviour of the true (typically male) perpetrator of the abuse and the structural inequalities that often confine women's options in these situations.

Birth alert documentation is another gendered mechanism of risk thinking and surveillance, which places the burden of blame and responsibility predominantly on women. Although birth alerts have been discontinued in the Canadian provinces of Ontario, British Columbia, and Manitoba (after data collection for this study was completed), they remain in use in other provinces. A birth alert is a formal document sent from child protection officials to healthcare agencies asking medical practitioners to notify the local CAS if they encounter the mother named on the alert. Birth alerts are typically completed when a child protection agency learns that a woman considered high risk is pregnant, as a means of ensuring immediate follow up upon the birth of the baby. In this way, birth alerts fundamentally serve to criminalize and regulate women as mothers before they have even had a chance to mother.

Mothering and the Healthcare System

Similar to the process of mother-blaming within the field of child protection, the health behaviours discourse within medical systems is another potentially harmful and stigmatizing concept that places the burden of risk to children predominantly on mothers. According to this discourse, poor health and disability are the result of poor decision making, whereas good health is purely a matter of individual agency and control (Reid and Tom).

This discourse plays out in the lives of mothers in relation to how often they interact with the healthcare system in regard to their children's needs. Again, because of patriarchal maternalist ideals, mothers enter into regular and recurrent contact with healthcare providers much more so than fathers (Reid and Tom). Throughout their interactions with the healthcare system, mothers encounter discourses that are not only stigmatizing but also "deeply misogynistic" and embedded in biomedical ideologies "entrenched in male dominated [notions]" of health, functioning, and childrearing (Jackson and Mannix 154; Young). Jackson and Mannix found that although it was the health needs of their child that brought mothers to the hospital, mothers themselves repeatedly felt judged by nursing staff. Many felt that nurses were assessing their "perceived rationality, intelligence and whether or not they [appeared] sensible" (Jackson and Mannix 156). The rampant blaming, stigmatization, and risk assessment of women as mothers in the context of their interactions with the healthcare system begins during pregnancy, setting a standard of good mothering even prior to a child's birth (Burton-Jeangros; see Ion this volume).

The Paradoxical Nature of Service Involvement

Feelings of judgment on the part of mothers are perhaps most pronounced for those involved with the criminal justice system. Shoshana Pollack emphasizes how despite almost constant surveillance, these women are essentially made invisible by virtue of being labelled and assessed based only on the opinions of service providers (Pollack; see Hawthorne and Richardson this volume). Describing this surveillance-invisibility paradox, Pollack states as follows:

> Women in this study pointed out that the correctional perspectives and categories through which their behaviour was evaluated allowed little space for the actualities of their experience. Somewhat paradoxically then, the intense scrutiny and surveillance to which criminalized women are subjected— the very visibility of their lives—actually rendered them invisible. (1270)

This surveillance-invisibility paradox is similarly embedded in the governance, documentation, practices, and policies of the child protection and healthcare systems in Canada. There is a significant focus on surveillance and compliance for mothers involved with the healthcare and child protection systems, with less and less space for recognizing the complex contexts and experiences of these women. Within these systems, standardized risk and liability-focused mechanisms flourish (Bolton; Connell 216; Schram and Silverman).

As discussed in the introduction to this anthology, neoliberal discourses and values related to economic efficiency, quality assurance, standardization, and accountability increasingly embrace a tick-box approach to assessing families that allows little to no room for the narratives of mothers or frontline social workers. Not only does such practice result in the deskilling and burnout of child protection workers, it sets mothers up to be viewed primarily through a risk lens. Such approaches are understood to alienate and dehumanize individuals, effectively casting them as "a collection of risk factors to be managed" (Brown 355; Gillies; Pollack).

Thus, while service users, particularly mothers, involved with both the child protection and healthcare systems face heightened scrutiny and regulation, their own voices and opinions—"the actualities of their experience" (Pollack 1270)—are paradoxically made absent from practice decisions and documentation via increasingly standardized and regulated neoliberal approaches to practice within these systems

"Layering of Stigma": Age and Indigeneity

Young and/or Indigenous mothers are particularly vulnerable to the profoundly oppressive and stigmatizing risk and deviancy discourses that exist within child protection and healthcare systems. Within state institutions and society at large, young and/or Indigenous motherhood are socially constructed and widely accepted as automatically existing as counter to dominant Western motherhood ideals. Essentially, being young and being Indigenous are treated as "objective" risk factors, and women who embody these identities are immediately "othered" mothers (see Choate and Lindstrom; Bekaert, this volume).

Existing literature speaks to how medical professionals commonly judge young mothers as problematic and immoral and as bodies that "went out of control and that demonstrated sexually deviant behaviour" (Greene 125). Young mothers are frequently regarded as being a detriment to their infants' care and wellbeing purely because of their age. Once "othered," they are often forced outside of the boundaries of typical care within state institutions (Breheny; Greene; McDermott and Graham).

Within the Canadian context, colonial images and stereotypes of Indigenous women and mothers as being immoral, irresponsible, and neglectful have resulted in the "inferiorization of Indigenous mothering" (Browne, "Discourses" 67; Cull; Gosselin; Mzinegiizhigo-Kwe Bedard; see Choate and Lindstrom this volume). Neoliberal risk discourses and colonial notions of what constitutes good mothering continue to inform Canadian child protection practice and policy. Consequently, in Canada, Indigenous children and youth currently account for over 50 per cent of children in state care, whereas they make up less than 8 per cent of the population (Statistics Canada).

Racist and colonial stereotypes regarding Indigenous women continue to inform not only the general Canadian consciousness but the views of medical professionals as well. Annette Browne observes that healthcare in Canada continues to "unfold against a backdrop of colonial relations" ("Clinical Encounters" 2169) and that harmful colonizing beliefs on the part of medical professionals perpetuate the violence experienced by Indigenous women within healthcare contexts. Judy Mill et al. echo this in their argument that being Indigenous is in itself a stigmatizing condition that results in Indigenous individuals experiencing "a layering of stigma" within the medical system (1470).

Methodology

This chapter emerges out of the first author's Master's of Social Work thesis project. Approved by the Research Ethics Board of McMaster University (Ontario, Canada), the study conducted semistructured interviews with four child protection workers employed at a child protection agency in Southwestern Ontario in 2017. The four interviews ranged in length from thirty to sixty minutes. Questions were open ended. All interviews were recorded and then transcribed verbatim. The data underwent a thematic analysis, whereby common ideas or experiences that emerged across the interviews were manually identified and explored.

It is necessary to acknowledge that this methodological approach does not directly engage with mothers. Instead, the voices and experiences of mothers are mediated through interpretations of child protection workers. We welcome further research that can directly engage with mothers who navigated intersecting child protection and healthcare systems.

Findings and Analysis

Four overarching themes emerged from the data: 1) the surveillance-invisibility paradox; 2) pressure to prioritize professional partnerships over a mother's needs; 3) deep concerns about birth alerts; and 4) intersecting notions of risk based on age and Indigeneity. It is worth stating here that we recognize that for every scenario cited below, there are counter examples of healthcare professionals that fully embrace a collaborative and relational approach to caring for new mothers and who do not conform to dominant conceptualizations of good mothering. Nevertheless, in a few interviews, child protection workers repeatedly speak about observing the problematic treatment of certain mothers within the healthcare system.

Theme One: The Surveillance-Invisibility Paradox

Although participants did not use the term "surveillance-invisibility paradox" explicitly, the interviewees' narratives repeatedly reflected Pollack's use of the term in relation to mothers intersecting healthcare and child protection systems. The heightened surveillance and scrutiny of certain mothers within the hospital setting manifested in reports being made to the local child protection agency, many of which did not pertain to child protection issues. Participants described receiving repeated calls from hospital staff about disagreement around mothering practices or the living situations and experiences of certain women rather than concerns about child maltreatment. At the same time, there appeared to be little to no concern about the subjective experiences as well as complex needs of mothers themselves.

Even more concerning, participants noted how some hospital staff making reports to the Children's Aid Society (CAS) appeared alarmingly hasty, cold, and resistant to mothers' questions or opinions. For example, one participant described a situation in which she received a call from a nurse that was concerned because a mother (who had been discharged herself but whose baby had to remain in the special care nursery for a period of time) had called the hospital at 3:00 a.m. to check in on her baby. The nurse had expressed to this participant social worker that she had not felt this was an appropriate time for this mother to have been calling the hospital. This worker interpreted the same event in a different way; she understood the mother's phone call as a positive effort on this woman's part, as she was actively expressing concern for her baby's wellbeing. The participant further described how instead of trying to encourage this new mother's involvement in, and confidence around, her baby's care, the nurse had also criticized this mother for the type of questions she was asking about her infant. As this participant described: "[The nurse] said to me that this mom's questions were not appropriate, but I thought good for her, good for this mom for trying to learn and be involved. She was a young, new mom trying her best." This is a prototypical example of the surveillance-invisibility paradox that Pollack discusses in that hospital staff were extremely attuned to this mother's behaviour and parenting (in)actions while simultaneously they appeared to criticize and disregard her questions and experience as a new mother trying to do her best.

Another participant provided an example of the surveillance-invisibility paradox when working with a woman who had recently given birth to a baby that also required care in the special care nursery. To visit her infant more frequently, this mother had decided to remain in the hospital overnight, although she had been discharged. Because there were no beds available at the time, she slept in a chair at the hospital. In this case, the nursing team contacted the CAS to express their concern over this mother's decision to sleep overnight at the hospital. This participant described how nursing staff continued to contact her to report several benign behaviours this mother engaged in while visiting her baby at the hospital. Despite this heightened surveillance, however, the experiences of this woman herself were invisible in the nurses' reports.

Participants in this study noted how interactions between medical professionals and these new mothers seemed to cause a sense of isolation and invisibility for many of the women they worked with— particularly first-time moms who were navigating a new and unknown experience. As one participant stated when speaking about a young mom she was working with: "I know it's not [the nurses'] job to social work through issues with families, but don't make it harder by ignoring these moms and not engaging with them really or answering their questions about their babies."

For some mothers, exclusion within the hospital also seemed to arise in a less direct manner. According to participants, several mothers with whom they had worked admitted to feeling uncomfortable and/or nervous asking questions of hospital staff for fear of being judged. As one participant stated: "Moms I've worked with have talked about how uncomfortable they are, how upset they are for feeling like staff are not helpful or are rude. Some of these moms have told me they were afraid to ask questions about their baby because of this."

These narratives highlight how harmful paradoxical dynamics in the context of state service involvement play out for certain mothers. When women do not adhere to the dominant patriarchal, maternal ideals of motherhood, they are habitually cast as a permanent other and are subsequently alienated, surveilled, and ultimately harmed in the healthcare context in a myriad ways (Savarese 89). As one participant noted: "I guess my general perception is they [the nurses] are cold towards the moms I've worked with, and they're very structured. Just go in, do what they need to do and leave, no talking, no helping, no answering any questions really. But then they are quick to approach or call [CAS] to report everything they think this mom is doing wrong."

These negative hospital experiences have the potential to result in profound and lasting harm for mothers by establishing a baseline of fear in seeking out healthcare services in the future for themselves or their child.

Theme Two: Prioritizing Professional Partnerships over Mothers' Needs

There was a general concern expressed by participants that any type of complaint or effort to address the structural biases they encountered within the healthcare system would not be well received at the administrative level of the child protection agency, even in cases when direct supervisors were in agreement with the participants' concerns. When asked what they could do to address their concerns regarding hospital staff members' behaviour towards some new mothers, a number of the participants expressed worry about potentially damaging relationships with hospital staff and/or disrupting the larger partnership between their agency and the local healthcare system. Although the participants were clear that they felt the issues described above need to be remedied, the possibility of placing stress on the working relationship between their agency and the local healthcare system was something that they wanted to avoid in order to preserve their own professional identity and safety. As one participant stated:

> I don't know if staff [concerns and/or experiences] would be supported over [organizational] partnerships. Because collaboration and working collaboratively is an agency focus, and so if you are pushing back against another community partner, I don't know if that's going to be positively received.... People may not know how to approach these difficult conversations, so they just don't do it. And then they're worried again—are they going to be supported ... if they do bring these issues up with nurses and other hospital staff?"

Interestingly, one participant spoke of the authority of the medical system and how at times even she felt overtly intimidated: "Hospital staff are hospital staff. They're on a different pedestal sometimes.... I probably wouldn't bring up any issues directly [with medical professionals] because I would be too scared of backlash. We have to work with these people. I will come across them again, so I wouldn't take this on myself. The agency could and should though."

As this participant astutely asserts, addressing biases on the part of medical teams cannot be left solely to the individual child protection workers but must be taken on at the system level. Through the interviews, it became clear that participants sometimes felt unsupported by management within their agency to take on what they see as problematic behaviours on the part of medical staff. This speaks to the immense power afforded those working in medical contexts. Just as new mothers' experiences were undermined by healthcare staff, child protection workers appeared to feel trepidation in their interactions with medical professionals. These problematic dynamics perpetuate the stigmatizing processes at play within and between these systems, as they ultimately serve to protect the interests of powerful service providers at the expense of mothers entrenched in extremely complex circumstances.

Theme Three: Concerns about the Institutionalized Practice of Birth Alerts

A key structural practice that emerged in relation to the harmful intersection of medical and child protection systems was birth alerts. There was a general sentiment from all participants in this study that birth alerts are problematic in that they appear to automatically set mothers up to be viewed negatively by hospital staff. One participant described birth alerts as "frustrating" and explained as follows: "There's the child protection piece of me that says for sure we need these when there's a solid, safety, and child protection reason, but then another piece of me knows how staff will judge families when an alert is sent out." This participant felt that the birth alert documents, by virtue of the information asked for, are "very judgmental and forensic." Another participant referred to birth alerts as "a necessary evil" and went on to state: "If we've sent a birth alert, [hospital staff] have already decided how things are going to go down it seems.... I don't think it's fair.... They've already made judgements about the family and about what child welfare should be doing just based on the alert."

These narratives expose the problematic nature of this documentation as well as concerns around how birth alerts are interpreted by hospital staff. Our analysis of participant narratives positions birth alerts as an institutionalized, oppressive, textual representation of a state sanctioned control mechanism between the child protection and medical systems. Participants' narratives suggest that birth alerts increase the likelihood that mothers will face intensified scrutiny and alienation in the hospital setting—almost to the point of inevitability. All of the participants acknowledged how this documentation prompts dynamics of judgement, exclusion, and harm within the hospital setting, before a woman has even attended to give birth. Again, it also helps to explain why some mothers may avoid state systems—medical, social, or otherwise—altogether.

Theme Four: Intersectionality in Relation to Age and Indigeneity

A theme that arose in each of the participant interviews had to do with intersectional or overlapping stigmas, particularly in relation to age and/or Indigeneity. It was participants' general impression that young mothers appeared to be regarded by hospital staff as being detrimental to their infants' care and wellbeing solely because of their age (see Bekaert's insights in this volume). Consequently, they were more apt to experience the surveillance-invisibility paradox in comparison to mothers who were older and, thus, regarded as more closely adhering to dominant ideals of good mothering.

Two participants described calls received from hospital staff where the expressed concern was solely related to a new mother's young age. As one participant stated: "Some staff when they call in, maybe because of their values, they look at a young mom automatically as a concern, and this isn't necessarily in and of itself a concern, but staff often see young age immediately as a child protection issue." Three of the participants felt that being a young mother automatically resulted in poorer treatment by hospital staff. As one worker described: "Hospital staff don't teach the younger moms.... They seem quite hard on them and just brush them off." Similarly, another participant stated: "The younger the mom, the more judgement there is from staff it seems. I worked with one mom who was quite young, and she had lice, and was having trouble breastfeeding so she was looked down upon almost right away."

Two participants in this study worked exclusively with Indigenous families. These participants were clear in naming colonialism and racism as a source of judgment and poor treatment by hospital staff. One participant spoke of a situation with a new mother who was voluntarily working with the child protection agency: "No matter what this mom did, the hospital would call me with a concern."

This participant attributed these constant reports of nonchild protection issues regarding this Indigenous mother to overt racist attitudes and stereotypes among hospital staff: "I strongly believe that some of these nonconcerns that are reported are coming from racism. I would be so bold as to say that ... some of this is from racism and colonialism that we've sort of bumped up against."

Another participant gave a startling example of what she felt were blatant racist stereotypes when a nurse informed her that she asks that any women who identify as Indigenous to complete urine drug tests upon admission to the hospital. According to this participant, the nurse justified this practice by explaining that this test would help the hospital differentiate between substances administered during a woman's hospital stay (i.e., legitimate drugs given by medical professionals) and those present prior to medical intervention (i.e., illegitimate substances). It was the understanding of this worker that this was this nurse's practice only when women identified as Indigenous.

It is significant to note that only the participants working at the Indigenous agency identified Indigenous identity as being stigmatizing for mothers within the healthcare system. Although our sample is small, further study is needed to determine if there is a potential lack of awareness on the part of some child protection workers around how race functions as a complex intersection in the lives and experiences of certain mothers and how state systems often perpetuate this.

Discussion: A Help-Harm Paradox

The findings reveal that what we conceptualize as a help-harm paradox operating within the lives and experiences of mothers encountering both child protection and medical systems. Child protection workers observed that the more mothers were identified as at risk, the more harm rather than help or support they experienced. By virtue of the regulatory and risk-focused mechanisms operating within state institutions, certain mothers are not only surveilled more and alienated from decision-making regarding the care of their children, they were harmed in the context of what are supposed to be supportive, care-based relationships. They were made to feel unimportant, inadequate, and invisible by healthcare professionals, who repeatedly turned to child protection authorities in circumstances where there were not child protection concerns.

The birth alert process, which was still in existence in Ontario when this research was conducted, led to pre-emptive judgmental, punitive, and invasive interventions that did not recognize the experiences, strengths, and general humanity of new mothers. Based on the narratives of participants, marginalized mothers, particularly young and/or Indigenous mothers, have good reason to avoid seeking help or support from medical and child protection systems: ageism, racism and colonialism continue to drive child protection referrals and actions. In cases where participants observed overt racism on the part of medical professionals, they felt that they had little agency and/or support to challenge these behaviours due to systemic power imbalances between child protection and medical professionals.

Child protection workers themselves are caught up in this help-harm paradox. Participants, all of whom work within the confines of a technocratic child protection systems, felt their professional allegiance to institutional partners within the medical system was often a bigger priority for their agency than supporting mothers navigating extremely complex circumstances. Child protection professionals were required to follow up on referrals made by medical staff even when their own professional ethics and judgment would suggest there was no need for concern. Considered together, these phenomena speak to the power binary that child protection workers must navigate: they are extremely powerful in their relations with families but often powerless within the systems they work. It is within this space that professionals must manoeuvre the complexities of maximizing help and reducing harm, which is an extremely complex (if not futile) task, given that child protection practice remains situated predominantly in a risk paradigm.

Limitations, Future Directions, and Recommendations

The main limitation of this study is that it did not engage the direct voices of mothers. Because of this, our findings are limited to perceptions of child protection workers working with mothers. We enthusiastically encourage further research that engages directly with women who have mothered at the intersections of the child protection and medical systems. Their voices and experiences will offer insights and nuances we simply cannot provide here.

In terms of future research and practice directions, our study indicates that there is a need for improved cooperation and communication between medical and child protection professionals. Providing opportunities for these professionals to collaborate and learn from one another outside of imminent crisis situations could be enormously helpful for all: healthcare and child protection workers as well as mothers, children and families. At a rudimentary level, this research has also revealed that there is still much work to be done in terms of embracing antioppressive, antiracist, and decolonizing practices and policies within and between the child protection and healthcare systems. We propose the following recommendations in an effort to begin mitigating harm of these institutions in the lives of mothers deemed "at risk".

1. Joint, Ongoing Education between Child Protection and Healthcare Staff

A good starting point would be for medical and child protection professionals to actively collaborate in a space where inequitable power relations can be acknowledged and an antioppressive, decolonizing, and ethical care lens can be explored. Professionals who frequently work together must have the opportunity to continuously build trusting, respectful relationships. Ongoing relationship building between these individuals and systems will help build trust and mitigate misunderstandings of the roles of different professionals while also addressing inequitable power relations between professionals.

2. Discontinuation of the birth alert system across Canada

We agree with the decision across most Canadian provinces to discontinue birth alert practices. Birth alerts are an inherent shortcut in practice that perpetuate colonizing and harmful risk-focused work within the child protection and healthcare systems. We are heartened that citizens and policymakers alike appear to be addressing this issue but troubled that birth alerts are still occurring in some Canadian jurisdictions.

3. Less Reliance on Standardized Risk-Focused Assessments

We call on the ministries that oversee the provincial child protection agencies to consider letting go of the colonial, neoliberal, risk-focused, and cumbersome and standardized assessment documentation. As it currently stands, this documentation is comprised primarily of tick-box questions that do not accurately capture the nuances and complexities of frontline practice or the lives of mothers. This type of standardized documentation deskills child protection workers and hyperindividualizes risk by ignoring systemic barriers and diminishing clients to "a collection of risk factors to be managed" (Brown 355). In their critique of the overwhelming administrative tasks associated with child protection work in the UK, Brid Featherstone et al. state the following: "From the perspective of the workers, the system constraints were devastating. Eighty-six percent of their time was spent on system driven tasks with only fourteen percent in direct contact, but even that percentage was problematic with dialogue dictated by the [standardized] forms and their need for data" (34). As these authors point out, child protection work is dominated by standardized documentation and the timelines associated with this (Featherstone et al.). Consequently, "... workers [do] not have the time to build the kinds of relationships that could support thoughtful assessments of risk", or that allow for deeper and more preventative work to be done with families. The considerable resources that go into completing the current standardized documentation could be much better used to support more time for child protection workers to build meaningful, care- and strengths-based relationships with mothers and families.

4. Including the Voices of Mothers and Child Protection Professionals in the Process of Reforming Child Protection Practice

Genuinely including the narratives and experiential knowledge of child protection workers and mothers is a vital next step in addressing the limitations of the current child protection system and other systems. Presently, there is an overreliance on the opinions and decisions of management, politicians, researchers, and state actors, who are removed from the realities of frontline practice. Addressing this void is critical in dislodging the marginalizing, colonizing, and patriarchal processes that intersect and flourish between these systems. For example, a task force comprised of child protection professionals and mothers could go a long way to resolving the help-harm paradox described above.

Along these lines, there is some inspiring work currently being done by First Voice Advocates in Ontario—a group of youth and former youth who are or have been in state care. Through establishing the Ontario Children's Advancement Coalition, this group has managed to get a seat at the policy table and is actively working with the provincial Ontario government to reform child protection practices in a way that addresses the needs and experiences of youth in care.

Conclusion

The child protection system, and people within it, are entangled in incredibly complex power dynamics related to state authority, surveillance, and privilege. Child protection practice in Ontario continues to emphasize risk and allow for "the imposition of standards of privilege in judging the adequacy of mothering done by those without privilege" (Mandell 244). This dynamic is intensified when the child protection system is encountered alongside other extremely powerful state institutions—in the case of this study, the healthcare system. The mothers whom child protection workers are theoretically there to support become entangled in a help-harm paradox, whereby the greater the need (which is defined as risk), the greater the potential for harm.

The unquestioned application of patriarchal, maternal ideals of motherhood alongside entrenched neoliberal risk-based processes within health and social services contribute to the continued oppression that certain mothers endure in their joint involvement with child protection and medical systems. The recommendations offered above outline concrete ways that the child protection and healthcare systems within Canada can begin to work to mitigate the harm that often occurs for certain mothers under the guise of support within these institutions. If this is to be accomplished in any meaningful and genuinely transformative manner, the voices and experiences of mothers and child protection workers must be foregrounded and prioritized over protecting professional partnerships. The work of First Voice Advocates in Ontario inspires an optimism that this is possible.

Works Cited

Bolton, Sharon. "'Making up Managers': The Case of NHS Nurses." *Work, Employment and Society*, vol. 19, no. 1, 2005, pp. 5-23.

Braedley, Susan, and Meg Luxton. *Neoliberalism and Everyday Life.* McGill-Queens University Press, 2010.

Breheny, Mary, and Christine Stephens. "Irreconcilable Differences: Health Professionals' Constructions of Adolescence and Motherhood." *Social Science and Medicine*, vol. 64, no. 1, 2007, pp. 112-24.

Brown, Debra. "Working the System: Re-Thinking the Institutionally Organized Role of Mothers and the Reduction of 'Risk' in Child Protection Work." *Social Problems*, vol. 53, no. 3, 2006, pp. 357-71.

Browne, Annette. "Clinical Encounters between Nurses and First Nations Women in a Western Canadian Hospital." *Social Science and Medicine*, vol. 64, 2007, pp. 2165-76.

Browne, Annette. "Discourses Influencing Nurses' Perceptions of First Nations Patients." *Canadian Journal of Nursing Research*, vol. 37, no. 4, 2005, pp. 62-87.

Burton-Jeangros, Claudine. "Surveillance of Risks in Everyday Life: The Agency of Pregnant Women and its Implications." *Social Theory and Health*, vol. 9, no. 4, 2001, pp. 419-36.

Dean, Hartley. *Short Introductions: Social Policy*. Polity Press, 2019.

Croghan, Rosaleen, and Dorothy Miell. "Strategies of Resistance: 'Bad' Mothers Dispute the Evidence." *Feminism and Psychology*, vol. 8, no. 4, 1998, pp. 445-65.

Cull, Randi. "Aboriginal Mothering Under the State's Gaze." *"Until Our Hearts are on the Ground": Aboriginal Mothering, Oppression, Resistance and Rebirth*, edited by Jeanette Corbiere Lavell and Dawn Memee Lavell-Harvard, Demeter Press, 2006, pp. 141-56.

Featherstone, Brid, Sue White, and Kate Morris. *Re-Imagining Child Protection: Towards Humane Work with Families*. Policy Press, 2014.

Fiske, Jo-Anne, and Annette Browne. "Aboriginal Citizen, Discredited Medical Subject: Paradoxical Constructions of Aboriginal Women's Subjectivity in Canadian Health Care Policies." *Policy Sciences*, vol. 39, 2006, pp. 91-111.

Gillies, Val. "Meeting Parents' Needs? Discourses of 'Support' and 'Inclusion' in Family Policy." *Critical Social Policy*, vol. 25, no. 1, 2005, pp. 70-90.

Gosselin, Cheryl. "They Let Their Kids Run Wild": The Policing of Aboriginal Mothering in Quebec. *"Until Our Hearts are on the Ground": Aboriginal Mothering, Oppression, Resistance and Rebirth*, edited by Jeanette Corbiere Lavell and Dawn Memee Lavell-Harvard, Demeter Press, 2006, pp. 196-207.

Greene, Saara. "Embodied Exclusion: Young Mothers' Experiences of Exclusion from Formal and Informal Sexual Health Education." *Atlantis*, vol. 32, no. 2, 2008, pp. 124-35.

Hooper, Carol-Ann. "Child Sexual Abuse and the Regulation of Women." *Regulating Womanhood: Historical Essays on Marriage, Motherhood and Sexuality*, edited by Carol Smart, Routledge, 1992, pp. 53-77.

Jackson, Debra, and Judy Mannix. "Giving Voice to the Burden of

Blame: A Feminist Study of Mothers' Experiences of Mother Blaming." *Journal of Nursing Practice*, vol. 10, 2004, pp. 150-58.

Krane, Julia, and Linda Davies. "Mothering and Child Protection Practice: Rethinking Risk Assessment." *Child and Family Social Work*, vol. 5, 2000, pp. 35-45.

Laychuk, Riley. "Brandon Mom 'in Absolute Shock' after 2-Day-Old Infant Apprehended in Hospital by Cfs." *CBC*, 9 Dec. 2020, www.cbc.ca/news/canada/manitoba/brandon-infant-apprehended-1.5833450.

Mahon, Rianne. "Varieties of Liberalism: Canadian Social Policy from the 'Golden Age' to the Present." *Social Policy and Administration*, vol. 42, no. 4, 2008, pp. 342-61.

Mandell, Deena. "Power, Care and Vulnerability: Considering Use of Self in Child Welfare Work." *Journal of Social Work Practice*, vol. 22, no. 2, 2008, pp. 235-48.

McCorkel, Jill. "Embodied Surveillance and the Gendering of Punishment." *Journal of Contemporary Ethnography*, vol. 32, no. 1, 2003, pp. 41-76.

McDermott, Elizabeth, and Hilary Graham. "Resilient Young Mother: Social Inequalities, Late Modernity and the 'Problem' of Teenage Motherhood." *Journal of Youth Studies*, vol. 8, no. 1, 2005, pp. 59-79.

McDonald-Harker, Caroline. "Mothering in the Context of Domestic Abuse and Encounters with Child Protection Services: From Victimized to "Criminalized" Mothers". *Criminalized Mothers, Criminalizing Motherhood*, edited by Joanne Minaker and Bryan Hogeveen, Demeter Press, 2015, pp. 323-54.

Mill, Judy E., et al. "Stigmatization as a Social Control Mechanism for Persons Living with HIV and AIDS." *Qualitative Health Research*, vol. 20, no. 11, 2010, pp. 1469-83.

Minaker, Joanne, and Bryan Hogeveen. "From Criminalizing Mothering to Criminalized Mothers: An Introduction." *Criminalized Mothers, Criminalizing Motherhood*, edited by Joanne Minaker and Bryan Hogeveen, Demeter Press, 2015, pp. 1-24.

Mzinegiizhigo-Kwe Bedard, Renee-Elizabeth. "An Anishinaabe-kwe Ideology on Mothering and Motherhood". *"Until Our Hearts are on the Ground": Aboriginal Mothering, Oppression, Resistance and Rebirth,* edited by Jeanette Corbiere Lavell and Dawn Memee Lavell-Harvard, Demeter Press, 2006, pp. 65-75.

National Inquiry into Missing and Murdered Indigenous Women and Girls. "Reclaiming Power and Place: The Final Report of the National Inquiry Into Missing and Murdered Indigenous Women and Girls." *Missing and Murdered Indigenous Women and Girls*, www.mmiwg-ffada.ca/final-report/. Accessed 3 June 2022.

O'Reilly, Andrea. "Introduction." *From Motherhood to Mothering: The Legacy of Adrienne Rich's Of Woman Born*, edited by Andrea O'Reilly, State University of New York Press, 2004, pp. 1-26.

Parton, Nigel. "Concerns About Risk as a Major Driver of Professional Practice." *Beyond the Risk Paradigm in Child Protection*, edited by Marie Connolly. Palgrave, 2017.

Pollack, Shoshana. "Labeling Clients 'Risky': Social Work and the Neo-Liberal Welfare State." *British Journal of Social Work*, vol. 40, 2010, pp. 1263-78.

Pollack, Shoshana, and Amy Rossiter. "Neoliberalism and the Entrepreneurial Subject: Implications for Feminism and Social Work." *Canadian Social Work Review*, vol. 27, no. 2, 2010, pp. 155-69.

Reid, Colleen, and Allison Tom. "Poor Women's Discourses of Legitimacy, Poverty, and Health." *Gender and Society*, vol. 20, no. 3, 2006, pp. 402-21.

Rich, Adrienne. *Of Woman Born*. W.W. Norton & Company, 1986.

Rogowski, Steve. "From Child Welfare to Child Protection/Safeguarding: A Critical Practitioner's View of Changing Conceptions, Policies and Practice."*Practice*, vol. 27, no. 2, 2015, pp. 97-112.

Rose, Nikolas. "Government and Control." *British Journal of Criminology*, vol. 40, 2000, pp. 321-39.

Ruddick, Sara. *Maternal Thinking: Toward a Politics of Peace*. Beacon Press, 1989.

Savarese, Josephine L. "Theorizing Soft Criminalization in the Child Welfare System: An Analysis of Re S.F." *Criminalized Mothers, Criminalizing Motherhood*, edited by Joanne Minaker and Bryan Hogeveen, Demeter Press, 2015, pp. 88-111.

Scourfield, Jonathan, and I. Welsh. "Risk, Reflexivity and Social

Control on Child Protection: New Times or Same Old Story?" *Critical Social Policy,* vol. 23, no. 3, 2003, pp. 398-420.

Schram, Sanford, and Basha Silverman. "The End of Social Work: Neoliberalizing Social Policy Implementation." *Critical Policy Studies,* vol. 6, no. 2, 2012, pp. 128-45.

Smythe, Elizabeth. "The Violence of the Everyday in Healthcare." *First, Do No Harm: Power, Oppression and Violence in Healthcare,* edited by Nancy Diekelmann, The University of Wisconsin Press, 2002, pp. 164-203.

Statistics Canada. "Reducing the Number of Indigenous Children in Care." *Statistics Canada,* www.sac-isc.gc.ca/eng/1541187352297/15 41187392851. Accessed 3 June 2022.

Webb, Stephen. *Social Work in a Risk Society: Social and Political Perspectives.* Palgrave MacMillan, 2006. Print.

Wrennall, Lynne. "Surveillance and Child Protection: De-Mystifying the Trojan Horse." *Surveillance and Society,* vol. 7, no. 3-4, 2010, pp. 304-24.

Young, Iris Marion. *Throwing Like a Girl and Other Essays in Feminist Philosophy and Social Theory.* Indiana University Press, 1990.

Chapter 4

Is Harm Reduction Safe? Exploring the Tensions between Shelter Staff, Mothers, and Children Working or Living in Shelters

Angela Hovey, Susan Scott, and Lori Chambers

Case Studies

Sally

Sally[1] is a twenty-nine-year-old mother of an eight-year-old boy who fled a difficult six-year relationship by seeking emergency shelter services. Her physically and emotionally abusive partner started injecting morphine during their relationship. Sally also began injecting illicit morphine as a means of coping with this relationship. She and her son arrived at a shelter that used harm reduction approaches such as distributing clean needle kits and the use of legal substances, such as alcohol and medical marijuana,[2] in designated places onsite (although she was not aware of this until after she arrived and learned this from another resident). Sally did continue to inject morphine while staying at the shelter, either in her room or the washroom. She injected while her son was sleeping or while he was at school to ensure that he would not know that she was using drugs. She did not tell the staff that she was injecting morphine during her stay. Sally was fearful that if she disclosed this to staff, they would be required to call the Children's Aid Society (CAS). She understood their legal obligation to report based on her own college training as a personal support worker (she worked in a long-term care facility while staying at the shelter). Sally understood that her substance use could be seen as neglectful of her child and therefore made explicit efforts to manage her use safely for her son. She was not clear about the rules of the shelter regarding women using and having children with them. Nonetheless, she did access the clean needle kits available upon request from shelter staff.

Julia

Julia, a thirty-seven-year-old mother of two, had a very different experience at this same shelter. Her thirteen-year-old daughter remained with her abusive partner, and her older son was living with an aunt while attending college. She was using prescription narcotics as a result of serious injuries sustained through physical assaults by her partner. She had previously used cocaine but was trying to abstain from illicit substance use. Julia was concerned about substance use, the impact of exposure on children, and the practices of the shelter. She witnessed another mother with two babies carelessly using crack. This triggered Julia's childhood trauma and the more recent loss of both of her parents to suicide and overdosing. It also challenged her own recovery from her cocaine addiction. When she brought her concerns about this mother (related to the safety of not only her babies but also other shelter residents and their children) to the shelter staff, her concerns were dismissed. She was told these babies would be exposed like this at home anyways, and if Julia was that concerned, she should call CAS herself. Shelter staff made it clear they were not going to make a call to CAS. This experience caused Julia so much personal trauma and concern that she returned to her abusive relationship rather than remaining in the shelter.

Introduction

The case examples are part of the stories of two mothers who were interviewed in our research study examining residents' experiences living in domestic violence shelters in Ontario, Canada that had implemented harm reduction practices. Examples of harm reduction practices observed in this project included providing safe use kits (e.g., clean needles and safe snorting), sharps disposal containers, room safes as well as allowing consumption of alcohol in their rooms and having no curfews. The first shelter, where we conducted most of the interviews (twenty-five), allowed alcohol consumption in rooms. The other four shelters, where an additional nineteen former residents were interviewed, did not permit the consumption of alcohol or illicit drugs on site. Instead, they embraced various approaches to substance use practices. One of these four other shelters had no tolerance for any substance use by residents, whereas the remaining three shelters differed in their policies and practices about substance use. For example, one shelter offered unsearched secure storage lockers for residents but required staff access to the locker area, whereas another shelter provided in-room lock boxes, which allowed independent access.

Throughout this chapter, we examine the challenges and tensions created when shelters attempt to support all mothers who experience intimate partner violence (IPV)[3]—some of whom do and some of whom do not use substances. These tensions can be exacerbated or ameliorated depending on several factors, including the following: the ways that domestic violence shelters respond to residents' substance use; the degree to which shelter practices prioritize the safety of residents' children; and the shelter's relationship with child welfare (including their approach to addressing IPV exposure and caregiver substance use).

Background on the Relationship between Child Welfare and Women's Shelter

To contextualize this discussion, we consider aspects of the shelter and child welfare movements that contribute to the tensions. During the 1970s and 1980s, feminists advocated that IPV exposure was harmful to children and that women needed safe places to escape this violence (Houston 107). Shelters for women and children in Ontario emerged as part of the feminist movement of the 1970s. The first Ontario shelter opened in 1972 in Toronto (Janovicek 5). Central to this feminist movement was the idea that violence against women was a social rather than an individual problem and therefore required social policy rather than individual solutions. In 1983, the federal government responded by designating the first funding for shelters and transition houses (Janovicek 7). Currently, Ontario has 112 emergency domestic violence shelters, of which ninety-five are funded by and legislated under the Ontario Ministry of Children, Community, and Social Services (MCCSS).

During the 1970s and 1980s, researchers and child welfare systems also began to pay attention to the issues related to children's exposure to IPV. Whereas the feminist social movement perspective considered both women and children as victims of IPV by men, the perspective of child welfare tended to be that mothers and children were separate and that the mothers had a responsibility to protect their children from potential harms in any form, including the male partner's violence against the women (Côté 142). In this way, mothers were, and often still are, held responsible to stop IPV by child welfare workers. It is not uncommon for child welfare workers to provide mothers with clear messages that they must leave their abusers and avoid any contact with abusers, or their children will be apprehended (Hughes et al. 1087). Such responses and interventions by child welfare workers became "an unintended consequence of the initial feminist position [on children's exposure to IPV]" (Houston 107). The real threat that child welfare workers in Ontario may apprehend a child or children of mothers who have experienced IPV but who do not leave their abusive partners remains a significant and ongoing concern for mothers.

These complexities inspired feminist advocates in the late 1990s and 2000s to reposition exposure to IPV as "not necessarily harmful to children," and it was asserted that removing children from their mother was potentially more damaging (Houston 106). However, some child welfare organizations are still inclined to equate IPV exposure with child maltreatment (Henry 84). As feminist-based organizations, many domestic violence shelters interpret child welfare intervention as separate from the needs of mothers and thus avoid aligning themselves "too closely with child protection," as it may negatively affect their relationship with mothers (Potito et al. 373). To complicate matters further for shelter staff, child welfare laws and practices have also evolved. Shelter staff are subject to mandatory reporting requirements of suspected child abuse and neglect (CYFSA s.125[6]).[4] The perceived competing priorities of child welfare and protection versus needs of abused mothers contributes to the tensions between child welfare and IPV services (Mennicke 51).

Substance use by mothers adds another layer of complexity to tensions between domestic violence shelters and child welfare systems. Similar to Sally and Julia, women who experience IPV are more likely to cope with this trauma by using or becoming dependent on substances (Macy et al. 882; Martin et al. 986; Peters et al. 2118; Schumacher and Holt 190). The extent of the problem is potentially underestimated (Schumacher and Holt 190) or unknown (Macy et al. 882). Mothers who use substances and have children in their care are often hesitant to seek shelter from IPV for fear of losing their children to protective services (BCSTH 19, 27; Macy et al. 892-893). Sally did not disclose her substance use to shelter staff because of this fear. Her concern is warranted, since problematic substance use commonly results in reports to child welfare authorities (Simon and Brooks 295). Furthermore, when children are exposed to IPV and their mother is "abusing" substances, child welfare involvement is far more likely (Lawson 37; Victor et al. 307). Co-occurrence of caregiver substance abuse and child exposure to IPV significantly increases the odds of child welfare involvement and the out-of-home placement of children (Lawson 37-38). This hesitance to seek support through the shelter system was further reinforced by the fact that, historically, domestic violence shelters often excluded women from entering shelters if they were noticeably impaired (Baker et al. 434; Martin et al. 990, 993-94; Rothman et al. 4). Sandra Martin et al. found some women were using while in shelter, regardless of the policies, and were simply not open about their substance use (993).

In recognition that all women deserve to be safe, Ontario women's shelters have begun to shift their practices with regard to substance use. Some shelters outside of Canada have also begun to implement practice changes by introducing harm reduction or substance use policies to eliminate past exclusionary practices (Morton et al. 340; Rothman et al. 4). In 2015, MCCSS introduced standards that require Ontario government-funded "shelters provide access to all women seeking shelter services, including women who use substances" (14). MCCSS did not, however, provide guidelines for how services would be provided to women who were using substances, nor did it provide enhanced funding to deal with the challenges such admissions might cause. This has resulted in varied shelter practices regarding substance use.

Despite the lack of direction from MCCSS, some Ontario shelters have started to adopt substance use practices that align with harm reduction philosophy. Harm reduction is an approach to practice, a set of practices, and, most importantly, a philosophy, in which one attempts to reduce risks associated with a potentially harmful behaviour, such as substance misuse (Beirness et al. 2). It is a public health approach intended to mitigate the problematic consequences of behaviours associated with use, such as unprotected sex (Logan and Marlatt 201; Skewes and Gonzalez 1), but does not require those who use substances to cease using (Logan and Marlatt 202; Pauly et al. 22; Ruefli and Rogers 2). Instead, substance use is acknowledged, not judged, and a neutral stance is adopted by staff working with those who use substances (Hawk et al. 2; Pauly 6; Vakharia and Little 66). Harm reduction promotes personal safety (Ruefli and Rogers 6; Vakharia and Little 66). It can also promote collective safety through appropriate disposal practices. Harm reduction encompasses values of respect, collaboration, and personal agency to allow incremental healing and recovery that may or may not include abstinence (Pauly 6; Skewes and Gonzalez 1; Vakharia and Little 66, 68). Influenced by responses to HIV/AIDS, harm reduction was subsequently applied to substance use, and can be further applied to a wide range of areas, including shelter and child welfare work.

Harm reduction approaches aid in increasing compliance with the MCCSS policy by eliminating the shelters' exclusionary practices to better support women with access to shelter. But it is not only women who are housed in domestic violence shelters; children are also present. Children's safety is one of the most commonly cited concerns about implementing harm reduction in such settings (BCSTH 19, 29; Morton et al. 338; OAITH 8; Rothman et al. 6). The safety of children within domestic violence shelters that adopt harm reduction practices is a source of tension. These tensions may arise between both child welfare and shelter staff as well as between using and nonusing mothers, whose children may or may not be with them in the shelter. Yet our findings indicate that it is possible that harm reduction approaches in shelters could mitigate some of these challenges.

Findings

To better appreciate these tensions and the ways harm reduction approaches could mitigate safety concerns for children, the next three sections highlight examples provided by the women we interviewed about their experiences with substance use practices and harm reduction approaches in shelters. The first section, "Shelter Staff," considers ways in which shelter staff supported or interacted with residents from the perspective of the women, including mothers. Major tensions revolved around the duty to report, but other tensions were also present (e.g., talking versus not talking with women about substance use, judging women regarding their parenting, and dealing with women's fears regarding substance use and being reported to child welfare). The second section, "Women Supporting Women," examines how women and mothers supported one another with parenting their children while in shelter, often in ways that increased safety for children while also making choices about their substance use. For women, major tensions also revolved around the duty to report, sometimes including their own duty to report. For this group, other issues also arose, such as the triggering of past trauma and/or substance use, safety of children, and fear of surveillance of parenting. The third section, "Women's Recommendations," draws upon participants' suggestions for shelters to address the tensions described.

Shelter Staff

Frontline staff are the first responders to women and children seeking support and shelter services. They are in the difficult position of enforcing rules or guidelines that residents may not appreciate, including making a call to child welfare authorities if a child in the shelter is considered to be at risk of abuse or harm. The staff's duty to report suspected child abuse and neglect contributes to considerable tensions between residents and staff. Some participants identified situations in which they supported staff calling CAS, while at other times it appeared to be unwarranted from the participants' perspectives. There were also situations in which participants believed staff should have called the CAS and did not, as identified in Julia's story.

Staff are required to implement all policies and practices of the shelter on a day-to-day basis, whether or not they agree with them, while also using their own judgment and interpretation to apply these policies. It became clear that that how staff managed this responsibility could negatively affect not only the tensions between staff and residents but also between staff. By the same reasoning, shelter staff also have the potential to resolve tensions between residents and staff while ensuring positive experiences of residents and safety of children residing in the shelter. Participants noted that some staff members were more capable of responding to conflictual situations arising than other staff members. One example emerged regarding child minding for mothers in the shelter.

Caring for and/or supervising children is considered the mother's responsibility throughout her stay in shelter. One key shelter support for mothers, which is common policy and practice for shelters, is the staff minding children when mothers have appointments to attend. Child minding does not extend to a mother who wants to use substances on or off the property. In these instances, shelter policy prohibits staff from providing childcare. However, some women identified examples of some staff monitoring children despite these policies and procedures. As Milly described:

> I don't have it [marijuana] around my kids, you know what I mean? So I didn't roll it in the room I was sharing with them....
> I would go in the bathroom, open the window, turn on the fan, roll a joint, and then I would go out for a walk, and if my kids were sleeping, I had the staff. They were phenomenal. They worked with me. They would watch my baby monitor while I would sit across the road [to smoke my joint], and if anything happened or my kids got up, they would come to the front and wave me over.... I can still get up every morning with my kids. My cupboards are full of food. My kids got clean clothes on their back. My house is clean. My bills are paid. I am not on the sidewalk jonesing. I am not turning tricks.

Milly's example demonstrated staff flexibility or possible dis-agreement with policy limiting child minding to appointments. The staff member appeared to ensure her children's safety and to support this mother with safe use of an illicit substance off-site.

When a woman arrived at a shelter intoxicated, staff often found ways to support the woman. For example, they may have the woman stay in a quiet room away from the other residents until she is no longer intoxicated. Many participants agreed that staff engaged fairly with women who were using. Sandy, a mother of two young children who did not drink often but decided to drink one day, indicated how she experienced the staff's fair approach: "[The staff] ... were good.... They didn't say anything to me. They just kind of laughed it off like my kids weren't in danger or anything.... I had full control over myself.... [Staff] keep just enough of an eye open and ... they are on guard but ... not do anything really." By responding in this manner, staff were nonjudgmental about her use and were also ensuring that *Sandy* did not feel the need to hide her situation. Staff could see that Sandy was parenting her children reasonably and the children were not at risk of harm. From a harm reduction perspective, staff respected Sandy's choices and acknowledged she had the capacity to be responsible for her children.

When issues related to substance use arose in the shelters and women brought them to the attention of staff, several approaches were described. One approach staff used was to hold a group meeting with all residents to review shelter rules, ensuring that the issue was discussed and resolved in a nonthreatening manner. Another approach was to meet one on one with the woman who was the subject of the issue to discuss and review shelter rules. By responding in this way, staff safeguarded mothers and their children while respecting the women involved in the situation. As Emma indicated: "That's what made it so good.... [Staff] would review the rules about it [the issue] and how to do it in a proper way so that I didn't have to feel worried for my children or for their wellbeing as well. And a lot of people applied/abide by it."

Interestingly, the use of harm reduction approaches also enabled staff to support mothers whose children engaged in substance use while in the shelter. For example, Deb felt well supported by staff when her teenaged daughter consumed alcohol for the first time and over-indulged. Although Deb's daughter was underage, she was at an age when youth typically experiment with alcohol. Staff accepted the daughter back into the shelter upon her return. They talked with both Deb and her daughter about what had happened and what they had learned from the experience, as *Deb* explained:

> They didn't belittle her.... They pretty much were able to counsel me you know; it's okay; she's a teenager; these kinds of things do

happen.... It was actually maybe a good place for the first time for her to drink to be because once I got her cleaned up, I brought her down, and I cuddled her, and we comfort her but she was able to also get counselling right away to deal with her anxiety.

The support staff provided was based on harm reduction principles. They were able to support both Deb and her daughter with respect and nonjudgment while also working to reduce the potential harm for the daughter.

Women Supporting Women

Domestic violence shelters are places of communal living. Many women and children are sharing space while being overwhelmed or traumatized after fleeing violence. The many personalities can clash or be quite supportive of one another. Some mothers were concerned about how their children experienced other women's substance use and/or their own use and attempted to protect their children from potential harm. Their concerns, similar to Julia's, included carelessness with use and loud or aggressive behaviours related to use. Sometimes women worked together to support one another and the children in the shelter.

Outside of formal arrangements with the shelter for child minding around appointments, mothers had little time without their children. At some shelters, some mothers supported one another by watching the other's children. Although this was positive and helpful in many circumstances, there were examples of more concerning situations depending on who was caring for children. Kate described a situation she observed in which a woman who had recently used substances was then minding another mother's child:

> ... she would babysit while the other one went to a meeting for something else.... Inside here, I don't think it would be a problem because the counsellors are here. I don't think anything stupid would happen.... the counsellors know if they are giving a needle [clean needle kit] to this person. That person they are giving the needle to ... should not be babysitting the kids in an hour right?

Both mothers and nonmothers worked together at times to ensure that children were fed when their mothers were unable to prepare food due to substance use. Sometimes situations arose in which the behaviour of a woman under the influence of a substance was problematic and affected others in shared spaces, such as the kitchen. A common scenario described by several women was when someone was intoxicated and attempted to make themselves something to eat in the kitchen when mothers were trying to feed their children and get them ready for school. Mothers' approaches to managing these moments differed. Some would remain and finish feeding their children, whereas others would remove their children from the kitchen and come back once the intoxicated woman was finished. Sara provided an example of how she and other women handled situations with another resident who was using substances and acting in an aggressive and unpredictable manner:

> Well, we would all kind of try to calm her and leave her, like you know, give her space…. No one yelled at her or anything like that. We kind of just, you know, talked to her calmly because … we never knew what she was going to be on [a particular substance]…. When I did get to meet this person when she was sober, she was a very kind person and you realize how tough [a time] a person can have in their life.

In some circumstances, staff were required to intervene by asking the intoxicated woman to finish up and leave the kitchen. Harm reduction approaches in these situations supported the women using but also did not necessarily impede mothers in appropriately caring for their children regardless of the circumstances they faced. In Sara's example, she illustrated this supportive approach but also demonstrated personal compassion and understanding for the challenges of her fellow resident. This was a theme we found in many of our interviews.

Women's Recommendations

Based on their experiences, women expressed ideas about how shelters could improve or might better address some of the issues that arise related to substance use and children's safety. The ideas most salient to the tensions and safety of children included suggestions about physical layout or room assignments, stronger staff adherence to shelter rules, and supports for communicating with children about substance use.

Many women recommended that shelters should alter living arrangements to accommodate children's needs and women's substance use needs. This would include having separate space and designated areas for women who use and areas for mothers with their children in order to provide better safety and support for both using women and children. Some focused more on keeping children separate from those without children. As Maya suggested: "[The shelter has] two apartments. Why can't they just put like families in one and all the singles in the other?"

Other women went so far as to suggest that the shelters that welcome children should not accommodate women who use and do not have children with them. As Tina offered: "If they [women who use substances] have kids I feel like yes [they should remain in shelter] ... If they don't have kids, they might need to go to another place, another shelter." The support for mothers whether using or not was clear as in Tina's message, but it also illustrates the tensions around responding to women who use. Some of these accommodation challenges may not be easily reconciled, but the message of supporting some safer space for children where possible within the shelters is important to consider.

Several participants believed it was important for staff to uphold rules or even involve child welfare when the use was excessive and affected the safe care of children. As described at the start of the chapter, Julia was so concerned about "an excessive amount of drug use" and the careless use behaviour by a mother with her babies that she left the shelter and returned to her abuser. Julia went on to explain that she had returned to the shelter a second time with her daughter. Again, she (along with another mother) had to endure extreme substance use and concerning behaviour by a resident who was actively using. On this occasion, Julia described that she and the other mother were "hiding our daughters in the rooms upstairs and having to listen to it carry on for forty-eight hours." These experiences informed her recommendation:

> I would have liked to have seen that when I came to staff and advised of the drug use with the, the mother using around her babies. I would have liked to have seen that situation dealt with differently. I would have liked there to have been some rules

around that I would have liked to have not been met with staff saying to me well. You call Children's Aid if you think it's something.... If there is going to be a shelter where harm reduction is going to be offered, then there should definitely be some strict guidelines that staff must obey and go by with no exceptions made.

Julia's second stay and previous experience at this shelter reinforced the idea that there must be clear parameters on what constitutes harm reduction and the responsibilities of staff to ensure that it does not become an "anything goes" approach. The importance of this was reiterated by several other participants in our study.

Women also advocated for programs that would support age-appropriate communication with children about substance use and its impacts. Deb explained her thoughts:

Most moms don't want their kids to know they are addicted to drugs or anything.... Maybe the moms and kids need counselling together, so the children understand why mommy is the way mommy is ... you'd have to find a child-based word. You know ... mommy sometimes uses this stuff to help her feel better, but ... this is not right, and mommy is trying to get better.... I just think it would be a good idea to explain to children why their parents are the way they are.

Such education would help children to understand things that they might see in shelter and from their own parents and to possibly prevent substance use by the children themselves in the future.

Despite acknowledging the tensions that harm reduction approaches can intensify in shelters, most women agreed with implementing them. The recommendations women provided, along with the experiences they shared in their interviews, were also supportive of shelters implementing harm reduction approaches. The women seemed to recognize that although the tensions and safety concerns for children in domestic violence shelters supporting the needs of women using substances are complex and challenging, carefully thought-out harm reduction approaches can help to mitigate their safety concerns.

Discussion

Our findings revealed complex tensions between the safety of children within domestic violence shelters and women seeking supportive emergency shelter. Central to this discussion are the relationships between shelter staff, using and nonusing mothers (who have or do not have their children in the shelter), and their direct or tangential relationship with child welfare workers. We identified several tensions; the most relevant to all parties (i.e., the staff, women residents, and children) were the tensions related to the duty to report possible child abuse and neglect to child welfare. Both staff and the women residents are subject to this legal duty. The duty to report also permeated many of the other tensions identified in our interview data, particularly when IPV and substance use issues were present for individual women. These tensions included surveillance of parenting, fear of being reported to child welfare, triggering of past trauma and/or substance use, communal and staff care of children, substance use and parenting capacity, impacts of use on children, and development of understandings of others (e.g., children of mothers who use, women of other women who use, staff aiding others in understanding, staff understanding). In the context of these tensions and safety concerns, the women we interviewed described experiences of how shelter staff can work to ensure children's safety in the shelter and how the women and mothers can support one another to keep children safe. We found it is possible for harm reduction approaches in shelters to mitigate some of these challenges.

Research indicates that when children are exposed to IPV and their mother is abusing substances, the odds of child welfare involvement and out-of-home placement of children are significantly increased (Lawson 37-38). In contrast, our findings suggest that the link between IPV and mothers' substance use does not necessarily warrant intervention by child welfare, especially in the form of apprehension of the child, when the mothers and children are residing in a domestic violence shelter. As described above, many positive and supportive experiences emerged for participants due to actions of shelter staff, other women/mothers in the shelter, and mothers who used substances in safe ways (e.g., Sally's story). The tensions and stakes around whether or not to call CAS appeared to be difficult to navigate for all involved. Although there were times when shelter staff thought a child needed protection and therefore called CAS, we also identified situations in which staff declined to call (e.g., Julia's story), leaving the duty to report suspected abuse or neglect to the resident who witnessed the situation.

The legal duty to report and the child welfare mandate to protect children from harm may place shelter staff in conflict with their feminist perspectives, seeming to require that they engage in surveillance of the residents regarding their parenting, thereby losing their perspectives of equality and solidarity with the women (Côté 139). In addition, it is clear that child welfare works from a different perspective, often from a medical model of practice, and is focused on the child's needs regarding psychosocial growth and development, which may be inconsistent with relationship-based practice among shelter workers (Côté 139).

To maintain their perspectives of their work, the duty to report appears to have positioned women's shelter staff to be able to prioritize supporting the mothers' needs and behaviours associated with IPV over the safety and protection needs of children (Potito et al. 372). This may partially explain the hesitancy of some shelter staff to report in some warranted situations. Although women fear apprehension of their children if they go to a shelter, our research and the literature suggest the fear may be misplaced. Children exposed to IPV with no other maltreatment issues are significantly less likely to be apprehended (Henry 85; Lawson 34) or even opened as cases for other child welfare services (Victor et al. 306). In Ontario, although exposure to IPV represented 45 per cent—the largest category of substantiated child maltreatment investigations (Fallon et al. 35), only approximately 3 per cent of investigations resulted with an out-of-home placement (Fallon et al. 32). Practice has evolved with this awareness for both shelter and child welfare staff, but the level of collaboration and cooperation between the two has remained somewhat problematic, sometimes impacting the levels of trust between the two agencies (Potito et al. 372). When a mother who has experienced IPV misuses substances, it complicates the decisions of shelter staff in terms of how they support mothers, ensure the children's safety, and reconcile their legal duty to report.

Conclusion and Recommendations

The need for greater collaboration between child welfare agencies and domestic violence shelters regarding how to support mothers who use substances and are escaping violence has been acknowledged in the literature (Morton et al. 345; Ogbonnaya et al. 85; Potito et al. 383; Rothman et al. 6). Collaboration would require that the different perspectives of child welfare and shelter workers be examined and bridged. Harm reduction approaches have the potential to provide a bridge while addressing the perspectives of shelter and child welfare workers and ensuring that children be well. Rather than working to ensure women abstain from substance use and from involvement with their abusive partners, both shelter and child welfare workers could apply harm reduction approaches in their work to enable women to ensure the safety and wellbeing of their children while continuing to use substances and/or remaining with their partners. Understanding that there is a range of responses to IPV among children—including that some children may not be harmed but may be able to act to ensure their own and others' safety in situations of violence—could also be helpful (Overlien and Holt 66). For example, collaboration between child protective services and a domestic violence shelter in Ireland that implemented harm reduction approaches has been important to the success of that shelter in keeping children safe (Morton et al. 345-346). The women we interviewed never used the word "collaboration" nor was this overtly brought up in interviews. However, ideas about implementing programs to support age-appropriate communication with children about parental substance use were put forwards as an opportunity for child welfare, substance use counselling agencies, and shelter program staff to constructively work together. At the same time, several participants advocated for stronger supervision by shelter staff concerning issues related to substance use and the use of child welfare to intervene when a mother's substance use becomes problematic in parenting children.

Child welfare authorities also need to reconsider their perspectives on substance use and parenting in light of the legalization of marijuana in Canada and the development of harm reduction approaches. Can a mother who has fled a violent relationship with her children to a domestic violence shelter and uses substances still be a good mother? Our findings indicate that while there can be issues, harm reduction approaches have the capacity to ensure children are protected and safe. We recognize that there may be some misinterpretation among shelter staff and misunderstanding by residents about the duty to report and when child welfare would likely intervene. However, the adoption of harm reduction principles and practices by shelters could benefit children, mothers, shelter staff, and child welfare officials, with potentially improved services for children and reduced child welfare caseloads.

We recommend that Ontario shelters and child welfare agencies collaborate to a greater extent and that harm reduction approaches embraced across both contexts. Child welfare could provide ongoing education to shelter staff and residents about child welfare, including the duty to report. Furthermore, child welfare should learn more about harm reduction, including from shelter staff, and particularly how it could be implemented to ensure that children are both safe and protected in situations of children's exposure to IPV and substance use, without the need for ongoing child welfare involvement. Ideally, forming collaborative partnerships to provide in-shelter services based on harm reduction philosophy and approaches could keep children safe while respecting mothers who use substances to make responsible decisions about how to ensure their children are safe.

Endnotes

1. The names throughout this chapter are all pseudonyms to represent women interviewed for two research studies conducted in Ontario women's shelters in order to protect their privacy, confidentiality, and anonymity. Both studies were approved by Lakehead University Research Ethics Board in accordance with Canada's Federal Tri-Council Research standards.

2. The study was completed prior to Canada legalizing marijuana on October 17, 2018, but during the period in which medically prescribed marijuana was legal.

3. We use the term "intimate partner violence" (IPV) throughout with the exception of describing shelters. "Domestic violence shelter" is commonly used when referring to emergency shelters for women fleeing from violence.

4. Members of the public also have a duty to report suspected child abuse or neglect.

Works Cited

Baker, Charlene K., et al. "Domestic Violence, Housing Instability, and Homelessness: A Review of Housing Policies and Program Practices for Meeting the Needs of Survivors." *Aggression and Violent Behavior*, vol. 15, 2010, pp. 430-39.

BC Society of Transition Houses (BCSTH). "Reducing Barriers to Support for Women Fleeing Violence: A Toolkit for Supporting Women with Varying Levels of Mental Wellness and Substance Use." *BCSTH*, 2011, bcsth.ca/sites/default/files/publications/BCSTH%20Publication/Women's%20Services/ReducingBarrier Toolkit.pdf.. Accessed 4 June 2022.

Beirness, Douglas J., et al. "Harm Reduction: What's in a Name?" *Canadian Centre on Substance Abuse*, 2008, www.ccsa.ca/sites/default/files/2019-05/ccsa0115302008e.pdf. Accessed 4 June 2022.

Children, Youth and Family Services Act. *Supporting Children, Youth and Families Act, 2017, S.O. 2017, c. 14 - Bill 89. Ontario*, 2017, www.ontario.ca/laws/statute/s17014. Accessed 4 June 2022.

Côté, I. *Les pratiques en mainson d'hébergement pour femmes victims de violence conjugale: 40 ans d'histoire*. Presses de l'Université du Québec, 2018.

Fallon, Barbara, et al. *Ontario Incidence Study of Reported Child Abuse and Neglect-2018 (OIS-2018)*. Child Welfare Research Portal, 2020.

Hawk, Mary, et al. "Harm Reduction Principles for Healthcare Settings." *Harm Reduction Journal*, vol. 14, no. 70, 2017, pp. 1-9.

Henry, Colleen. "Exposure to Domestic Violence as Abuse and Neglect: Constructions of Child Maltreatment in Daily Practice." *Child Abuse & Neglect*, vol. 86, 2018, pp. 79–88,

Houston, Claire. "The Trouble with Feminist Advocacy Around Child Victims of Domestic Violence." *Women's Rights Law Reporter*, vol. 39, no. 2, 2018, pp. 85-121. HeinOnline.

Hughes, Judy, et al. "'They're not My Favourite People': What Mothers Who Have Experienced Intimate Partner Violence Say about Involvement in the Child Protection System." *Children and Youth Services Review*, vol. 33, 2011, pp. 1084-89.

Janovicek, Nancy. *No Place to Go: Local Histories of the Battered Women's Shelter Movement*. University of British Columbia Press, 2007.

Langenderfer-Magruder, Lisa, et al. "Getting Everyone on the Same Page: Child Welfare Workers' Collaboration Challenges on Cases Involving Intimate Partner Violence." *Journal of Family Violence,* vol. 34, 2019, pp. 21-31.

Lawson, Jennifer. "Domestic Violence as Child Maltreatment: Differential Risks and Outcomes Among Cases Referred to Child Welfare Agencies for Domestic Violence Exposure." *Children and Youth Services Review,* vol. 98, 2019, pp. 32-41.

Logan, Diane E., and G. Alan Marlatt. "Harm Reduction Therapy: A Practice-friendly Review of Research." *Journal of Clinical Psychology,* vol. 66, no. 2, 2010, pp. 201-14.

Macy, Rebecca J., et al. "Partner Violence and Substance Abuse Are Intertwined: Women's Perceptions of Violence–Substance Connections." *Violence Against Women,* vol. 19, no. 7, 2013, pp. 881-902.

Martin, Sandra L., et al. "Substance Abuse Issues Among Women in Domestic Violence Programs." *Violence Against Women,* vol. 14, no. 9, 2008, pp. 985-97.

Mennicke, Annelise, et al. "'It's Tricky ...': Intimate Partner Violence Service Providers' Perspectives of Assessments and Referrals by Child Welfare Workers." *Journal of Family Violence,* vol. 34, no. 1, 2019, pp. 47-54.

Morton, Sarah, et al. "Implementing a Harm Reduction Approach to Substance Use in an Intimate Partner Violence Agency: Practice Issues in an Irish Setting." *Partner Abuse,* vol. 6, no. 3, 2015, pp. 337-50.

Ogbonnaya, Ijeoma Nwabuzor, et al. "The Role of Co-occurring Intimate Partner Violence, Alcohol Use, Drug Use, and Depressive Symptoms on Disciplinary Practices of Mothers Involved with Child Welfare." *Child Abuse & Neglect,* vol. 90, 2019, pp. 76-87.

Ontario. Ministry of Children, Community and Social Services. "Violence Against Women Emergency Shelter Standards." *MCCS,* 2015, www.MCCS.gov.on.ca/MCCS/open/vaw/vaw_Manual.aspx. Accessed 4 June 2022.

Ontario Association of Interval & Transition Houses (OAITH). *Harm Reduction in VAW Shelters: Realities of Service.* OAITH, 2013, www. oaith.ca/news/training-news/2014/03/29/oaith-harm-reduction-report/. Accessed 4 June 2022.

Overlien, Carolina, and Stephanie Holt. "Letter to the Editor: Research on Children Experiencing Domestic Violence." *Journal of Family Violence*, vol. 34, 2019, pp. 65-67.

Pauly, Bernadette. "Harm Reduction Through a Social Justice Lens." *International Journal of Drug Policy*, vol. 19, 2008, pp. 4-10.

Pauly, Bernadette, et al. "Turning a Blind Eye: Implementation of Harm Reduction in a Transitional Programme Setting." *Drugs: Education, Prevention and Policy*, vol. 25, no. 1, 2018, pp. 21-30.

Peters, Erica N., et al. "Associations Between Expectancies of Alcohol and Drug Use, Severity of Partner Violence, and Posttraumatic Stress Among Women." *Journal of Interpersonal Violence*, vol. 27, no. 11, 2012, pp. 2108-27.

Potito, Christine, et al. "Domestic Violence and Child Protection: Partnerships and Collaboration." *Australian Social Work*, vol. 62, no. 3, 2009, pp. 369-87.

Rothman, Emily F., et al. "Rhode Island Domestic Violence Shelter Policies, Practices, and Experiences Pertaining to Survivors with Opioid Use Disorder: Results of a Qualitative Study." *Substance Abuse: Research and Treatment*, vol. 12, 2018, pp. 1-6.

Ruefli, Terry, and Susan J. Rogers. "How Do Drug Users Define Their Progress in Harm Reduction Programs? Qualitative Research to Develop User-Generated Outcomes." *Harm Reduction Journal*, vol. 1, no. 8, 2004, pp. 1-13.

Schumacher, Julia A., and Deobrah J. Holt. "Domestic Violence Shelter Residents' Substance Abuse Treatment Needs and Options." *Aggression and Violent Behavior*, vol. 17, 2012, pp. 188-97.

Simon, James D., and Devon Brooks. "Identifying Families with Complex Needs After an Initial Child Abuse Investigation: A Comparison of Demographics and Needs Related to Domestic Violence, Mental Health, and Substance Use." *Child Abuse & Neglect*, vol. 67, 2017, pp. 294-304.

Skewes, Monica, and Vivian M. Gonzalez. "Attitudes Toward Harm Reduction and Abstinence Only Approaches to Alcohol Misuse among Alaskan College Students." *International Journal of Circumpolar Health*, vol. 72, 2013, pp. 1-5.

Vakharia, Sheila P., and Jeannie Little. "Starting Where the Client Is: Harm Reduction Guidelines for Clinical Social Work Practice." *Clinical Social Work Journal,* vol. 45, 2017, pp. 65-76.

Victor, Brian G., et al. "Domestic Violence, Parental Substance Misuse and the Decision to Substantiate Child Maltreatment." *Child Abuse & Neglect,* vol. 79, 2018, pp. 31-41.

Chapter 5

When Theoretical Frameworks Are Not Good Enough: Deconstructing Maternal Discourses in Child Protection Responses to Mothers Experiencing Intimate Partner Violence

Angelique Jenney

Introduction

Intimate partner violence (IPV) is prevalent, affecting almost 30 per cent of women globally, and includes experiences of physical, sexual, and psychological violence, stalking, or coercive control by a former or current intimate partner (WHO). Experiences of IPV have multiple consequences for women, including physical and psychological harm, increased risks of poverty and isolation, and effects upon experiences of mothering in the context of violence. They also face increased scrutiny by child protection authorities. This chapter will frame this discussion by considering the sociohistorical context of discourses around mothering that have framed the current approach of child protection to the issue of mothering in the context of violence.

The Sociohistorical and Political Context of the Maternal Discourse

> Women who deviated visibly from the norms of maternalism, women who worked, drank, yelled, were dirty, remained unmarried—these women were not only considered bad mothers, they were cast outside the boundaries of true womanhood. They were denied sympathy, let alone help.
>
> —Linda Gordon (252-53)

Social work has a long, complicated history in the social control of mothering, particularly in child protection practice. This history began by leveraging the value of the experience of motherhood—the maternalism construct—as an ideology that guided the work of early social reformers, laying the groundwork for what we know as social work practice today (Abrams). Evelyn Nakano Glenn states that mothering "has always been contested terrain" (2), referring to the ways in which mothering, as distinctly gendered, has long been a "social, rather than biological construct" (3). Women throughout history have been defined by their status as mothers (or not). Motherhood as a patriarchal construct has been used to control, legitimate, and oppress women through policies directed at keeping women in, and responsible for, the home (O'Reilly). It is within this patriarchal context that the gendered social work profession was born. At a time when the value of a woman was entirely dependent on her existence as a wife and mother, engaging in social work practice was historically a way for women without children to justify their societal value. This work provided them with not only a legitimate nurturing role but also social acceptance.

In this way, maternalism has ironically became one way of legitimizing the entry of women into paid work as well as public and political life. Believed to be naturally caring and nurturing, women took on leadership roles in the development of social services—first in the philanthropic/voluntary sector and later at a government level as welfare states came into being. In these roles, women were important supporters of institutionally supported caregiving (e.g., creches, children's homes, and orphanages) when mothers needed to work outside the home or could not care for their children for other reasons (e.g., death, illness, and extreme poverty).

Seth Koven and Sonya Michel were the first to refer to a "maternalistic discourse," defined as the ways in which women "transformed motherhood from women's primary private responsibility into public policy" (2). With the establishment of welfare states (rooted in the traditional conceptualization of the nuclear family), social workers came to play a more institutionalized role around the practice of mothering as well as advocating for material supports for motherhood, such as a mother's allowance. However, since these institutions of social welfare were founded on white settler colonialism, they became "instruments through which such racialization toward, and policing of, non-white bodies [were] realized" (Ramsay 252). Social work practice then entered a regulatory framework around motherhood through the establishment of child protection systems, which aimed to identify and protect at-risk children. Today, this regulatory role is personified by the child protection investigator, who is typically qualified as a social worker and registered with a professional college of social workers. In recent years, and largely through existing child protection systems, many argue that the profession has become more focused on the regulation of motherhood (Abramovitz), specifically identifying and intervening with so-called bad mothers (Swift).

Critically Engaging with Maternalism in Social Work Practice

My academic work, as well as my experience as a social worker engaged with women who have experienced IPV, informs this critical deconstruction of maternalism in child protection systems. I assert that maternalism acts as a patriarchal, colonial, and gendered mechanism of social control that contributes to the proliferation of the good mother narrative, inevitably leading to the bifurcation of mothers' needs from those of her children. Matricentric feminism—a theoretical orientation which "understands motherhood to be socially and historically constructed and positions mothering more as a practice than an identity" (O'Reilly 16)—is proposed as one alternative framework through which to inform social work practice with mothers experiencing IPV.

A critical analysis of maternalism however needs to consider that these constructs were developed and maintained within a context of white supremacy. As I write this chapter, I am aware of my own social location and identity as a white, cisgendered female, social worker, and how these very words are a result of my direct engagement with texts and ideologies presented by white settler feminists. In a time when racialized children, particularly Black and Indigenous children, remain overrepresented in child protection services, a critique of the ways in which child protection systems have been created is incomplete without taking into consideration the context of white supremacy and colonialist approaches to this development (Mohamud et al.). Maternalism has also been critiqued as the maternal methods of settler colonialism; in the role of social workers, white women "participate in respectability politics by enforcing the norms of whiteness upon multiply marginalized and colonized communities" (Haley 216). Cindy Blackstock describes "a white noise barrier" that exists in child welfare work, and Carole Zufferey reflects on whiteness not being interrogated as difference and therefore being privileged as the standard. It is within this context that the theorists in this chapter need to be viewed, as "scholarship on the history of social work has largely ignored the role of race and racialization throughout the development of the profession" (Haley 219).

Maternalism and Defining the Good Enough Mother

Mothering and motherhood are social constructions, rooted in early definitions of what constitutes "good-enough mothering." This term—developed by Donald Winnicott through combining the two concepts of the "ordinary devoted mother" and the "good-enough environment" (Johns)—describes the provision of a selfless and nurturing physical and psychological space in which optimal child development takes place. Central to the traditional maternalism construct is the idea that women are generally more empathic and relational than men—furthering the idea that being a good mother is natural to women and should be the primary focus of her identity rather than a practice in which she actively engages with and finds meaning (O'Reilly).

At the same time, maternalism has been used as a tool to achieve the support of the state for the activity of mothering (e.g., a mother's allowance, income splitting, and maternity leave), a sociohistorical and political strategy for advancing the rights of women as mothers (Koven and Michel; Abrams), a tool of oppression (aligned closely with paternalism in terms of power differentials across gender, race, and economic lines) (Michel), and as a theoretical construct and methodology for analyzing the problem of privileged women speaking on behalf of "othered" women (Waaldijk; Plant). Traditional, gendered maternal ideals remain deeply embedded in child protection work today and essentially pathologize mothers that diverge from the maternal ideal.

In her ethnographic research on African refugee settlement in Australia, Georgina Ramsay identifies challenges faced by families experiencing child apprehension and in particular the role of the state in "governing motherhood" (25). She asserts that the assessment of refugee parents and the perception of parenting style are subjective and that cultural, linguistic, and identity remain relatively misunderstood and misaligned in child protection work that is "embedded with a cultural bias of whiteness" (Ramsay 246). She goes on to state that such systems "are instruments through which such racialization toward, and policing of, non-white bodies are realized" (Ramsay 252).

Critically Reflecting on Power Relations Rooted in Maternal Ideals in Practice

It is important for professionals to critically question the theoretical assumptions and history informing contemporary practice (Roberts). In her work examining case records in social work practice, Karen Tice notes how "professional power shaped the interpretation, narration, and representation of social reality and clients' lives" (Tice 9). Implicit, taken-for-granted maternal discourses defining "good" and "bad" mothering may be used by state structures, such as child welfare, to judge and/or regulate mothers' behaviour (DiQuinzio). This results in what Ramsay terms a "paradox of protection," which becomes "a kind of benevolent cruelty," wherein support is "conditional on their subjugation to forms of neoliberal governance." (257)

It is not a coincidence that women dominate social service work, specifically in child protection, and that interventions are over-whelmingly focused on women (Scourfield; Humphreys). Child protection work has always been about the policing of mothering through the evaluation of maternal capacity, which is not an objective process but rather one that involves interpreting maternal behaviour through "prevailing cultural constructions of good enough mothering" (Krane 38).

There is a need for social workers to recognize "their own social locations in relation to mothering" (Krane 36). Although child protection workers face a host of complex challenges, their privileged and powerful position in relation to families needs to be acknowledged. This inevitably influences how they (within the confines of the child protection system itself) conceptualize, and respond to, the mothering of women within a mandated child protection framework. Furthermore, child protection workers need to understand "how maternal subjectivity is affected by women's experiences of violence" (Krane 36). For a worker who has not experienced violence, this can be a difficult subjectivity with which to engage and may result in an overreliance on problematic formulations of victimhood as well as constructs of good mothering.

This is the narrative within child protection practice that activates a continuum of service response and delivery. This narrative determines the level of intrusion in women and children's lives through a coded system. Such issues as substance use and domestic violence directly correspond to different levels of risk based on an objective coding mechanism that flags the area of concern. In the case of domestic violence, the main areas of concern are the impact of exposure to violence on children and the capacity of mothers to parent in the context of abuse.

Mothering in the Context of IPV

Despite the documentation of family violence issues in child protection files since the nineteenth century, it was not formally considered an issue of child maltreatment until the late 1990s (Gordon). Legislative changes and shifting societal attitudes rooted in didactic ideas about child development repositioned a mother's experiences of IPV as a child maltreatment concern. Experiencing violence is now flagged as an indicator of diminished parenting capacity in that mothers are unable to protect their children from harm (witnessing violence). Over the past few decades, the debate within child protection systems involvement in domestic violence cases has been based on whether children's exposure to domestic violence should be considered a form of maltreatment in itself as opposed to an additional risk factor for child maltreatment. Research examining the intersection between childhood exposure to intimate partner violence (CEIPV) and child protection systems found that involvement with the system was largely influenced by whether or not the domestic violence occurs in isolation or with another form of child maltreatment (Black). It seems that Gordon was particularly prescient when she stated, "Concern with family violence has been a weathervane identifying the prevailing winds of anxiety about family life in general" (Gordon 2).

Gordon further describes how society's concerns about the wellbeing of women remain entrenched in gendered roles (e.g., being a good wife and a good mother) and responsibilities (e.g., not exposing yourself or your children to violence). The consistent thread from the nineteenth century to the present is the silence in our data about the role of men who harm (Jenney). Growing awareness of CEIPV resulted in changes to child protection legislation across Canada, which has led to an opportunity for enhanced service provision. Such services include differential response models, which allow for workers to refer families to community support services as opposed to child protection, and specialized IPV teams within child protection offices with specialized skills and training who work in collaboration with local violence against women organizations. This situation has created opportunities for improved community-system collaborations and protocols between sectors (Trocmé; Beeman; Edleson) and increased public awareness that domestic violence is not socially acceptable (Nixon).

Early studies in this area highlighted the negative effects of IPV on mothering (Buchbinder; Casanueva; Ateah; Lapierre). For example, the literautre indicated that pregnant women affected by IPV report "more negative representations of their infants and themselves as mothers" than women who did not experience IPV (Huth-Bocks 79). This literature also noted that mothers are often caring for young children (holding them in their arms or otherwise tending to them) when violence occurs. The impact of trauma on the parent-child relationship —particularly a mother's ability to be emotionally available in order to provide sensitive and responsive care—highlighted capacity issues for women experiencing IPV related to struggles to manage experiences of shame and self-blame (Levendosky and Graham-Bermann). Furthermore, concerns about mothers' abilities not only to recognize danger towards themselves but also to miscalculate those safety concerns that would prevent them from providing the level of emotional safety necessary for optimal child development were raised (Levendosky and Graham-Bermann; Haight).

Research framed in this way has likely fuelled the "failure to protect" discourse accusing mothers of positioning children's needs as secondary to their own (Buchbinder and Eisikovits 362), even as their own narratives explicitly "justified their preferred actions as being for the sake of the children" (Jenney 35). The "failure to protect" rationale has unfortunately led to an unnecessary transformation of the mother-child relationship into a "conflictual one in terms of needs, interests and mutual perceptions" (Buchbinder 364). This rationale fails to understand the needs of mothers who experience IPV and their children as inevitably intertwined. This is certainly cause for concern, particularly when interventions designed to prevent child abuse and neglect have been found to be less successful with mothers who are experiencing domestic violence (Eckenrode). However, this should speak more to the need to provide additional supports rather than increased intrusion and surveillance.

IPV: Shifting from a Focus on Child Outcomes to the Experience of Mothers and Their Children

IPV has consistently been problematized on the grounds that it contributes to deleterious psychological issues and behaviours for children across the lifespan, including anxiety, aggression, as well as poor school performance and social skill development (Holt; Evans, Davies, and DeLillo; Kitzmann). At the same time, it has been widely recognized that some children who experience CEIPV do not demonstrate any adverse effects (Martinez-Torteya; Jaffe). The extent of impact has been linked to children's developmental levels and the context in which such violence occurs (Jenney). More recent research indicates that there may also be racial/ethnic differences in the impacts of CEIPV as well as differential risk factors for child welfare–supervised children and investigation practices, which need to be more fully considered (Costello; King et al.).

Positioning CEIPV as a form of maltreatment has led to ongoing concerns that abused women are being held responsible for violence they cannot control. In this way, many interventions themselves (most of which are intrusive and backed by the coercive powers of the state) are not relevant, appropriate, or supportive (Nixon). More specifically, many of the child protection approaches rely solely on what has been referred to as "the leave ultimatum" (Douglas; Nixon), which stresses termination of the relationship with the abuser as the main ingredient for safety. In reality, evidence has repeatedly shown that risk to a mother and her children often escalates when she leaves an abusive relationship (Jaffe). Without adequate infrastructure to ensure abused mothers and their children's material, physical, and social wellbeing, these interventions themselves may contribute to "collective harms from the overt failure to hold abusers accountable" (Strega 238).

Numerous researchers have identified how the confluence of increased reporting of CEIPV without corresponding institutional supports has created unintended negative consequences for families and communities (Alaggia et al.; Jaffe). In a simple sense, it would be the most helpful (and least harmful) way to ensure every mother who experienced domestic violence and sought support had immediate access to a system that would focus on holding her abusive partner accountable and creating safe living conditions for both women and children in this process. Despite increasing awareness of child protection authorities over the years of the negative effects of CEIPV and the need to hold perpetrators directly accountable, in practice, mothers continue to bear the consequences of these harms.

These patterns in child protection intervention, which are underscored by maternalistic approaches, continue to have a devastating effect on mothers experiencing violence. Although there has been some positive movement in terms of using strengths-based rather than deficit-based language (e.g., being a survivor of trauma or successfully ending an abusive relationship), maternalistic narratives around capacity are still salient even within sectors devoted to working from a feminist standpoint. For example, a study with shelter workers found that workers labelled "residents as ineffective, self-centered, indifferent, abusive, or loveless mothers" while simultaneously excusing such challenges to maternal capacity by attributing those feelings to the experiences of trauma (Peled 1229). Donileen Loseke argues that such definitions lead to "collective representations," wherein the labels given to abused women come to signify the ways in which social services respond to them.

Women who have experienced violence have often found themselves judged as either deserving or undeserving victims by the system, and in this way, good and bad mothering are also defined. This attention to women's parenting in the context of violence has resulted in a wave of research that once again prioritizes mothers over fathers in terms of investigation and intervention. As Simon Lapierre sagely notes, it is important to locate the difficulties women face in these circumstances in a comprehensive understanding of the social organization of mothering and of the high expectations that are placed on women as mothers because these elements influence both women's identities and the conditions in which they perform their mothering (Lapierre 459-60).

The effect that domestic violence has on parenting and children is a well-established area of research that has unfortunately focused on the capacity of mothering within the context of experiencing violence. Maternalistic constructs continue to reinforce mothers as the primary care providers, thereby assuming responsibility for CEIPV rests with them.

Challenging the Assumption That Unprotected Mothers Are Unprotective Mothers

Viewed through the lens of maternalism, the research examining mothering has privileged a narrow view of mothering and contributed to condescension in service provision that is at the heart of the current struggle. Although such initial research was largely deficit based, some researchers have found little to no differences between abused and nonabused women's mothering. Others have focused on the finding that many women, in an attempt to compensate for the violence their children are experiencing, may in fact "mobilize their resources to respond to the violence on behalf of their children" (Levendosky and Graham-Bermann 266), in particular by being more sensitive and responsive to them (Levendosky, Lynch, and Graham-Bermann).

Other researchers have pointed out that women are managing these complex issues despite the burden of the impact of a partner's destructive actions (Levendosky and Graham-Bermann) without the system taking this dynamic into account (Lapierre; Kelleher). Furthermore, when mothers and their children become safe from violence, negative parenting behaviours decrease (Lapierre), which suggests that support for interventions designed to assist women in managing the stress of the abusive partner should be the focus of our efforts (Casanueva).

Eli Buchbinder and Zvi Eisikovits suggest that "research on abused women's motherhood inevitably raises such questions of competing values and loyalties" (359) when findings illustrate mothering in a negative light. However, recognizing how gender inequity itself may influence these findings as well as the components at play (particularly abuser absence from our narratives) is one way of encouraging a more "politically responsible research agenda" (Jenney 38).

Limitations of Existing Research

Research on mothering in the context of violence has been limited by the use of self-reporting measures, retrospective interviews, clinical populations, and small, nonrepresentative samples. Furthermore, there is an inability to distinguish between those who are currently experiencing abuse and those who are not (Levendosky and Graham-Bermann; Haight). Some researchers have criticized the studies in this area as being centred on deficits so that in effect more is known about "these women's depression than their happiness, more about their difficulties as parents than their competencies," which, in turn, influences interventions (Sullivan 55).

This conflicting discourse about women's abilities to recognize (or acknowledge) their own level of risk and, as a result, their children's level of risk makes it difficult for child protection workers to ascertain the true risks involved (Jenney). However, this is an area rife with complexity and child protection workers continue to enact maternalistic approaches when they do not take diverse experiences of motherhood into account.

Intersecting Needs of Mothers and Their Children

> By pitting the interests of the child against the interests of
> mothers rather than seeing them as interdependent, decisions
> are often made that limit women's capacity to mother and
> children's opportunity to be mothered.
>
> —Lorraine Greaves (101)

Maternalism's overreliance on what has been termed "essential
motherhood" emphasizes the best interests of the child approach
(O'Reilly), which ostensibly divides child wellbeing from maternal
wellbeing, even though the two cannot be considered mutually
exclusive. This inherent division of need is deeply problematic for
mothers who are experiencing IPV and engaged with child protection
systems, as their needs and those of their children are actually the
same—safety in the broader familial context and stability in their
relationships with each other. Until the approach to service privileges
the mother-child relationship as the key avenue to intervention, we
will not be able to make the necessary changes in child protection
systems to improve outcomes for families.

Social workers are not the only proponents of the good-enough
mothering paradigm. Mothers who have been involved with child
protection systems also internalize similar societal narratives when
discussing their own expectations of motherhood (Stewart). It is
important to pay attention to the ways in which these shared social
constraints influence the interactions between social workers and
mothers (Sinai-Glazer) while recognizing the potential opportunities
for change.

Child Protection Practice Then and Now: Possibility and Potential

Matricentric feminism is a mother-centred framework that offers a
means of moving away from patriarchal and harmful discourses of
motherhood, such as maternalism, in order to emphasize maternal
wellbeing. It highlights maternal agency as a way to bring about the
required social changes to optimize the health and safety of children in

our society (O'Reilly). Matricentric feminism emphasizes motherhood as a practice rather than an identity, but at the point of child protection involvement, it still falls short of considering the site of the mother-child relationship, rather than the individual child, as the most important point of intervention. When violence has been perpetrated against mothers, it is ultimately perpetrated against the mother-child relationship, and this should be our focus. The real question becomes how interventions can best support mothers in the difficult, complex, and time-intensive work that is necessary for repairing and strengthening relationships with their children after violence has occurred.

Although there has been a significant shift in the ways (and intentions) in which workers practice child protection, the reality is that in child protection, workers are inevitably vested with the authority to investigate allegations and remove children from homes (Waldfogel); therefore, there will always be a stark power differential. Ann Fleck-Henderson has gone so far as to suggest that the child protection worker "who strives to be empowering to a victim of domestic violence is implicitly in a paradoxical position" (337). As most abused women are involved with child protection involuntarily, as the result of an external report, the relationship is established within adversarial, invasive conditions from the outset (Aron). However, it also opens up an opportunity to illustrate that although child protection workers can assert authority over families, they are powerless within what can be considered an oppressive system itself. Berteke Waaldijk considers this contrast as an area for growth and suggests that an approach that recognizes that women on the frontline of child protection may also help implement change while working within the confines of legislation and policy to support clients in the best ways possible. This is echoed by Jennifer Haley who maintains that "White social workers have an ethical responsibility to explicitly confront systems and structures of racism and capitalism for the impact of our actions to be anti-oppressive" (22). Furthermore, in order to foster such change, Blackstock challenges us to collectively bring awareness to "harmful and colonial philosophies and practices that are embedded in social work itself" (36).

As individuals, many of whom are also mothers, child protection workers are not "entirely deaf and blind to their clients' subjectivity"

(Waaldijk 95), and perhaps that is how we recognize that the creation of both the client and social worker occurred simultaneously within this maternalistic discourse. Lara Campbell echoes this sentiment, arguing that mothers "employed a language of maternalism that reflected their own particular needs for adequate wages, less-humiliating methods of welfare provisions and government provision of social welfare to support, nurture and protect the role of motherhood and familial life" (103). In this way, research using the voices of women being investigated by child protection systems has led to more respectful measures of investigation and a move towards more responsive service provision, albeit still within a maternalistic discourse. For example, child protection approaches over the decades have evolved to include policies (e.g., differential response) that have allowed social workers some voice and choice in determining how they would service families—for example, determining whether or not to investigate families versus making a referral to community-based resources (Trocmé; Alaggia et al.)—to more client-centred approaches such as the signs of safety (SoS) model, which is a strength-based approach that works with families and understands them as experts in their own family dynamics (Turnell).

As Emily Keddell points out, when social workers and clients interact, they consider the moral implications of the positions offered them (good or bad). This is part of the attraction of the SoS model, as it "encourages social workers to offer multiple subject positions that give parents a wider range of subjectivities," (73) beyond the good-bad mother dichotomy. This model operationalizes collaboration in ways that differ from traditional maternalistic frameworks in which mothers are invited to contribute to the narrative of their own caregiving and suggest what would be most helpful for their family context. This is accomplished through allowing clients to voice their own strengths and worries about the reason for child protection involvement. Allowing space in which the good mother identity can be expanded to include mothers who are struggling results in lowering the need for maternalistic discourse to promote workers as experts in defining both problems and solutions for families. In this way, social workers may work collaboratively with families as they mutually navigate complex challenges alongside a complex system.

The Absence of Fathers in Child Protection Investigations

> Whether acknowledged or not, fathers who are caring, dangerous, poor, occasional, violent, strong, resourceful and alcoholic and who may have many other qualities, exist in the lives of women and children.
>
> —Leslie Brown et al. 30.

At the root of the current child protection approach is a continued absence of attention to men's use of violence and the understanding of how such violence is itself an attack on the mother-child relationship. The violent behaviour of male partners makes many mothers the key subject of child protection work; women become the focus of child protection interventions for issues over which they have little control. When investigations are broken down into factors that affect the mother-child relationship, the majority of these are directly related to actions by perpetrators of violence (Katz), once again missing the opportunity to intervene directly with the individual responsible. Throughout the investigation process, mothers are judged and made responsible for the behaviours of their partners (Heward-Belle), which serves to contribute to patriarchal expectations of the performance of motherhood (Stewart).

File reviews from social service agencies over the past several decades indicate that women have been repeatedly judged for the actions of their partners, and services have been provided or withheld depending on perceived deservedness (Tice; Gordon; Jenney). Abusive partners are typically absent throughout the process of investigation and intervention (Brown et al.; Thiara). Whether this is because men are difficult to engage with or are simply ignored by social workers is not always clear. It seems evident that the maternal construct continues to be at play in a highly gendered workforce, in which women are not always seen as having the power to influence the behaviour of men (Landsman; Strega). In this way, mothers become the target of intervention by default and are often held to a higher level of accountability of managing their abusive partners than the system itself (Johnson; Brown et al.).

Conclusion

Although maternalism has played an important role in welfare states addressing the needs of women and children, maternalistic ideas and values limit the progressive possibilities for mothers who have experienced IPV and are engaged in state-sanctioned, child protection systems. As stated by Michel, maternalism's "acceptance of the existing gender order, although strategically necessary, also hindered the expansion of women's roles and rights" (27), which effectively confines them within maternal roles (Michel 27). This knowledge should lead social workers to question themselves and their own work through a feminist lens. Reflecting on the dominance of maternalism, it seems that the popular views of motherhood have not changed as much as one would hope or expect. Maternalism continues to contribute to a discourse that devalues women's work and results in women-dominated professions, such as social work, being seen as expected progressions of women's natural instincts of nurturing and mothering behaviours. Despite major demographic shifts in family structures and the myriad changes in child protection work with abused women, traditional ideas continue to undermine progressive practice and policy changes. The paternalistic constructs of motherhood, the bifurcation of child and mother needs, the lack of discourse around the role that men/fathers play in the lives of these children, and an overreliance on a patriarchal view of motherhood all serve to oppress mothers rather than to support them. Without directly engaging with abusive men as the point of intervention, social workers cannot move past holding women responsible for the safety of themselves and their children.

It may be helpful, as Andrea O'Reilly suggests, to view maternalism as functioning as a standpoint and performed on a continuum rather than as a static concept. Matricentric feminism may then be used as a construct through which to consider how some of these complex and competing discourses may be shifted into a new framework for dialogue. O'Reilly's matricentric feminism maintains a discourse that considers mothering as a practice, but these practices may still be considered negative or positive in child protection work and steeped in systemic racism. Beyond my attempt to do so here, matricentric feminism has not yet been applied to the issue of mothering in the context of IPV. We need theory that considers the diversity, humanity, and dignity of women as mothers. At the heart of the harms done to women who have experienced violence and their children is the attack on the relationship between mother and child. This relationship is damaged by repeated acts of abuse (Katz; Lapierre), and we must ensure our systems respond with opportunities for repair.

Rather than consider either the mother or the child as the subject of our interventions, the relationship between mother and child must become the focus. By doing so, we ensure systems act to restore maternal integrity, respond to behaviours with empathy and understanding, recognize a mother's suffering is inextricably connected to her child's suffering, and work alongside her to strengthen and rebuild what has been so purposefully dismantled through acts of IPV. By taking this path, our systems can positively contribute to an active repair of relationships. They can work towards social justice and equity for families who have experienced IPV.

Works Cited

Abramovitz, Mimi. *Regulating the Lives of Women: Social Welfare Policy from Colonial Times to the Present*. South End Press, 1996.

Abrams, Laura S., and Laura Curran. "Between Women: Gender and Social Work in Historical Perspective." *The Social Service Review*, vol. 78, no. 3, 2004, pp. 429-46.

Alaggia, Ramona, et al. "Does Differential Response Make a Difference: Examining Domestic Violence Cases in Child Protection Services." *Child and Family Social Work*, vol. 20, no. 1, 2013, doi: 10.1111/cfs.12058.

Alaggia, Ramona, et al. "In Whose Best Interest? A Canadian Case Study of the Impact of Child Welfare Policies in Cases of Domestic Violence." *Brief Treatment and Crisis Intervention*, vol. 7, no. 4, 2007, pp. 275-90.

Aron, Laudan Y., and Krista K. Olson. "Efforts by Child Welfare Agencies to Address Domestic Violence." *Public Welfare*, vol. 55, no. 3, 1997, pp. 4-13.

Ateah, Christine A., et al. "Mothering, Guiding, and Responding to Children: A Comparison of Women Abused and Not Abused by Intimate Partners." *Journal of Interpersonal Violence*, vol. 34, no. 15, 2019, pp. 3107-26.

Beeman, Sandra K., and Jeffrey Edleson, L. "Collaborating on Family Safety: Challenges for Children's and Women's Advocates." *Journal of Aggression, Maltreatment, & Trauma*, vol. 3, no. 1, 2000, pp. 345-58.

Beeman, Sandra K., Annelies K. Hagemeister, and J. L. Edleson. "Child Protection and Battered Women's Services: From Conflict to Collaboration." *Child Maltreatment*, vol. 4, no. 2, 1999, pp. 116-26.

Blackstock, Cindy. "The Occasional Evil of Angels: Learning from the Experiences of Aboriginal Peoples and Social Work." *First Peoples Child & Family Review: A Journal on Innovation and Best Practices in Aboriginal Child Welfare Administration, Research, Policy & Practice*, vol. 4, no. 1, 2009, pp. 28-37.

Brown, Leslie, et al. "Manufacturing Ghost Fathers: The Paradox of Father Presence and Absence in Child Welfare." *Child and Family Social Work*, vol. 14, no. 1, 2009, pp. 25-34.

Buchbinder, Eli, and Zvi Eisikovits. "Reporting Bad Results: The Ethical Responsibility of Presenting Abused Women's Parenting Practices in a Negative Light." *Child and Family Social Work*, vol. 9, no. 4, 2004, pp. 359-67.

Campbell, Lara. "'Respectable Citizens of Canada': Gender, Maternalism and the Welfare State in the Great Depression." *Maternalism Reconsidered: Motherhood, Welfare and Social Policy in the Twentieth Century*, edited by Marian van der Klein et al., Berghahn Books, 2012, pp. 99-120.

Casanueva, Cecilia E., et al. "Quality of Maternal Parenting among Intimate-Partner Violence Victims with the Child Welfare System." *Journal of Family Violence*, vol. 23, no. 6, 2008, pp. 413-27.

Costello, Lauren Fries, and Sacha Klein. "Racial/Ethnic Differences in Determinants of Trauma Symptomatology among Children in the U.S. Child Welfare System Exposed to Intimate Partner Violence." *Journal of Family Violence*, vol. 34, 2019, pp. 33-45.

DiQuinzio, Patrice. "The Politics of the Mothers' Movement in the United States: Possibilities and Pitfalls." *Journal of the Association for Research on Mothering*, vol. 8, no. 1-2, 2006, pp. 55-71.

Douglas, Heather, and Tamara Walsh. "Mothers, Domestic Violence and Child Protection." *Violence Against Women*, vol. 16, no. 5, 2010, pp. 489-508.

Eckenrode, John, et al. "Preventing Child Abuse and Neglect with a Program of Nurse Home Visitation: The Limiting Effects of Domestic Violence." *Journal of the Association for Research on Mothering*, vol. 284, no. 11, 2000, pp. 1385-91.

Edleson, Jeffrey L., and Neena M. Malik. "Collaborating for Family Safety: Results from the Greenbook Multisite Evaluation." *Journal of Interpersonal Violence*, vol. 23, no. 7, 2008, pp. 871-75.

Evans, Sarah E., C. Davies, and D. DiLillo. "Exposure to Domestic Violence: A Meta-Analysis of Child and Adolescent Outcomes." *Aggression and Violent Behaviour*, vol. 13, no. 2, 2008, pp. 131-40.

Fleck-Henderson, Ann. "Domestic Violence in the Child Protection System: Seeing Double." *Children and Youth Services Review*, vol. 22, no. 5, 2000, pp. 333-54.

Glenn, Evelyn Nakano. "Social Constructions of Mothering: A Thematic Overview." *Mothering: Ideology, Experience, and Agency*, edited by Evelyn Nakano Glenn, Grace Chang, and Linda Rennie Forcey, Taylor & Francis Group, 1994, pp. 1-29.

Gordon, Linda. *Heroes of Their Own Lives: The Politics and History of Family Violence*. Viking, 1988.

Greaves, Lorraine, et al. *A Motherhood Issue: Discourses on Mothering under Duress*. Status of Women, 2002.

Haight, Wendy L., et al. "Mothers' Strategies for Protecting Children from Batterers: The Perspectives of Battered Women Involved in Child Protective Services." *Child Welfare*, vol. 86, no. 4, 2007, pp. 41-62.

Haley, Jennifer M. "Intersectional and Relational Frameworks: Confronting Anti-Blackness, Settler Colonialism, and Neoliberalism in U.S. Social Work." *Journal of Progressive Human Services*, vol. 31, no. 2, 2020, pp. 210-25.

Heward-Belle, Susan. "Exploiting the 'Good Mother' as a Tactic of Coercive Control: Domestically Violent Men's Assaults on Women as Mothers." *Affilia: Journal of Women and Social Work*, vol. 32, no. 3, 2017, pp. 1-16.

Holt, Stephanie, Helen Buckley, and Sadhbh Whelan. "The Impact of Exposure to Domestic Violence on Children and Young People: A

Review of the Literature." *Child Abuse & Neglect*, 32, no. 8, 2008, pp. 797-810.

Humphreys, Cathy, and Deborah Absler. "History Repeating: Child Protection Responses to Domestic Violence." *Child and Family Social Work*, vol. 16, no. 4, 2011, pp. 464-73.

Huth-Bocks, Alissa C., et al. "The Impact of Domestic Violence on Mothers' Prenatal Representations of Their Infants." *Infant Mental Health Journal*, vol. 25, no. 2., 2004, pp. 79-98.

Jaffe, Peter G., Claire V. Crooks, and David A. Wolfe. "Legal and Policy Response to Children Exposed to Domestic Violence: The Need to Evaluate Intended and Unintended Consequences." *Clinical Child and Family Psychology Review*, vol. 6, 2003, pp. 205-13.

Jaffe, Peter G., et al. *Risk Factors for Children in Situations of Family Violence in the Context of Separation and Divorce.* Department of Justice, 2014.

Jenney, Angelique. *Doing the Right Thing: Negotiating Risk and Safety in Child Protection Work with Domestic Violence Cases.* University of Toronto, 2011.

Johns, Jennifer. "Good-Enough Mother." *International Dictionary of Psychoanalysis*, edited by Alain de Mijolla, vol. 2, Macmillan Reference, Gale eBooks, 2005, p. 688.

Johnson, Susan P., and Chris M. Sullivan. "How Child Protection Workers Support or Further Victimize Battered Mothers." *Affilia: Journal of Women and Social Work*, vol. 23, no. 3, 2008, pp. 242-58.

Katz, Emma. "Coercive Control, Domestic Violence, and a Five-Factor Framework: Five Factors That Influence Closeness, Distance, and Strain in Mother-Child Relationships." *Violence against Women*, vol. 25, no. 15, 2019, pp. 1829-53.

Keddell, Emily. "Theorising the Signs of Safety Approach to Child Protection Social Work: Positioning, Codes, and Power." *Children and Youth Services Review*, vol. 47, 2014, pp. 70-77.

Kelleher, Kelly J., et al. "Self-Reported Disciplinary Practices among Women in the Child Welfare System: Association with Domestic Violence Victimization." *Child Abuse & Neglect*, vol. 32, no. 8, 2008, pp. 811-18.

King, Bryn, et al. "Factors Associated with Racial Differences in Child

Welfare Investigative Decision-Making in Ontario, Canada." *Child Abuse & Neglect*, vol. 73, 2017, pp. 89-105.

Kitzmann, Katherine M., et al. "Child Witnesses to Domestic Violence: A Meta-Analytic Review." *Journal of Consulting and Clinical Psychology*, vol. 71, no. 2, 2003, pp. 339-52.

Koven, Seth, and Sonya Michel, editors. *Mothers of a New World: Maternalist Politics and the Origins of Welfare States*. Routledge, 1993.

Krane, Julia, and Linda Davies. "Mothering and Child Protection Practice: Rethinking Risk Assessment." *Child and Family Social Work*, vol. 5, no. 1, 2000, pp. 35-45.

Landsman, Miriam J., and Carolyn Copps Hartley. "Attributing Responsibility for Child Maltreatment When Domestic Violence Is Present." *Child Abuse & Neglect*, vol. 31, 2007, pp. 445-61.

Lapierre, Simon. "Mothering in the Context of Domestic Violence: The Pervasiveness of a Deficit Model of Mothering." *Child and Family Social Work*, vol. 13, no. 4, 2008, pp. 454-63.

Levendosky, Alytia A., and Sandra A. Graham-Bermann. "Parenting in Battered Women: The Effects of Domestic Violence on Women and Their Children." *Journal of Family Violence*, vol. 16, no. 2, 2001, pp. 171-92.

Levendosky, Alytia A., S. M. Lynch, and S. A. Graham-Bermann. "Mother's Perceptions of the Impact of Woman Abuse on Their Parenting." *Violence against Women*, vol. 6, no. 3, 2000, pp. 247-71.

Loseke, Donileen R. "Lived Realities and Formula Stories Of "Battered Women." *Institutional Selves: Troubled Identities in a Postmodern World*, edited by Jaber F. Gubrium and James A. Holstein, Oxford University Press, 2001, pp. 107-26.

Martinez-Torteya, Cecilia, et al. "Resilience among Children Exposed to Domestic Violence: The Role of Risk and Protective Factors." *Child Development*, vol. 80, no. 2, 2009, pp. 562-77.

Michel, Sonya. "Maternalism and Beyond." *Maternalism Reconsidered: Motherhood, Welfare and Social Policy in the Twentieth Century*. Mariam van der Klein et al. Berghahn Books, 2012, pp. 22-37.

Mohamud, Faisa, et al. "Racial Disparity in the Ontario Child Welfare System: Conceptualizing Policies and Practices That Drive Involvement for Black Families." *Children and Youth Services Review*, vol.

120, 2021, p. 105711.

Nixon, Kendra L. "Leave Him or Lose Them? The Child Protection Response to Woman Abuse." *Reclaiming Self: Issues and Resources for Women Abused by Intimate Partners*, edited by Leslie M. Tutty and Carolyn Goard, Fernwood Publishing & RESOLVE, 2002, pp. 64-80.

Nixon, Kendra L., Colin Bonnycastle, and Stephanie Ens. "Challenging the Notion of Failure to Protect: Exploring the Protective Strategies of Abused Mothers Living in Urban and Remote Communities and Implications for Practice." *Child Abuse Review*, vol. 26, no. 1, 2015, pp. 63-74.

Nixon, Kendra L., et al. "Protective Strategies of Mothers Abused by Intimate Partners: Rethinking the Deficit Model." *Violence against Women*, vol. 23, no. 11, 2017, pp. 1271-92.

O'Reilly, Andrea. *Matricentric Feminism: Theory, Activism, and Practice.* Demeter Press, 2016.

Peled, Einat, and Rachel Dekel. "Excusable Deficiency: Staff Perceptions of Mothering at Shelters for Abused Women." *Violence against Women*, vol. 16, no. 11, 2010, pp. 1224-41.

Plant, Rebecca Jo, and Marian van der Klein. "Introduction: A New Generation of Scholars on Maternalism." *Maternalism Reconsidered: Motherhood, Welfare and Social Policy in the Twentieth Century*, edited by Marian van der Klein et al., Berghahn Books, 2012, pp. 1-21.

Ramsay, Georgina. "Benevolent Cruelty: Forced Child Removal, African Refugee Settlers, and the State Mandate of Child Protection." *PoLAR: Political and Legal Anthropology Review*, vol. 40, no. 2, 2017, pp. 245-61.

Roberts, M. "Critical Thinking and Contemporary Mental Health Care: Michel Foucault's "History of the Present." *Nursing Inquiry*, vol. 24, no. e12167, 2017, pp. 1-7.

Scourfield, Jonathan B. *Gender and Child Protection*. Palgrave Macmillan, 2003.

Sinai-Glazer, Hagit. "Who Else Is in the Room? The Good Mother Myth in the Social Worker-Mother Client Encounter." *Social Policy & Society*, vol. 15, no. 3, 2016, pp. 351-67.

Stewart, Stacey. "A Mother's Love Knows No Bounds: Exploring

'Good Mother' Expectations for Mothers Involved with Children's Services Due to Their Partner Violence." *Qualitative Social Work*, vol. 21, no. 3, 2021, doi.org/10.1177/1473325020902249. Accessed 11 June 2022.

Strega, Susan. "Failure to Protect: Child Welfare Interventions When Men Beat Mothers." *Cruel but Not Unusual: Violence in Canadian Families*, edited by Ramona Alaggi and Cathy Vine, Wilfrid Laurier Press, 2006, pp. 237-66.

Sullivan, Chris M., et al. "Beyond Searching for Deficits: Evidence That Physically and Emotionally Abused Women Are Nurturing Parents." *Journal of Emotional Abuse*, vol. 2, no. 1, 2000, pp. 51-71.

Swift, Karen J. *Manufacturing "Bad Mothers": A Critical Perspective on Child Neglect*. University of Toronto Press, 1995.

Thiara, Ravi K., and Cathy Humphreys. "Absent Presence: The On-going Impact of Men's Violence on the Mother-Child Relationship." *Child and Family Social Work*, vol. 22, no. 1, 2015, pp. 137-45.

Tice, Karen W. *Tales of Wayward Girls and Immoral Women: Case Records and the Professionalization of Social Work*. University of Illinois Press, 1998.

Trocmé, Nicolas M., D. Knoke, and C. Roy, editors. *Community Collaboration and Differential Response: Canadian and International Research and Emerging Models of Practice*. Centre of Excellence for Child Welfare, 2003.

Turnell, Andrew, and Steve Edwards. *Signs of Safety: A Solution and Safety Oriented Approach to Child Protection Casework*. W.W. Norton & Company, 1999.

Waaldijk, Berteke. "Speaking on Behalf of Others: Dutch Social Workers and the Problem of Maternalist Condescension." *Maternalism Reconsidered: Motherhood, Welfare, and Social Policy in the Twentieth Century*, edited by Marian van der Klein et al., Berghahn Books, 2012, pp. 80-98.

Waldfogel, Jane. "Rethinking the Paradigm for Child Protection." *Future of Children*, vol. 8, no. 1, 1998, pp. 104-19.

Winnicott, Donald. *The Maturational Processes and the Facilitating Environment: Studies in the Theory of Emotional Development*. International Universities Press, Inc., 1965.

World Health Organization. *Intimate Partner and Sexual Violence against Women: Fact Sheet.* WHO, 2014.

Zufferey, Carole. "'Not Knowing That I Do Not Know and Not Wanting to Know': Reflections of a White Australian Social Worker." *International Social Work*, vol. 56, no. 5, 2012, pp. 659-73.

Chapter 6

Challenging Systemic Bias towards Indigenous Mothers Arising from Colonial and Dominant Society Assessment Methodology through a Lens of Humility

Peter W. Choate and Gabrielle Lindstrom

Introduction

Throughout Canada, Indigenous families are the most over-represented population within child intervention systems (Choate 1085). Mothers, far more than fathers or other caregivers, are subject to the scrutiny and overview of child intervention (Strega, et al.) for reasons that are most often related to both the history of colonial assimilation and the unacknowledged ways that colonial ideologies continue to influence the attitudes and practices of policymakers and social workers. Given the overrepresentation of Indigenous children in care, it would appear Indigenous mothers are particularly overmonitored. This creates an ongoing prejudicial review of the mother and ensures existing assessment approaches do not consider the oppressive colonial legacy in which Indigenous mothers exist. To some degree, this analysis is informed by our own subjective positions in the world. Peter Choate is a settler colonial, who grew up on the traditional lands of the Musqueam, Squamish, and the Tsleil-Waututh First Nations. A Blackfoot woman from the Kainaiwa First Nation in Southern Alberta (the largest reserve in Canada), Gabrielle Lindstrom (née Weasel Head) is keenly aware of how deeply embedded colonial ideologies in education, legislative, and social systems have affected Indigenous communities. With both her parents having attended Indian residential schools and her family system disrupted by ongoing colonization, she is dedicated to illuminating and challenging colonial ideologies in curriculum, education, and policy. Mount Royal University, where we both work, is on the traditional lands of the Niitsitapi, Blackfoot Confederacy and the peoples of Treaty 7, which include the Siksika, the Piikani, the Kainai, the Tsuut'ina, and the Stoney Nakoda First Nations. In addition, the City of Calgary is homeland to Métis Nation Region 3.

Drawing on both the results of our previous work (Choate and Lindstrom, "Inappropriate Application"; Choate and Lindstrom, "Parenting Capacity Assessment"; Lindstrom et al.; Lindstrom and Choate) and our professional and cultural positioning as Indigenous and settler scholars, we emphasize our significant concerns with current child intervention assessment methodology, as these processes were neither developed with nor by Indigenous people. The assessment tools are not normed relative to Indigenous culture, which is further exacerbated by the fact that functional definitions of "good enough parenting" are also entrenched in Eurocentric norms and values. For example, the context of assessment is to determine whether a mother is good enough to raise her child based upon Euro-normative definitions of mothering, the needs of a child, and the dyadic nature of the mother-child relationship. Another example is attachment theory, which draws upon individualistic cultural definitions of attachment, which are then imposed on Indigenous peoples, particularly mothers (Choate et al. 70). More generally, the ways Indigenous peoples are conceptualized by non-Indigenous members of society have direct bearings on the statistics and anecdotal evidence that are used to measure, define, and understand the overrepresentation of Indigenous children in the child welfare services. This evidence is often framed within a deficit perspective regarding Indigenous peoples, and it becomes difficult to conceptualize Indigenous issues as anything more than problems to be solved (Greidanus and Johnson; Ponting and Voyageur). Consideration is not given to the relational nature of Indigenous cultures and ways of knowing.

In this chapter, we illuminate Indigenous ways of knowing and propose means through which current practices based on colonial definitions can be reframed, such as utilizing Indigenous constructed assessments that are premised on culturally determined definitions, align with Indigenous knowledge systems and considers the impacts of the colonial legacy on Indigenous people. A related example of this is the use of the principles of the *Gladue* assessments from the criminal justice system, which require that matters related to assimilation be included in the review. We go further by arguing for approaches and definitions relating to both capacity and strength in caregiving systems that are rooted in Indigenous knowledge along with decision making constructed by Indigenous ways of knowing. Finally, we challenge the current legislative definitions calling for changes in both law and the role of the courts. We begin by first highlighting the disparate clashes between Indigenous ways of knowing and Eurocentred constructions of Indigenous peoples.

Ontological Orientation

In this section, we advance a much needed discussion aimed at illuminating the tensions between two knowledge systems—the Indigenous and Western paradigms—by offering critical points for reflection. These are intended to provide a conceptual frame of reference that enables one to identify the specific and obvious ways that Eurocentred assessment approaches imposed on Indigenous families are in direct misalignment with Indigenous definitions of family and parenting. Interrogating the Western paradigm embraced in state-sanctioned child intervention systems is a necessary endeavour, since our current social, economic, political, and cultural contexts are embedded within a taken-for-granted system of thought that emerges from a distinct cultural perspective (one that does not originate from the lands of what is now called Canada). Blackfoot scholar Leroy Little Bear reminds us that "Culture comprises a society's philosophy about the nature of reality, the values that flow from this philosophy, and the social customs that embody these values" (Littlebear). Indeed, Willie

Ermine and other Indigenous scholars (Bastien; Battiste; Cajete) have critically problematized the naturalization of the Western knowledge system as a universal "God's eye" view on reality that suffocates other ways of knowing. Critically understanding the differences between Indigenous and Western knowledge systems not only leads to a more balanced analysis of current social issues but also recognizes the validity and strength of Indigenous paradigms given that no matter "how dominant a worldview is, there are always other ways of interpreting the world" (Little Bear). We must critically recognize that our current Canadian social context is premised within a distinct cultural philosophy that emerges from the Western paradigm. According to Little Bear, "One of the problems with colonialism is that it tries to maintain a singular social order by means of force and law, suppressing the diversity of human worldviews." Concepts such as truth, justice, morality, and freedom are culturally determined, and it is not realistic to assume these can be universally applied and/or that they are individually experienced in the same ways. Indeed, the values that flow from Western philosophy are entrenched in our governance, legal, and social structures, which have, in turn, been imposed upon the Indigenous families. We must consider that failures to achieve parity with Western definitions of "good parenting" and "care" are not the failings of Indigenous families but rather are reflective of power imbalances and the social contexts of oppression (Haskell and Randal 52, 81) resulting from these conflicting worldviews. As Ermine argues:

> The situation, and very often the plight of Indigenous peoples, should act as a mirror to mainstream Canada. The conditions that Indigenous peoples find themselves in are a reflection of the governance and legal structures imposed by the dominant society ... it is not really about the situation of Indigenous peoples in this country, but it is about the character and honor of a nation to have created such conditions of inequity. It is about the mindset of a human community of people refusing to honor the rights of other human communities. (200)

Situations currently affecting Indigenous communities—such as poverty, addiction, and overrepresentation within social systems—are complex conditions deeply embedded in historical colonial practices, which have contributed to the current systemic oppressions. We argue that these conditions cannot be reduced to explanations premised solely on Western values. This discussion also serves to strengthen our contention that understanding and adopting Indigenous-defined approaches to assessment offer opportunities to shift colonial attitudes embedded in child intervention policies, theories, tools, and practices. This requires a paradigm shift within child intervention services. At the level of individual non-Indigenous, Eurocentric social workers, shifting one's paradigm involves critically attempting to learn about and understand the complexities of another thought system while simultaneously being critically aware of how one's own judgments, assumptions, and biases stand in the way of a meaningful and authentic interpretation of Indigenous cultural practices and beliefs (Mitchell and Moore). Hence, such a shift involves a process of unlearning common definitions of family, parenting, and child attachment that are constructed from a colonial paradigm. It also involves a willingness to learn from Indigenous peoples—whether those are clients or Indigenous Elders and scholars—with respect to values, beliefs, and practices. More than this though, a paradigm shift requires embracing humility, which is a value that is not often emphasized, let alone taught, in social work curriculum and pedagogy.

Indeed, it is our contention that humility is a necessary element for transforming the relationship between child intervention and Indigenous families, given that the methodologies currently adopted by child intervention services and applied to Indigenous families do not incorporate the complexities of Indigenous thought systems and how these continue to shape the familial structure and parenting approaches of Indigenous peoples. In response to indifferent and unresponsive and uncaring political and social systems, Indigenous Elders, scholars, and community members have been concerned with advancing an understanding of Indigenous ways of knowing. It is at the epistemological level that Indigenous peoples have been most misunderstood. Indeed, since colonial settlers have been coming to these lands, Indigenous peoples have been attempting to convince political and social system leaders that Indigenous culture matters, how Indigenous culture is experienced matters, and how others perceive Indigenous culture matters. All of this defines the parameters through which a person or system can meaningfully respond to the needs and concerns of Indigenous people. Indigenous peoples have also been concerned with defining and dialoguing about what it means to be a human being, since as Māori scholar Linda Tuhwai-Smith argues, they are so keenly aware of what it means to be stripped of that humanity (20). These are but a few of the reasons why a discussion on epistemology is warranted. Societal definitions of humanness and how we understand ourselves as moral, just, and good human beings occur at a conceptual site—that of epistemology. At the individual level, and especially for practicing social workers, exploration and insight into one's own knowledge (i.e., humility) and its origins are equally warranted, given the relational components that are involved with client interactions.

Western knowledge emerges from a distinct Eurocentric worldview that encompasses a linearity of time, standardized approaches, and understandings of self that are diametrically opposed to Indigenous paradigms. Eurocentric understandings of relationship are limited in the sense that the individual self is seen as the centre of the universe. Theological foundations afford man the transcendent authority to rule above all other living creatures and the natural world, which is one fraught with danger and one which must be tamed in order to harness its power for the benefit of man. Social hierarchies are made possible through abstract theories that justify power over the natural environment. Little Bear critiques Eurocentric values as: linear and singular, static, and objective ... in terms of a social organization that is hierarchical in terms of both structure and power." He continues: "Socially, it manifests itself in terms of bigger, higher, newer, or faster being preferred over smaller, lower, older, or slower. Singularity manifests itself in the thinking processes of Western Europeans in concepts such as one true god, one true answer, and one right way." In today's world, we see linearity in our education, social services, as well as in our justice and government structures. Typically, abstract engagement with theory and experimentation, as well as documentation and writing, is privileged over direct experience within relational networks. Furthermore, the pursuit of documentation, narrowly defined to meet the child intervention system needs, erodes the space for meaningful relationships. Hence, it is within this limited and limiting framework of humanity that the long-established attempts at assimilating Indigenous nations into Western settler society has served as the defining feature between Indigenous and non-Indigenous relations in Canada. This situation has led to a state of dependency on

Western systems for the vast majority of Indigenous communities. Betty Bastien argues that this concept of dependency rests within the Eurocentric ideal of power, which "automatically victimizes Indigenous peoples since these conceptions continually reconstruct powerlessness, victimization, deficiency or inferiority as characteristics of Indigenous peoples" (16). One need only look at government statistics on Indigenous peoples to understand how the national narrative reproduces Indigenous peoples within a deficit frame of reference, wherein they continually lag behind the rest of the general population in health, education, economics, and other social determinants (Reading; Greenwood and de Leeuw). Challenging deficit thinking involves reframing how Indigenous peoples are conceptualized within social policy and government systems. For example, instead of labelling Indigenous peoples as being overrepresented in the child intervention systems, this could be reframed to depict an overrepresentation of hegemonic state systems in the lives of Indigenous peoples. The framing of Indigenous people's place in society enables the normalization of definitions, such as "good parenting" and "healthy families." These are then imposed on Indigenous families and used as a method to further justify and perpetuate the assimilation and oppression of Indigenous children.

Although one could argue that the statistics are merely numbers that offer a baseline for better understanding problems that need to be solved, these problems are defined from a Eurocentric perspective (Henrich). Dawn Mahi argues that as a society, "we measure what we value" (51), and if settler societies continue to focus on measuring and recording the deficiencies of Indigenous peoples, then that becomes the defining story of Indigenous peoples. Recognizing the critical need to challenge Eurocentric definitions of good parenting, attachment theory, and family, we argue that within the child intervention system, there must be a movement towards reframing and redressing how assessments are applied against Indigenous peoples. An important part of this involves better understanding the complexities of Indigenous paradigms, including relational ways of being with human and more-than-human worlds.

Indigenous scholars have emphasized how Indigenous knowledge emerges from a relational epistemology (e.g., Bastien; Deloria; Ermine). Individual identities are constructed from participation and experience in the context of connections to everything around them. These are not simply person-to-person relationships but to other living entities, such as water and the energies of the universe: hence, we apply the phrase "all my relations" (Deloria). The natural world and all living things therein are a part of kinship alliances. As we asserted in previous work (Lindstrom et al.; Lindstrom and Choate; Choate and Lindstrom, "Inappropriate Application"), Indigenous families are not narrowly defined within bloodlines which typifies the Eurocentric definition of the nuclear family. Instead, family is broadly conceptualized—first or second cousins are considered brothers and sisters; aunts and uncles are no different than one's biological mother or father; and grandfathers and grandmothers also include community Elders. Although this notion of family may not apply to all Indigenous people within Canada, it is nonetheless vital that child welfare systems adjust their assessment practices, based on the above-mentioned definitions, for those Indigenous people who still define their identities within this relational structure.

However, the colonial legacy remains firmly entrenched within child welfare systems and buttresses the current frame of reference. As Mahi suggests, our cultural positioning dictates how we measure things and how we apply what we think we know about ideas (53). For example, the dominant Eurocentric hegemony embraces narrow ideas about healthy child development. Yet the cultural lens used to design research and filter interpretations around healthy child development is rarely acknowledged, let alone critically questioned or challenged as emerging from a specific Eurocentric cultural frame of reference. Indeed, the paradigm that has constructed this frame of reference is deeply embedded within various systems, policies, and practices and is reproduced in power relations between child intervention and Indigenous families. What appears to be needed is a critical understanding that whenever we encounter an exchange of knowledge or the creation of knowledge, we are doing so from a particular social and cultural location. However, child intervention overall uses universal Eurocentric ethics, definitions, research methodologies, assessments, and practices that are simply not relevant and applicable to all people of various cultural backgrounds. This is particularly true for Indigenous people's worldviews, whose emphasis on relational ways of knowing and being often stand in direct contradiction to Eurocentric values of independence and self-sufficiency.

Assessment

The ultimate question before child intervention is whether a parent is or can become good enough to raise their own children (Choate and Engstrom 368). Mothers are often seen from a deficit view, which fails to consider the oppressive economic and social realities they try to manage and overcome (Strega et al.). The challenge is what constitutes good enough (Choate and Engstrom 378). In our view, Eurocentric views, definitions, and constructs dominate the discussion, leaving Indigenous peoples marginalized in how successful parenting might appear from their cultural perspective (Lindstrom and Choate 55).

When the various recommended processes for parenting capacity assessment are examined in detail, Indigenous mothers are set up for failure (Choate 1094). This concern arises from the reality that no assessment process has been normed using Indigenous peoples. When we examined this question in the Nistwatsiman project (Lindstrom and Choate 52-53), we found that how family is constructed in the Blackfoot peoples of Alberta varies across several important dimensions. Although we do not presume to know how that would be expressed in Indigenous cultures across Canada, we are confident that Indigenous peoples define family, raising children, support systems, and transitions to adulthood quite differently than Eurocentric systems. We wish to note several key areas of difference:

- Who is family?—Eurocentric approaches think of the nuclear family as the basic unit of society. Thus, parent(s) and children are the basic structure. Extended family is seen as sitting outside the place of primary responsibility for raising the next generation. Furthermore, family is defined through biological lineage or legal constructs, such as blended families, adoption or foster care, single parent units, or family units constructed by a variety of means including surrogacy. Indigenous cultures do not app-roach caregiving in these legal or biological frames. Rather, community, culture, Elders, and people who hold position in the raising of the child simply through participation in the family are seen as vital to the successful raising of a child. For example, a child may live with a grandparent for extended periods of time— not because the parents cannot handle them or do not want to parent but because there is an understanding and deep appreciation of the wisdom and care the child will experience through being immersed in that relationship. Community members beyond the mother and father (including but also beyond the biological family) may play similar, central, and valuable roles in a child's upbringing.

- Attachment—this is an area of significant difference yet one that privileges a Eurocentric understanding of relationship. Drawing upon the work of John Bowlby, Mary Ainsworth, and Mary Main (see discussion in Choate et al.), child intervention has been framed as preserving a dyadic attachment relationship, typically rooted in the mother-child relationship, and then gradually extending out to other significant people in the child's life. The notion is that security is rooted in a primary relationship. Choate et al. have argued that such an approach is discriminatory to collectivistic cultures, such as most Indigenous cultures in Canada. In the latter examples, the child is seen not as belonging to the parent but to the members of a cultural group, who will all contribute to the raising of the child. Attachment is to the system not a single person.

- Psychometrics—these tools are used commonly throughout the parenting capacity assessment processes. Choate and McKenzie examined the set standardized tools to see if they reflect Indigenous understandings. Not surprisingly but of urgent concern, the authors concluded there is a dearth of valid psychometrics for Indigenous peoples. This was true with both personality and parenting tools. Thus, an Indigenous mother assessed for mental health and/or "parenting capacity" with psychometrics is systemically set up to be deemed inadequate.

- Observational techniques—a cornerstone of assessment is to observe the child with the parent. This allows for an understanding of the ways in which the two interact, what sort of relationship they have, and how the parent is attuned to the needs of the child and does such things as instruct and set boundaries. Careful consideration of each of these observations show that they are deeply rooted in cultural values. When a collectivistic culture is involved, aspects of these roles may fall to other caregivers. For example, in the Nistawatsiman project (Lindstrom and Choate

52-53), Elders spoke of their roles at times to discipline or rebuke a behaviour so as not to disrupt the relationship with the parent and child. In other circumstances, certain teaching roles fall to others for skills, such as hunting, ceremony, and cultural teachings. When observation occurs, the parent may not step into what they believe is not their role. An example is allowing the greater latitude to make errors. This is common in many Indigenous cultures. Children are thought to learn many important lessons through making mistakes, which directly challenge a Eurocentric control-oriented (risk prevention) model. Structured observational systems that we have examined do not have these constructs developed in a way that will see strength in the Indigenous approach. Furthermore, child intervention constructs of what parents are expected to do are racially biased and often fail to consider the structural, historical, and contextual realities of parents, instead focusing on individual risk factors (Stokes and Schmidt 1118).

• Adverse childhood experiences (ACEs)—ACEs have received a significant amount of attention in the childcare, health, and child intervention literature. A recent search on Google Scholar brought up over 933,000 citations of which 235,000 showed some child intervention connection (as of September 22, 2019). ACEs have become a pervasive part of the child intervention discourse and assessment process. This discourse harms colonized peoples (Czyzewski), as they are ultimately held responsible for the legacy of their oppression (Luther 78). A mother who is connected to the intergenerational traumas of Indian residential schools, the Sixties Scoop, the Millennial Scoop, and the present overrepresentation of Indigenous children in the Canadian child intervention systems will almost inevitably have a high ACE score. These are predeterminative risk factors, which fail to consider collective and individual efforts to achieve success. ACE scores keep people in the damaged paradigm of victim-survivor. But as Elders continue to tell us, Indigenous peoples continue to not only survive but thrive and grow. There is, thus, a great deal of strength and perseverance among Indigenous peoples that remains both devalued and invisible. Indeed, a vital distinction between Indigenous and Eurocentric worldviews is around the conceptualizations of the purpose and outcome of human suffering. Generally, the Eurocentric perspective considers the outcomes of suffering within a trauma framework, which is then imposed on Indigenous mothers using risk factor analysis. Hence, Eurocentric ideas of ACE become yet another way of enforcing a deficit view of mothers rather than an opportunity to celebrate cultural and communal strength. However, Indigenous perspectives understand that suffering is as much a part of the human condition as happiness or good health. Thus, we argue, that a mother should be considered beyond the borders of ACE, as seen in Figure 2.

• Resiliency—Strength-based discourses in social work, such as empowerment theory, may offer an understanding of Indigenous peoples using resilience as part of the foundation for analysis, yet these discourses are constructed through a Eurocentric paradigm. This, too, is problematic, since common notions around resilience are insufficient in helping social workers reframe deficit thinking, given that the ways used to measure resilience reduce human experiences of suffering and strength to person-centered, individually conceptualized protective and/or risk factors. These discourses continually marginalize the voices of Indigenous peoples in the very development of resilience-based frameworks of analysis. In relation to the previous point around ACE studies, Indigenous mothers' ability to achieve good enough parenting is measured within Eurocentric assessment frameworks, which, given the distinct ways Indigenous peoples understand suffering, are insufficient in authentically capturing what success and resilience could mean from a uniquely tribal perspective informed by lived experience and oral traditions.

In our view, a mother must be considered in the broader view of Figure 2 to demonstrate where growth has occurred. We go further, however, to argue that when a mother is connected to culture, this creates a web of resources, supports, and understandings that reflect a vibrant strength that Eurocentric parenting assessment tools are ontologically unable to capture.

Alternatives to Judicial Views—Do They Offer Hope?

If assessment of parenting capacity is to have validity, then it must be considered from a cultural perspective. If this does not occur, then the colonialism of child intervention will continue. There are two significant court cases in Canada that direct us towards alternatives, although they come from the criminal justice system. The more recent is a Supreme Court of Canada (2018 SCC 30) decision regarding a Métis inmate (*Ewert*) who claimed that the psychometric assessment tools used to classify him were not validated with an Indigenous population. The majority opinion of the court agreed. This decision adds to the argument that when an Indigenous mother is assessed by child intervention workers, it must be done using culturally valid methods and tools. A 1999 Supreme Court of Canada case regarding *Gladue* (1 SCR 688) saw the court rule that Aboriginal offenders required a new approach to sentencing that would consider "the particular cir-cumstances of Aboriginal offenders (para. 93(2)) looking at systemic and background factors that are unique" (para. 93[6]). The relevance in the current discussion is that the Supreme Court of Canada has held that the unique perspectives of Indigenous peoples do matter. However, whereas *Ewart* appears to be leading to a reconsideration of the application of psychometrics to people for whom they have not be validated, *Gladue* has proved to be a disappointment, given that it has not led to a reduction of the Indigenous populations in Canada's prison system (Roach 503). Yet they do provide a forum for contextualized knowledge and the alternative ways risk for an Aboriginal offender may be considered (Maurutto and Hannah-Moffat 463-64). Child intervention lacks any such legal directive. In *Racine v. Woods* (1983), the Supreme Court of Canada weighed into the intersection between colonialism and Indigenous parenting in the child welfare context when it held that attachment or bonding is more important than culture, thus diminishing the value of the presence of the child in the cultural systems that may be natural to the child.

Although some progress has resulted from the *Ewart* case (see also Choate and McKenzie), the alternative *Gladue* assessments have failed. *Racine* remains the highest judicial view on culture and parenting. Some researchers assert that race itself may be a confounding factor in risk assessment if space is not created for it (Hannah-Moffat and Maurutto 469), which is reinforced with the introduction of predictive analytics into child intervention. Race data negatively influence such systems (Eubank; Keddell). Indeed, the Canadian Mental Health Association (CMHA) has identified "Aboriginal status" as a risk factor in the social determinants of health in relation to the Canadian population (CMHA).

However, we argue that *Gladue* can illustrate how society needs to address systemic oppression by creating room for Indigenous thought, worldviews, and perspectives. A strong lesson from *Gladue* is to create space for Indigenous peoples to in turn create solutions, since solutions not developed from Indigenous ways of knowing and being can, and very often do, fail to address the needs of Indigenous communities.

Other Ways Forwards

Culturally relevant and specific approaches are needed to understand Indigenous parenting practices. This is not the task of the colonial systems but rather of the Indigenous peoples who possess the specific ways of knowing that comprehend and elucidate how a child is raised successfully within and connected to culture (de Leeuw et al. 292).

Elder Roy Bear Chief from the Siksika First Nation has worked with knowledge passed on to him from his older brother Clement Bear Chief. As seen in Figure 3, the model uses the spider web. He tells the story of how the Ani to Pisi (i.e., the spiderweb) can explain the intricate connections involved in the care of people. Creator asked the spider to make a web and surround the people with this protective web. If there was a disturbance in the thread (which Roy referred to as a "vibration"), Creator would be there to help calm the vibration and restore balance. The spiderweb can be used to map out support systems and resources.

Vibrations (disturbances) can be quelled by the assistance of the supports that make up the web. In this adaptation, the relational connections involved in the raising and care of an Indigenous child are seen. This diagram might not represent all Indigenous views but is a mechanism to demonstrate the complexities of the relationships built within one's culture. It also shows that Indigenous peoples may see problems differently. An example is seeing an issue from a circular versus a hierarchical perspective.

Case Planning

When assessment is done with the mother, and with her culture and connections intact, case planning becomes a connected and cooperative approach. This differs greatly from the traditional view of case planning where problems are identified and then the social worker develops a plan of corrective action. Within the standard model that typifies current assessment approaches, the goal is often articulated as empowering the client to take charge of their lives so that child intervention can step away. We believe there are several errors in such thinking:

- It is grounded in the power being held by the social worker. Empowerment is, at its core, the transfer of power from one party to the other. It is not rooted in the belief that the parent is powerful enough to sort out a direction. It also runs counter to the essential construct that Indigenous mothers can and do find needed supports within culture, but child intervention seeks to use extracultural methods rooted in colonialism. This is not surprising given that social work is grounded in colonial theories, methods, and practices (Choate et al.).

- It does not recognize the multiple elements of Ani to Pisi or the complexity of supports that would exist if Ani to Pisi were the basis of understanding the child caring system.

- It makes the mother hold the determination of success. It is not the system of care that acts as the basis of determining how the child can be raised. This affirms the Eurocentric view of attachment, childcaring, family systems, and other elements of raising a child.

When case management is done from a cultural perspective, then the child is seen as being cared for across a system—such as the elements of the web.

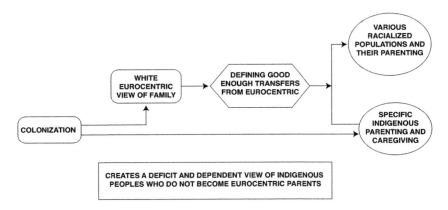

Figure 1. Linkage between definitions of good enough and colonial Eurocentric views of parenting

Incorporating definitions that emerge from a distinct cultural paradigm challenges social and systemic discourses that represent Indigenous peoples within a deficit perspective and advances the need to reframe the outcome of human suffering as a unique experience of resilience that is premised on Indigenous philosophies of perseverance in the face of historical traumas and ongoing colonization. In Figure 2 (see below), we highlight a model that moves Indigenous peoples from a victim-survivor positioning—one that is imposed on Indigenous peoples within Western trauma-resiliency frameworks—to one that emphasizes current strengths. This movement is crucial not only because it makes room for self-determination in defining trauma and resilience but also because it challenges the basic assumptions in social work theory, such as empowerment. Within social work programs, buttressing commonly used approaches with all clients is the notion of empowerment; the social worker becomes the catalyst for clients to discover their own sense of agency. As Leavelle Cox argues, "The strengths perspective is an empowerment approach. The client is viewed as having the ability to solve his or her problems. The focus is on the client's strengths, rather than problems and/or pathology" (305). Empowerment theory provides social workers with a lens through which to examine the strengths of their clients and build upon those points of strengths. Marc Zimmerman maintains that empowerment theory is values based and reflective of a need to organize community life: "The value orientation of empowerment suggests goals, aims, and strategies for implementing change. Empowerment theory provides principles and a framework for organizing our knowledge. The development of empowerment theory also helps advance the construct beyond a passing fad and political manipulation" (43). However, there is an underlying assumption that the values that orient empowerment as a model for change are ones that are shared among all communities. Finally, empowerment theory practitioners seem to presume that as a conceptual lens, it can be effectively applied to all clients regardless of the client's values or cultural orientation. However, for Indigenous peoples, individual autonomy and the right to determine one's own path in life—that is, the right to be self-determining—are values that existed long before colonization and are ones that endure to this day. Although it appears to be couched in benevolence, empowerment theory assumes that Indigenous peoples are unable to help themselves. We argue that such a theory enables child services to adopt a paternalistic approach. It offers neither a critical entry point to dismantle the ideologies that have disempowered Indigenous peoples, nor does it encourage individual social workers to confront how the social work system upholds colonial paternalism.

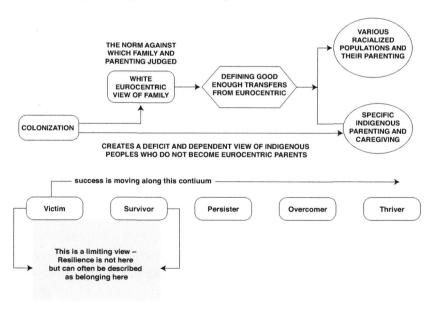

Figure 2. A continuum of progress from intergenerational and personal trauma that moves beyond the deficit and dependence view of an indigenous mother and not bound by ACE scores

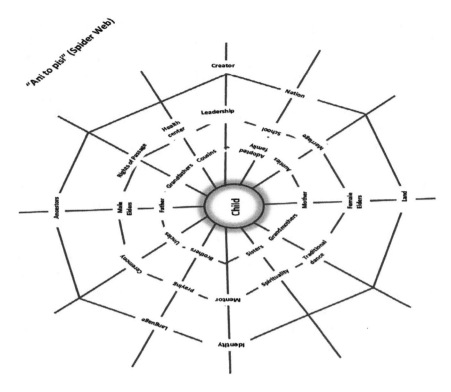

Figure 3. Ani to Pisi—A web that surrounds and interconnects the care of the child across multiple dimensions (Source: Elder Roy Bear Chief)

Conclusions

In this chapter, we have shown that colonialism has had direct effects on the perceived parenting capacity of Indigenous mothers. We have foregrounded our arguments and claims by unpacking the tensions inherent in Eurocentric and Indigenous perspectives—an important but often overlooked endeavour, which not only serves to contextualize colonial social work practices, such as assessment, but also adds critical depth to our suggestions. Inter- and multigenerational trauma has impaired the transmission of parenting practices and Indigenous knowledge. Contrary to ACE predictions, however, Indigenous communities have survived and continue to thrive. Such strength is seen not only in the continuing existence of Indigenous peoples themselves but also in the ongoing legacies of their ways of knowing and ceremony.

Mothers involved with child intervention often carry the extra burdens related to childcare as well as managing the deprivations resulting from resource deprivation and the residual impacts of trauma. The mothers are also held liable for protecting not only themselves from abusive relationships but also the child (see Jenney, this volume). This requires the mother to manage her own and the child's ongoing relationships while manoeuvring around and within colonial and oppressive sociopolitical realities.

When Indigenous mothers are involved with child intervention, they are faced with needing to show they are good enough. In this chapter, we show that Eurocentric assessment criteria used to determine the good enough mother systematically disadvantages Indigenous mothers. The methodology, philosophy, theories, and practice parameters of social work are rooted in colonial, Eurocentric knowledge that continues to systemically oppress Indigenous people. We suggest that the only safe way forwards for Indigenous peoples is to embrace Indigenous knowledge and ways of knowing in defining good mothering. Indigenizing existing social work approaches does not go far enough to interrogate the foundational knowledge and biases in the field. The Truth and Reconciliation Commission calls to action for child intervention cannot be satisfied through modification. There is a fundamental need to restructure and rethink how it is possible (or if it is possible) to determine a good enough mother.

It is ironic that the ability of Indigenous peoples to take charge of their own child intervention and to apply their own epistemology requires the legal permission of colonial governments. Even those agencies delegated to provide child intervention for their children (i.e., existing Indigenous Children's Aid Societies) do so mostly under the authority of the provincial or territorial legislation. However, unless Indigenous communities can manage and deliver child intervention from their own cultural and legalistic frame, we are dubious that Indigenous mothers will be seen from their own cultural positioning and strengths, resulting in their children still being brought into care.

Acknowledgment

We would like to acknowledge the support of Ms. Cari Merkley, librarian, Mount Royal University.

Works Cited

Bastien, Betty. "Indigenous Pedagogy: A Way Out of Dependence." *Aboriginal History: A Reader,* edited by Kristen Burnett and Geoff Read, Oxford University Press, 2016, pp. 15-25.

Battiste, Marie. *Indigenous Knowledge and Pedagogy in First Nations Education: A Literature Review with Recommendations. Indian and Northern Affairs Canada*, 2002, www.afn.ca/uploads/files/education /24._2002_oct_marie_battiste_indigenousknowledge andpedagogy _lit_review_for_min_working_group.pdf. Accessed 5 June 2022.

Cajete, Gregory. *Look to the Mountain: An Ecology of Indigenous Education.* Kivaki Press, 1994.

Canadian Mental Health Association. "Social Determinants of Health." *CMHA,* 2021, ontario.cmha.ca/provincial-policy/social-determinants/. Accessed 5 June 2022.

Choate, Peter. "The Call to Decolonize: Social Work's Challenge for Working with Indigenous Peoples." *British Journal of Social Work,* vol. 49, no. 4, 2019, pp. 1081-99.

Choate, Peter, and Amber McKenzie. "Psychometrics in Parenting Capacity Assessments—A Problem for First Nations Parents." *First People's Child and Family Review,* vol. 10, no. 2, 2015, pp. 31-43.

Choate, Peter, and Gabrielle Lindstrom. "Inappropriate Application of Parenting Capacity Assessments in the Child Protection System." *Imagining Child Welfare in the Spirit of Reconciliation,* edited by Dorothy Badry et al., University of Regina Press, 2018, pp. 93-115.

Choate, Peter, and Gabrielle Lindstrom. "Parenting Capacity Assessment as a Colonial Strategy." *Canadian Family Law Quarterly,* vol. 37, 2018, pp. 41-59. Canadian Business & Current Affairs, https://search.proquest.com.

Choate, Peter, and Sandra Engstrom. "The Good Enough Parent: Implications for Child Protection." *Child Care in Practice,* vol. 20, no. 4, 2014, pp. 368-82.

Choate, Peter, Natalie St-Denis, and Bruce Maclaurin. "At the Beginning of the Curve: Social Work Education and Indigenous Content" *Journal of Social Work Education*, vol. 58, no. 1, pp. 96-110.

Choate, Peter, et al. "Rethinking Racine v Woods from a Decolonizing Perspective: Challenging Applicability of Attachment Theory to Indigenous Families Involved with Child Protection." *Canadian Journal of Law and Society*, vol. 34, no. 1, 2019, pp. 55-78.

Cox, Leavelle. "BSW Students Favor Strengths/Empowerment-Based Generalist Practice." *Families in Society: The Journal of Contemporary Human Services*, vol. 82, no. 3, 2001, pp. 305-13.

Czyzewski, Karina. "Colonialism as a Broader Social Determinant of Health." *The International Indigenous Policy Journal*, vol. 2, no. 1, 2011, doi:10.18584/iipj.2011.2.1.5

Deloria, Barbara, et al., editors. *Spirit and Reason: The Vine Deloria Reader.* Fulcrum, 1999.

Ermine, Willie. "Ethical Space of Engagement." *Indigenous Law Journal*, vol. 6, no. 1, 2007, pp. 193-203.

Eubanks, Virginia. *Automating Inequality: How High-Tech Tools Profile, Police and Punish the Poor.* St. Martin's Press, 2017.

Ewert v. Canada. 2 S.C.R. 165. *Supreme Court of Canada*, 2018, scc-csc. lexum.com/scc-csc/scc-csc/en/item/17133/index.do. Accessed 5 June 2022.

Greenwood, Margo, and Sarah de Leeuw. "Social Determinants of Health and the Future Well-Being of Aboriginal Children in Canada." *Pediatrics and Child Health*, vol. 17, no. 7, 2012, pp. 381-84.

Greidanus, Elaine, and J. Lauren Johnson. "Knowledge as Medicine: The Use and Efficacy of a Youth Treatment Program Integrating Aboriginal Cultural Education." *Indigenous Perspectives on Education for Well-Being in Canada*, edited by Frank Deer and Thomas Falkenberg, ESWB Press, 2016, pp. 107-22.

Hannah-Moffat, Kelly, and Paul Mauruto. "Re-Contextualizing Pre-Sentence Reports." *Punishment and Society*, vol. 12, no. 3, 2010, pp. 262-86.

Haskell, Lori, and Melanie Randall. "Disrupted Attachments: A Social Context Complex Trauma Framework and the Lives of Aboriginal Peoples in Canada." *Journal of Aboriginal Health*, vol. 5, no. 3, 2009, pp. 48-99.

Henrich, Joseph. *The WEIRDest People in the World: How the West Became Psychologically Peculiar and Particularly Prosperous.* Farrar, Straus, and Giroux, 2020.

Keddell, Emily. "Substantiation, Decision-Making and Risk Prediction in Child Protection Systems." *Policy Quarterly*, vol. 12, no. 2, 2016, pp. 41-60.

Leeuw, Sarah de, et al. "Deviant Constructions: How Governments Preserve Colonial Narratives of Addictions and Poor Mental Health to Intervene into the Lives of Indigenous Children and Families in Canada." *International Journal of Mental Health and Addiction*, vol. 8, no. 2, 2010, pp. 282-95.

Lindstrom, Gabrielle, and Peter Choate. "Nistawatsiman: Rethinking Assessment of Aboriginal Parents for Child Welfare Following the Truth and Reconciliation Commission." *First Peoples Child and Family Review*, vol. 11, no. 2, 2016, pp. 46-70.

Littlebear, Leroy. "Jagged Worldviews Colliding." *Learn Alberta*, 2000, www.learnalberta.ca/content/aswt/documents/fnmi_worldviews/jagged_worldview s_colliding.pdf. Accessed 5 June 2022.

Luther, Alexander. *Developing a More Culturally Appropriate Approach to Surveying Adverse Childhood Experiences among Indigenous Peoples in Canada.* MSc. University of Windsor, 2019.

Mahi, Dawn. "Children of Kalihi." *Reclaiming Children and Youth*, vol. 22, no. 1, 2013, pp. 50-54.

Maurutto, Paula, and Kelly Hannah-Moffat. "Aboriginal Knowledges in Specialized Courts: Emerging Practices in Gladue Courts." *Canadian Journal of Law and Society*, vol. 31, no. 3, 2016, pp. 451-71.

Mitchell, Richard. C., and Shannon A. Moore. "Transdisciplinary Child and Youth Studies: Critical Praxis, Global Perspectives." *World Futures*, vol. 74, no. 7-8, 2018, pp. 450-70.

Ponting, J. Rick, and Cora Voyageur. "Challenging the Deficit Paradigm: Grounds for Optimism among First Nations in Canada." *Canadian Journal of Native Studies*, vol. 21, no. 2, 2001, pp. 275-307.

R. v. Gladue. 1 S.C.R. 688. *Supreme Court of Canada*, 1999, scc-csc. lexum.com/scc-csc/scc-csc/en/item/1695/index.do. Accessed 5 June 2022.

Racine v. Woods. 2 SCR 173. *Supreme Court of Canada*, 1983, scc-csc. lexum.com/scc-csc/scc-csc/en/item/2476/index.do. Accessed 5 June 2022.

Reading, Charlotte. "Structural Determinants of Aboriginal Peoples' Health." *Determinants of Indigenous Peoples Health*, edited by Margo Greenwood et al., 2nd ed., Canadian Scholars Press, 2018, pp. 3-17.

Roach, Kent. "One Step Forward, Two Steps Back: Gladue at Ten and in the Courts of Appeal." *Criminal Law Quarterly*, vol. 54, 2009, pp. 471-505.

Smith, Linda Tuhiwai. *Decolonizing Methodologies: Research and Indigenous Peoples.* 2nd ed. Zed Books, 2012.

Stoakes, Jacqueline, and Glen Schmidt. "Race, Poverty and Child Protection Decision Making." *British Journal of Social Work*, vol. 41, no. 6, 2011, pp. 1105-121.

Strega, Susan, et al. *Failure to Protect: Moving Beyond Gendered Responses.* Fernwood, 2013.

Zimmerman, Marc. A. "Empowerment Theory." *Handbook of Community Psychology*, edited by Julian Rappaport and Edward Seidman, Springer, 2000, pp. 43-63.

Chapter 7

A Window into the System: A Feminist Analysis of the Construction of Teenage Mothers in Serious Case Reviews in the United Kingdom

Sarah Bekaert and Brooke Richardson

Introduction

This chapter examines serious case reviews (SCRs) of child protection cases in the United Kingdom (UK) involving teenage mothers. It explores whether child protection workers, professionals, and systems respond differently to teenage mothers compared to older mothers in a safeguarding and child protection context. Safeguarding is understood here as the professional and organizational activities to identify and prevent harm before it occurs, whereas child protection refers to the legislative and organizational systems, and practitioners therein, that respond to children identified as experiencing harm. Both concepts are indicative of the risk paradigm in child protection, which is future oriented, precautionary, and understood to be objectifiable through forensic measures (Parton 6). This chapter is part of a wider exploration of the contemporaneous positioning of teenage mothers in society and how teenage mothers fare in this context (Bekaert; Bekaert and Bradly; Bekaert and SmithBattle).

SCRs are multidisciplinary reviews (operating outside of the criminal justice system) that are conducted when a child who has been involved in child protective services has died or been seriously injured in the UK. The aim of SCRs—which are housed in the publicly accessible National Society for the Prevention of Cruelty to Children (NSPCC) database—is to facilitate transparency and establish what lessons can be learned in relation to how practitioners and systems work to protect children. The UK government sets out its duty to protect children from harm and abuse through the Children Act of 1989 and 2004. When these protective systems fail and a child is seriously injured or dies, there is an inquiry to draw together the chronology of events prior to the death/injury of the child with the goal of learning from the incident and preventing such occurrences in the future. In 2011, professor Eileen Munro from the London School of Economics and Political Science was commissioned by the UK Department of Education to write a report answering the following question: "What helps professionals make the best judgments they can to protect a vulnerable child?" (6). In this report, Munro notes that practice recommendations identified in SCRs "tend to take the form of admonishments to professionals of what they 'should,' 'need, or 'must' do in specific situations in the future," which reinforces "a prescriptive approach towards practice" (60). Building upon this insight, a review of the SCRs by Peter Sidebotham highlights communication, lack of professional confidence, and inadequate professional support as recurring themes (190). What SCRs appear to not have instantiated, and the Munro Report calls for, is "moving from a system that has become over-bureaucratized and focused on compliance to one that values and develops professional expertise" (6). In this chapter, we take a closer look at how teenage mothers and professionals are implicated in existing SCRs. We also look beyond the family-professional re-lationship, which is repeatedly evidenced in the SCRs, and we begin to consider how the child protection system, contrary to its stated aims, often compromises effective support for teenage mothers by profess-ionals.

Sociopolitical and Cultural Context: Teenage Parenthood in the UK

In the UK, the Children Act 1989 and 2004 conceptualize young people as children until the age of eighteen. Young people are legally obliged to be in education or training until that age. Compared to a generation ago, an increasing number of young people delay full-time employment to attend college or university. In this way, becoming a teenage mother catapults young women into an adult world that, socioculturally speaking, they are not supposed to be entering. Stable employment and economic self-sufficiency are the assumed pre-requisites for starting a family (Bekaert and Bradly 4). Ironically, such social and economic norms are at odds with the biological reality that the late teens and early twenties are prime childbearing years for women.

There has been a dramatic reduction in teenage parenthood over recent decades in the UK. Evidence suggests that this is in part due to the multifaceted and sustained approach of the Teenage Pregnancy Strategy 1999–2010 (SEU), which saw the teenage conception rate drop by 51 per cent (Hadley, Ingham and Venkatramen 1). Although this policy has resulted in fewer teenage parents, those that do exist are consequently more likely to be culturally constructed as "other" and to be perceived as less fit to parent (Aldred 85). Not surprisingly, teenage mothers are less likely to engage with antenatal care, are more likely to live in poverty (Whitworth and Cockerill 323), and are dispro-portionately diagnosed with postnatal depression (Hall and Williams 11). In this chapter, we explore how teenage mothers—who are already under the suspicious moral gaze of society for being a young mother—are positioned by the child protection system in the UK, which is en-trenched in a risk paradigm (Connolley; Parton; Parton et al.).

Theory and Method: Feminist Discourse Analysis

This study is rooted in a feminist theoretical framework, as we attempt to "view the world in more complex, context-based ways" (White et al. 267). We embrace the idea that good care is a social responsibility, whereby its gendered and undervalued nature is problematic and indicative of hegemonic power relations (Tronto). In doing this research, we aim to create space for a gendered understanding of social phenomena and use these insights to advocate for social change (Wilkinson 1; Wilkinson 493).

Another key premise of this project is that gendered, hegemonic power relations play out at both the discursive and material level and that identifying when and/or where this occurs is necessary to make resistance and change possible (Lazar). In this chapter, we identify the discursive construction of hegemonic power relations in relation to teenage mothers involved in SCRs in the UK. Building on this, we explore new, more equitable ways of thinking about teenage mothers, child protection workers, and the broader systems in which they are located.

Practically guiding our analysis is the listening guide developed by Andrea Doucet and Natasha Mauthner. Although this guide was originally developed for the purpose of analyzing interview data, we have adapted its principles and process to a feminist discourse analysis of SCRs. The listening guide requires four readings of the data. The initial reading is for the plot, or the overall story. The second reading takes a closer look at the subjectivity of the "I" in the story. The third observes key relations and/or networks in which the subject exists (i.e., how she is positioned in relation to her parents, her partner, and more formal relations with professionals). Finally, the fourth reading examines the wider social structures and cultural contexts relevant to the subject.

It is important to point out that even though SCRs are an official review of the facts, they are written by a person, who likely occupies a position of authority and/or privilege. In this way, it is interesting to note a marked absence of "I" in the SCRs. With no assertion of "I," SCRs take on an objective, forensic tone, when the reality is that the SCR will inevitably reflect the reviewer's perspective/subjective understanding to some degree. Instead of positioning the writer as a subjective actor in a position of privilege, SCRs frequently paraphrase the voices of the professionals who were involved in the case to make their points. Such an approach tends towards downloading responsibility for supposed error to individual workers rather than providing a critical reflection on system-level processes.

Although most SCRs state the importance of including the family members' voices as part of the review, they were notably absent in the

SCRs reviewed, particularly mothers (which is consistent with Lucy Baldwin's findings). The voices of children in senior school (between eleven and sixteen years old) were occasionally included, whereas younger children's views were absent in all the documents reviewed. In some cases, legal frameworks formally prohibited the inclusion of mothers' voices. For instance, if there was an ongoing criminal investigation mothers could not be interviewed. Even though it is standard practice to invite mothers to give their account of events, our analysis revealed that few took up this offer, which is likely due to a sense of disempowerment throughout their engagement with the child protection system. Existing literature suggests that mothers feel that what they say will not make a difference and ultimately cannot change the outcome for them and their children (Cameron and Hoy). In a case where their child has been seriously injured or died, there is likely even less motivation to reengage with child protection processes.

We are also mindful that it is not simply the content of the SCRs but the actual existence of these documents that is worthy of analysis. A SCR enters the field as an agent in its own right and within a wider hegemonic social system. Lindsay Prior suggests that documents represent a set of discursive practices that exist beyond the document (3). In this instance, SCRs are part of an evolving systemic and multidisciplinary risk focus and are recruited as allies for wider hegemonic child protection discourses. Formal documents function not merely as simple repositories of facts and detail about subjects; they also actively construct the publicly available subjectivities of those involved, often without their consent or participation (Prior 91).

Data Collection

The support of the curators of the NSPCC was elicited to search the database with the following keywords and phrases: teen pregnancy, teenage parenthood, and young parenthood. Fifty-two cases were identified that were relevant to teenage parenthood—ranging in publication years from 2011 to 2017. Of the fifty-two cases reviewed, the reasons stated for the review included death (twenty-three), injuries (seventeen), neglect (two), and specific conditions (two: sudden infant death and a congenital neurological condition). In eight cases, the specific reason for the review was not stated. The high incidence of death and injury is notable, with acute events leading to death being more common than neglect. In the majority of the death cases, the child was less than one year old.

One of the key stated purposes of the SCR is to identify what the system could have done better rather than a forensic search for culpability. Yet most SCRs do clearly identify a perpetrator. The SCRs concluded that the perpetrator was the mother in three cases, the father in twelve, a partner in two, and an "other" (e.g., an uncle or a friend) in a further three cases. The parenting unit was identified as jointly responsible in eleven cases. In twenty-one cases, no perpetrator was identified. The reviews show that child death or serious injuries are rarely a result of one act done by one person at one point in time. It is almost always the complex intersection of several factors at the micro, meso, and macro level that cumulate across time, including the mother's (who is often still legally a child herself) own childhood experiences.

Thematic Findings and Analysis

Five themes were identified from the data: 1) young maternal age being viewed as an objective risk factor; 2) the mothers' overwhelming histories of hardship positioned as risk; 3) infantcentric professional practice, in which the infant's needs were seen as separate from and more important that the mother's needs; 4) mother-blaming; and 5) blaming individual child protection workers.

Theme One: Youth as a Risk Factor

It quickly became clear that being young was viewed by professionals as a risk factor. Frequently, the mothers and/or fathers were referred to as "vulnerable young parents" (Child M, Dorset) often without further qualification. Being young was noted first, followed by a list of other risk factors in their lives. For example, one SCR read: "They were teenage parents with a complex history, had missed appointments, there was some drug use, there were some concerns about housing conditions and father's mental health and domestic violence" (Child J, Oxfordshire). Being a teenage parent appeared to hold a common sense understanding of vulnerabilty and risk. Yet the evidence listed suggests, the contrary, that it is not being a teenager itself that is a concern but rather a history of complex, traumatic life events that have accumulated across many of these young parents' lives. This tension was noted, albeit without resolution, in one review specifically referring to teenage mothers: "There has been considerable debate over whether poor outcomes for teenage mothers and their babies are a consequence of the mother's age, or of her often disadvantaged circumstances" (Children R, S, and W, Lewisham).

Observations of the teenage mothers were frequently linked to what was viewed as typical adolescent behaviour. In one case, "adolescent ambivalence" in engagement with professionals (Child G, West Sussex) was cited as a key problem within the mother rather than something professionals had a responsibility to address. Another report claimed that the "mother's lack of compliance [with social workers and community supports] was mainly as a product of her youth," and later concluded "adolescents are often difficult to engage" (Child G, West Sussex). In one case, the mother was described as self-absorbed and not interested in her newborn, demonstrating "typical" adolescent behaviour: "She spent her time texting on the phone. She did not attend to his needs, she did not talk or try and reassure him" (Baby M, Buckinghamshire).

In some cases, SCRs acknowledged a need for critical reflection on the implicit assumption that age is a risk factor. In the case of Charlie and Charlotte (Durham), the reviewer expressed concern that the "Parents [were] seen as manipulative with no reflection on why." Challenging the idea that young parents are ontologically deficient, other SCRs explicitly noted that childhood trauma and/or lack of positive parenting experiences in these parents' lives is a greater consideration than age itself. It was the "effect of childhood experience on their own development and hence their parenting capacity" (Child C and N, Tyneside). Despite some SCRs noting the limitations of the deficient teenage parent (typically the mother) discourse, the matter was left without resolution, whereby being young appeared to somehow explain the serious occurrence.

One observation that was particularly troubling in relation to this youth-as-risk discourse was how despite an almost universal assumption of risk by dint of age, responsibility for preventing the occurrence was placed almost entirely on mothers. Words and phrases, such as "manipulation" and "lack of compliance" placed the responsibility for constructive engagement with the system solely on the teenage mother (and occasional father) rather than acknowledging that practitioners have a professional responsibility to tailor their practice in a way that builds trust and engagement. As noted above, mothers were sometimes described as "selfish," behaving like "typical teenagers." Such a description of mothers let child protection workers and other professionals off the hook in terms of persisting in their work with the mother. As one social worker is quoted, she was "sick of trying to sort her [the mother] out" (Sibling 1, 2 and Baby G, Lincoln). In another case, lack of engagement on the part of the teenage mother led to the case being closed rather than exploring more meaningful ways of engaging.

Ironically, child protection workers failing to meaningfully engage with young mothers mirrors how professionals describe the behaviour of teenage mothers—that is, they are criticized for failing to engage with their infants. In both cases, the person in the position of caregiver disengages. A double standard is created whereby young parents are positioned as being inadequate and hurtful in relation to their infant, but professionals are simply able to close the case with few to no consequences. Furthermore, it appears justifiable to understand the mother's lack of engagement as rationale for doing so, despite their often complicated family situations and the professional's duty to protect. However, we are mindful that we must not simply shift the blame from the mother to the professional. Perhaps most interestingly of all, in both cases, the reviews rarely consider how the structural conditions in place (or the lack of structural conditions in place) meet the needs of the mothers and/or professionals. The lack of supportive social infrastructure—not just within child protection services but increasingly skeletal social services such as housing, childcare, mental health services—is left unproblematized.

Theme Two: Overwhelming Histories of Hardship Positioned as Risk

It became apparent in reading the SCRs that the teenage parents involved in these cases had histories of trauma and struggle in their lives. One fifth (21 per cent) had been or were (at the time of the SCR) in state care themselves. The SCRs demonstrated that workers were mindful that many of the young parents' role models had been poor, often referring to a lack of a "parenting compass" (Child D, Haringey). However, a lack of positive parenting figures was still positioned as an individual risk factor, again situating the problem within the individuals rather than the complex social situations these young parents were navigating. Identifying and alerting professionals to a need for support through recognizing a lack of a parenting compass is only helpful if there is immediate access to supportive services. Without this, a lack of a parenting compass just becomes yet another risk factor for the already vulnerable mother who has Likely already experienced trauma. And even in cases where services are required as a result of compounding risk factors, access to these services can also become problematic if it leads to increased scrutiny of their mothering. This review suggests that services are rarely offered as a result of the mother's expressed needs. Rather these services are imposed on her through standard checklists, risk assessments, and preconceived professional cultural understandings of risk. In addition, the offered services are then withdrawn when there is a perceived lack of engagement with the prescribed support.

The life circumstances of the young mothers also reflected other major hardships. Homelessness was experienced by 11 per cent of parents and intimate partner violence (IPV) by 34 per cent. Eight per cent of the young mothers were parenting with a partner who was significantly older; for four of the couples, the male partner's age was between eight and seventeen years older, increasing the likelihood of a power imbalance in the relationship (Oudekerk, Guarnera, and Reppucci 1242). In this way, an overall lack of basic stability in these young parents' lives, alongside possible power differentials between parents, may go further in explaining their challenges than dismissing them as "typical teenagers". There was also a high prevalence of learning disability in the young parent population: 10 per cent of the young mothers and 15 per cent of the fathers identified as having, or were diagnosed as having, a learning difficulty, such as autism, attention deficit hyperactivity disorder, attention deficit disorder and dyslexia. Fifteen per cent of mothers and 6% per cent of fathers or partners were noted to have engaged poorly with school or to have been excluded from school. Mental health concerns—such as depression, self-harm, and anxiety—were noted in 26 per cent of mothers and 15 per cent of fathers/male partners. Drugs and alcohol were identified as a problem for 11 per cent of mothers and 30 per cent of fathers/male partners. Violence was perpetrated by 8 per cent of mothers and 22 per cent of fathers/male partners, and crime was noted for 2 per cent of mothers and 17 per cent of fathers/male partners. Again, these complex challenges, often rooted in systemic oppression, were presented as deficits solely of the individual parent rather than systemic problems in need of social policy solutions.

Certain events were notable around the pregnancy and birth of their children, particularly not seeking medical care (see Berrouard and Richardson, this volume). Eleven per cent of young mothers self-discharged from antenatal and/or postnatal care, and 10 per cent presented late for antenatal care or concealed their pregnancy, a few doing so until birth. Although SCRs tended to label avoidance of medical systems as "irresponsible teenage behaviour," it is much more likely that these behaviours reflect the mothers' justified fear of state-sanctioned systems in a society that disapproves of teenage parenthood. A fear of systems is likely more pronounced for the youth who themselves were in state care at the time of the injury or death of their child. Furthermore, medical and social systems tend to pathologize normal human responses within abnormal, extremely complex life circumstances—particularly for groups that do not adhere to dominant, sociocultural norms and values (see Choate and Lindstrom this volume). When this occurs, human beings are objectified, which is a terrible dehumanizing feeling for anyone and something feminism has long sought to address. Instead of pathologizing and blaming young mothers for their trepidation in seeking medical care and social support, it may be more useful to ask how these systems can become safer spaces for young mothers.

The family situations described in the SCRs reflect findings within the broader literature, which reveal that the intersection of poverty, young age, disability, and being a former ward of the state is consistently linked to earlier parenthood (Smith Battle 30; Arai 21; Fallon and Broadhurst 14). Even though this fact is generally known by child protection workers and systems (which is visible in young parents' automatic inclusion in many risk assessments by dint of age alone), in no SCR was there any evidence that the traumatic history of young mothers was honoured and/or given space to be explored. A trauma history tended to be noted in relation to assessing risk for the mother's child rather than meeting the needs of the family unit.

Theme Three: Infantcentric Professional Practice

Perhaps most troubling in the analysis was the lack of recognition of teenage parents as a unique and worthy group of humans in their own right. There appeared to be little acknowledgment that the teenage mother is often still legally a child with unique needs, and in some cases, the mother herself is/was a ward of the state. Indeed, contemporary understandings of adolescence recognize that biological and social development occur well into the mid-twenties (Sawyer et al.). The tension between supporting the teenage parent as adolescent *and* protecting their child was only noted by a few of the reviews. For example, one SCR called for "the need to consider young people under 17 as a child in their own right, and to include an assessment of their own needs as well as those of the unborn child" (Sibling 1, 2, and Baby G, Lincoln). Only the police (who tend to operate within a more established, formal, and legal framework) were identified as recognizing teenage parents as children in their assessment of capacity. One SCR (Baby H, Lancashire) stated: "The police gave formal consideration to the age of mother and her partner when interviewing them following the death of baby H ... deciding whether either was vulnerable within the meaning of legislation or required an appropriate adult."

Across the reviews, it was notable that even when teenage parents were recognized as children themselves, it did not appear to influence the practice of child protection workers. One review observed that there was "no assessment despite mother's age and father's disability" and called for "professional rigour regarding teenage parents [who are] young and potentially vulnerable." (Nolan and family, Bedfordshire). In reviewing the SCRs, we observed a tension between the child protection worker's acknowledgment of the legal status of the child as parent and the expectations for them to take up the adult responsibilities of parenthood. This tension tended to result in infantcentric practices to the exclusion of the young mother's needs. This appeared to arise from established ways of practicing within a risk framework that renders the mothers, whatever their age, solely responsible for the protection of their child. Such an approach dichotomizes the needs of a mother and her child, precluding the possibility that a young mother's needs are perhaps not all that different and/or separate from her child.

Theme Four: Mother-Blaming

Young mothers were held disproportionately responsible for abuse/neglect in the SCRs reviewed. Even though fathers were often present and in many cases were the perpetrators of abuse and neglect, an analysis of the SCRs revealed that the overwhelming focus of child protection workers was on the mothers' parenting. For example, in a case where the father was actively involved, one SCR stated, "Mother missed Nolan's paediatric review" (Nolan and family, Bedfordshire). In relation to IPV, another SCR noted: "The mother knew enough of the father's aggressive or volatile behaviour to have been able to make a reasonable judgement that he was not a safe, sole carer for her new-born baby, and hence she did not act with levels of protection deemed reasonable for a mother" (Liam, Brighton and Hove).

The teenage mother's subjective experiences, including fear of both her partner (if relevant) and the child protection authorities, was never mentioned in SCRs. There was occasional acknowledgment of the difficult situation the young mother was in due to stressful and traumatic life events, yet the mother-as-protector expectation stood firm: "Child D's mother did not harm her, but she was less able to protect the baby because of her troubled background and LD [learning difficulty]" (Child D, Luton). In one case, this expectation could even result in formal charges: "Mother was charged with causing or allowing a child to be harmed" (child LC, Lancashire).

Nigel Parton, David Thorpe, and Corrine Wattam have noted that child protection workers may take an approach of working with mothers to fulfil their responsibilities or blame them for their failure (120). This study reinforces the latter approach. Gendered practice prevailed, placing undue responsibility and sanctions on the teenage mother for the protection of the child from a male perpetrator. This approach allows men's violence to be ignored and go unchallenged. The bottom line is that the mother is positioned as the primary caregiver, who may now have the added responsibility of convincing authorities that the risks to the infant or child do not meet the threshold of intervention.

Theme Five: Blaming Child Protection Workers

The other group sometimes positioned as risky in our review of SCRs, particularly in relation to young mothers with complex trauma histories, was the child protection workers themselves. "Naïve optimism" on the part of child protection workers was cited in several cases. Some child protection workers in the SCRs were described as wanting to support young parents with positive goals of starting again. Indeed, empirical research does suggest that the birth of a child can provide an impetus for a fresh start for young mothers (e.g., family reconciliation and returning to education) (Herrman 249; SmithBattle 531). The SCR reviewers, with the benefit of hindsight, pathologized this optimism and called it "start again syndrome." A syndrome is by definition "a group of signs and symptoms that occur together and characterize a particular abnormality or condition" (Merriam-Webster). Professional optimism is not an abnormality or disorder; it is a strengths-based approach to practice that could be considered an act of resisting from within a liability-focused system. However, embracing optimism for a youth who is in the state care system, or a homeless mother, or for a mother who self-harms must be balanced with appropriate systemic supports to ensure young parents/mothers have their needs met. In this way, a strengths-based approach to practice remains rhetorical unless there is immediate access to material and emotional support. Responsibility here lies in ensuring all citizens have access to what they need to have the opportunity to be well (e.g., respite care, counselling, and decent work). Instead of diagnosing child protection workers with start again syndrome, it is necessary to ask them whether they have the tools and resources they need to work positively and meaningfully with young mothers. And of course, the mothers themselves must be given the time, space and voice to identify and express needs.

Conclusion

An analysis of the SCRs revealed that teenage motherhood is over-whelmingly associated with risk and vulnerability, whereby there is little to no space to see or understand teenage mothers as anything other than inadequate. Although there was occasionally an acknow-ledgment in the SCRs of the unique position of teenage mothers regarding their own development and legal status, it became apparent that this acknowledgment rarely influenced practice. Given the deeply entrenched risk paradigm in child protection—and the stated purpose of the SCRs to learn from these cases to prevent future harm—the language used in the SCRs indicated a surveillance, rather than support, approach to engaging young mothers. For example, the reports often referred to the mothers as being non-compliant and described their behaviour as resistant or manipulative. In cases where teenage parents voiced a desire to improve circumstances, and child protection workers took that at face value, the practical, community-based supports necessary to work towards these goals were notably absent. Even worse, workers were construed as pathological in their optimism (i.e., 'start again syndrome') and blamed (alongside parents) for the harm brought to the child.

It was also not uncommon for mothers' situations to be constructed as individual "choices" rather than the inevitable effect of ongoing, systemic trauma and/or oppression. This observation held true even for teenage parents who themselves were current or former wards of the state. This reflects a tension for health and social care professionals positioned as both advocates for communities and client-centered care while at the same time implementers of policy that denies these values and positions them as the "border police" of who is fit to parent. It is difficult, if not impossible, for any mother to feel cared for by the systems and people who are assessing her parenting and backed by the legal authority to take away her child. Similarly, it is difficult for child protection workers to care for a mother they feel is fundamentally making "choices" that put her child at risk of harm.

What has become very clear in this analysis of SCRs, and has been indicated elsewhere (e.g., Baldwin 2015) is that young mothers appear to be denied their voice, subjectivity and therefore the opportunity to define their needs. No SCR asked how social or healthcare systems could have been more accommodating for teenage mothers. Our findings reveal that the child protection process tends to offer services on a "take it or leave it", all or nothing, basis which does not adequately recognize or honour the complexities of these young mothers' lives (Parton, Thorpe, and Wattam 171). It is not unreasonable that young mothers should have access to a safe place to live and responsive, consistent, equitable relationships where their subjective experience is honoured. This would likely go a long way to ensuring her child is well cared for. To not put the social infrastructure in place to enable this, and instead allocate resources to micro-managing and/or surveying these young mothers' lives, perpetuates the hegemonic social order whereby she is likely to adopt an understanding of herself as unimportant, troublesome, hopeless, and irresponsible. SCRs appear to reinforce a mother-blaming narrative. It is no wonder she is unlikely to want to participate in a process (the SCR) whereby there is a vested interest in holding her responsible.

Our review of SCRs may provide more questions than answers. We can clearly see that young mothers involved in SCRs are resistant to social and/or medical services and that this may have fatal consequences for their children. What is left unexplored is a critical examination of why. It is possible that she feels the supports provided are meaningless, externally prescribed interventions. In this way, her lack of engagement is not evidence of the young mother's hopelessness/irresponsibility, but illustrative of her determination to define her own needs and life course.

None of this was given adequate weight in the SCRs reviewed. Mothers were ontologically positioned as inadequate by virtue of their age, and their trauma and struggle was equated with risk. They were directly or indirectly blamed for not meeting the needs of their child with no acknowledgment of their own complex needs. This is particularly surprising given many of the mothers in the SCRs were still legally children themselves.

It should not be this way. Rather than pinpointing individual decisions that, in retrospect, lead to a serious occurrence, this analysis of SCRs suggests that a systemic approach that prioritizes need over risk may go further in ensuring children, and children's children's, needs are met. Young mothers may feel more motivated if they felt their lives, and not just their children's lives, mattered. Similarly, they are worthy of having practical, material and emotional resources that provide them with real options (e.g., returning to school, decent work, and respite care). Having one's worth equated with adherence to compliance-based measures, some of which are next to impossible (for example, protecting their child from an abusive partner) is dehumanizing. Rather than blaming mothers and/or looking to individual workers to make better decisions amidst impossible conditions of scarcity and suffering, there is a systemic responsibility to ensure young mothers, and therefore their children, have access to tangible support, offered without condition or judgement. This responsibility lies with all of us, though government and/or political/policy is necessary.

Works Cited

Alldred, Pam. *"Fit to Parent": Psychology, Knowledge, and Popular Debate.* Ethos, 1999.

Arai, Lisa. *Teenage Pregnancy: The Making and Unmaking of a Problem.* Policy Press, 2009.

Baldwin, Lucy, editor. *Mothering Justice: Working with mothers in criminal and social justice settings.* Waterside Press, 1999.

Bekaert, Sarah. *Exploring the Influences on Teenage Pregnancy Decision Making Using the Listening Guide Data Analysis Method.* SAGE Publications Ltd, 2020.

Bekaert, Sarah, and Joelle Bradly. "The Increasingly Leaky Stigma of the 'Pregnant Teen': When Does 'Young Motherhood' Cease to be Problematic?" *Studies in the Maternal*, vol. 11, no. 1, 2019, pp. 1-9.

Bekaert, Sarah, and Lee SmithBattle. "Teen Mothers' Experience of Intimate Partner Violence: A Metasynthesis." *Advances in Nursing Science*, vol. 39, no. 3, 2016, pp. 272-90.

Cameron, Gary, and Sandy Hoy. "Mothers and Child Welfare." *Creating Positive Systems of Child and Family Welfare: Congruence with the Everyday Lives of Children and Parents*, edited by Gary Cameron et al., University of Toronto Press, 2013, pp. 44-66.

Children Act. HMSO, 1989.

Children Act. HMSO, 2004.

Connolley, Marie, editor. *Beyond the Risk Paradigm in Child Protection.* Palgrave, 2017.

Doucet, Andrea, and Natasha Mauthner. "What Can Be Known and How? Narrated Subjects and the Listening Guide." *Qualitative Research*, vol. 8, no. 3, 2008, pp. 399-409.

Fallon, Debbie, and Karen Broadhurst. *Preventing Unplanned Pregnancy and Improving Preparation for Parenthood for Care-Experienced Young People.* Coram, 2016.

Hadley, Alison, et al. "Implementing the United Kingdom's Ten-Year Teenage Pregnancy Strategy for England (1999–2010). How Was

This Done and What Did It Achieve?" *Reproductive Health*, vol. 13, no. 139, 2016, pp. 1-11.

Hall, David, and Jonathan Williams. "Safeguarding, Child Protection, and Mental Health." *Archives of Disease in Childhood*, vol. 93, no.1, 2008, pp. 11-13.

Herrman, Judith. "The Voices of Teen Mothers: The Experience of Repeat Pregnancy." *MCN: The American Journal of Maternal/Child Nursing*, vol. 31, no. 4, 2006. pp. 243-49.

Lazar, Michelle, editor. *Feminist Critical Discourse Analysis : Gender, Power and Ideology in Discourse.* Palgrave Macmillan, 2005.

Munro, Eileen. *Munro Review of Child Protection: A Child Centred System.* Department for Education. 2011.

Oudekerk, Barbara A., Lucy A. Guarnera, and N. Dickon Reppucci. "Older Opposite-Sex Romantic Partners, Sexual Risk, and Victimization in Adolescence." *Child Abuse & Neglect*, vol. 38, no. 7, 2014, pp. 1238-48.

Parton, Nigel. "Concerns about Risk as a Major Driver of Professional Practice." *Beyond the Risk Paradigm in Child Protection*, edited by Marie Connolley, Palgrace, 2017, pp. 3-14.

Parton, Nigel, et al. *Child Protection: Risk and the Moral Order.* Palgrave Macmillan, 1997.

Parton, Nigel, David Thorpe, and Corrine Wattam. *Child Protection: Risk and the Moral Order.* Macmillan International Higher Education, 1995.

Prior, Lindsay. *Using Documents in Social Research.* Sage, 2003.

Sawyer, Susan M., et al. "The Age of Adolescence." *The Lancet Child & Adolescent Health*, vol. 2, no. 3, 2018, pp. 223-28.

Sidebotham, Peter. "What Do Serious Case Reviews Achieve?" *Archives of Disease in Childhood*, vol. 97, no. 3, 2012, pp. 189-192.

SmithBattle, Lee. "Gaining Ground from a Family and Cultural Legacy: A Teen Mother's Story of Repairing the World." *Family Process*, vol. 47, 2008, pp. 521-35.

Social Exclusion Unit. *Teenage Pregnancy Strategy.* HMSO, 1999.

"Syndrome." *Merriam-Webster*, www.merriam-webster.com/dictionary /syndrome. Accessed 6 June 2022.

Tronto, Joan. *Caring Democracy: Markets, Equality, and Justice.* New York University Press, 2013.

White, Jacquelyn, et al. "Feminism and the Decade of Behavior." *Psychology of Women Quarterly,* vol. 25, no. 4, 2001, pp. 267-79.

Whitworth, Melissa, and Ruth Cockerill. "Antenatal Management of Teenage Pregnancy." *Obstetrics, Gynaecology, & Reproductive Medicine,* vol. 20, no. 11, 2010, pp. 323-28.

Wilkinson, Sue. "Feminist Social Psychologies: A Decade of Development." *Feminist Social Psychologies. International Perspectives,* edited by S. Wilkinson, Open University Press, 1996, pp. 1-2.

Wilkinson, Sue. "The Role of Reflexivity in Feminist Psychology." *Women's Studies International Forum,* vol. 11, No.5, 1988, pp. 493-50.

Chapter 8

Mothering Children with Fetal Alcohol Spectrum Disorder (FASD): Child Protection and Contested Spaces

Dorothy Badry, Kelly Coons-Harding, Robyn Williams, Bernadette Iahtail, Peter Choate, and Erin Leveque

Introduction

We write this chapter as researchers from both Canada and Australia who share a concern about the intersection of fetal alcohol spectrum disorder (FASD) and the child welfare system and the overrepresentation of Indigenous children in care. We are Indigenous (Williams and Iahtail) and settler scholars (Badry, Coons-Harding, Choate, and Leveque), and three of us have extensive experience with the child welfare system (Badry, Iahtail, and Choate). We are writing from an intersectional space on FASD with a goal of unsettling the discourse on FASD, mothering, child welfare, and Indigeneity. We are aware of the stigma that is associated with alcohol use and pregnancy as well as the subsequent engagement with the child protection system that often follows for so many mothers. In this chapter, we focus mainly on Canada and identify the Parent Child Assistance Program (PCAP) as a critical intervention model, which exists in both Alberta and Washington State. We also raise the discourse about gaps in Australia, where PCAP does not exist; however, mother mentoring services are often being provided from a maternal health framework including midwifery (Marsh et al. e2). A common concern in both Canada and Australia is effectively meeting the needs of mothers, children, and families for whom FASD is a concern, as child welfare interventions, particularly child removal, leave mothers with a staggering sense of loss and grief that often goes unrecognized. Christine Marsh et al. take up the concern of assumption of care—which is the removal of newborns by Family and Community Services (FACS) in Australia—and argue that this topic has received minimal attention in the literature (e2). Through the voices of mothers, social workers, and midwives, a narrative emerged suggesting that inter-generational trauma is a contributing factor to substance use and pregnancy. As one young mother explained: "The whole time I was pregnant I was really scared. I wanted to stop using but I was really frightened to get help because I thought they'd call FACS, which ultimately, that went against me anyway" (qtd. in Marsh et al. e4). The voice of this young woman sets the stage for our chapter.

In this chapter, we discuss the nuances of mothering, child protection, and FASD from a trauma-informed lens. The focus of this chapter is on challenging the space that contributes to the disem-powerment and disenfranchisement of mothers who are engaged in the child protection space, despite their personal desire to have a better life for themselves and their children. Through understanding the effects of trauma and disenfranchisement, this chapter will also investigate and further humanize the pressing issue of the disproportionate representation of Indigenous children in Canadian (Brownell et al.; Fallon et al. 16) and Australian child welfare systems (Tilbury 57).

Trauma-informed practice and care is a critical construct, as awareness of the impact of trauma is critical to formulating effective interventions. Nancy Poole and Lorraine Greaves identify the devastating effect of early life experiences, such as abuse, neglect, witnessing violence, and other losses that can "undermine or damage people's sense of safety, self and self-efficacy, as well as the ability to regulate emotions and navigate relationships ... there is compelling evidence that mental health and substance use problems are connected to people's experiences of violence, abuse and trauma" (xi-xiii). Natalie

Clark calls attention to the concern that in the Indigenous context, viewing trauma as an individual health problem minimizes the impact of historical violence and trauma associated with colonization. Thus, situating the problem in individuals does not hold a system to account that for decades has failed to protect children. Clark advocates for going beyond trauma-informed to violence-informed and intersectional work that "locates the source of girls' challenges within structural and systemic processes such as racism, poverty, sexism, and the intersections of these in their lives" (11).

Grounding FASD in a Child Protection Context

The 2008 Canadian Incidence Studies of Reported Child Abuse and Neglect (CIS) revealed that FASD was a concern in approximately 3,177 substantiated child welfare investigations across Canada (Public Health Agency of Canada 39). Risk factors in the home leading to child protection involvement included alcohol use in approximately 35 per cent of cases, drug and solvent use in over 40 per cent of cases, and mental health issues in over 35 per cent of cases (Goodman et al. 2). The CIS is currently undergoing a new cycle of data gathering, and what is important to note from the CIS data is that the risks for child protection involvement for children with FASD remains high and is an ongoing concern. This concern highlights the need for training on FASD for all child protection workers, and professionals working alongside child protection, training that is not yet available for most child protection workers (Badry and Choate 21). Our position is that training and increasing knowledge about FASD is critical to make informed care decisions and to support effective interventions.

Alcohol Use and Pregnancy, Disability, and Mothering

Kenneth Jones and David Smith were among some of the first North American researchers to identify and describe the characteristic facial features and physical anomalies associated with fetal alcohol syndrome (Jones and Smith; Jones et al.). FASD is the current diagnostic term used to describe impacts on the brain and body of individuals prenatally exposed to alcohol (Harding et al. 3). Since the first research on FASD, the medical community now explains that alcohol acts as a teratogen (toxin) to the developing fetus and actively discourages any alcohol/ substance use during pregnancy. Messaging about the risks of alcohol consumption during pregnancy and FASD in the media tends to position FASD as a result of individual mothers' choices rather than viewing it as a systemic, public health concern. Whereas some researchers posit that FASD is a result of "moral panic" (Armstrong and Abel 276), others demonstrate the role and impact of stigma in this public health issue (Corrigan et al. 1166). Ann Dowsett Johnston has identified drinking and pregnancy as "the last taboo" (173), and Janet Christie in the same book is quoted as stating that drinking and pregnancy "may be the most stigmatized area of a very stigmatized subject" (173). Elizabeth Armstrong illuminates how surveillance of mothers of children with FASD is related to the notion that their lives must be filled with "social disorder" and suggests that FASD has been constructed through a "one dimensional etiology"—exposure to alcohol during pregnancy (*Conceiving Risk* 151). Svetlana Popova and Christina Chambers have identified FASD as a preventable disability and a global health problem (1). Deepa Singal et al. in a study on psychiatric morbidity of mothers of children with an FASD diagnosis report a "high burden of psychiatric illness during their pregnancies, during which they consumed alcohol ... including anxiety and depression" (53) and suggest the need to recognize "higher rates of postpartum psychological distress" (540).

Alcohol use and pregnancy has significant risks, and it is estimated that globally almost 10 per cent of pregnancies are alcohol exposed (Popova et al. 237). In Australia, Sylvia Roozen et al. estimate prevalence at 10.82 of one thousand births (18). Even more alarming, parental substance use is a factor in between 50 and 79 per cent of child welfare cases in which young children are removed from parental care (Grant et al. 11). Mothers who use substances are positioned as a risk to their child and are frequently under surveillance, and it is not uncommon for children whose mothers use substances to enter into the care of the child protection system at birth because of child protection concerns (Marsh et al. e 2). Furthermore, women who give birth to a child with FASD often have other alcohol-exposed pregnancies without supportive interventions (Grant et al. 17). Such programs as the PCAP offer specific interventions aimed at prevention of FASD and support for women who have given birth or are at risk of giving birth to a child with FASD. This program was originally created at the University of Washington and was established in Alberta, Canada in 1999, and has since been provincially funded at over thirty sites, including First Nations and Métis communities. PCAP offers intensive long-term mentoring relationships and case management with a goal of preventing further births of alcohol-exposed pregnancies through holistic, intensive, and harm reduction-focused supports. In this way, PCAP is uniquely focused on mothers involved in the child welfare system. It is critical to acknowledge, recognize, and humanize mothers who use alcohol and other substances as a form of self-medicating to cope with complex sociohistorical and ongoing trauma (Choate and Badry 23)

The PCAP program was developed in response to the concerns of mothers, including intergenerational trauma and substance use, childhood abuse, incomplete high school education, and early substance use in adolescence (Grant et al. 12). In an effort to interrupt this intergenerational cycle, the PCAP program seeks to connect with these women and their families. A primary foundation of this work is relational-based approaches with women and offering mentoring supports for up to three years. Mentors receive advanced training and ongoing supervision working with fifteen families or more and engage in ongoing home visits bimonthly for up to three years. The key supports offered to women include identifying goals and maintaining ongoing support and coaching to reach these aspirations. Furthermore, a critical goal of PCAP is to prevent further alcohol-exposed births through completing substance use treatment, using family planning, remaining substance abstinent, engaging in work or training, and having their children reside in their own families. Therese Grant notes that "78.1% of the mothers had not delivered subsequent birth (SB) during the three-year intervention, 9.6% had a SB not exposed to alcohol or drugs and 12.3% had a SB exposed to substances" (15). Another well-known program is Mothercraft's Breaking the Cycle (BTC) in Toronto, which began in the 1990s and delivers services and outreach to mothers and children who are seen as clients and are offered theoretically grounded care. The key theories informing the work are developmental theory, attachment theory, trauma theory, relational theory, and harm reduction (Motz et al. 10). Specifically "pregnant substance involved women tell us that the services they prefer should include: the ability to affiliate with other women in similar circumstances ... a small group where they do not feel like their stories are overlooked or lost; and a specialized program with relapse prevention and prenatal components" (Motz et al. 25). The use of a relational framework to engage with women is at the centre of supportive interventions in the Pregnancy Outreach Program offered through BTC, including supporting women in maintaining positive relationships with other service systems, such as child welfare.

Contested Spaces

Mothers of children with FASD have distinct challenges and their lives are often fraught with risk. Armstrong identifies the issue of diagnosing "moral disorder" as society's way to hold women accountable for alcohol use during pregnancy ("Making Sense" 68). Mothers frequently face multiple barriers to parenting, including being single mothers, experiencing traumatic histories, such as intergenerational trauma, experiencing violence, living with mental health issues, living in poverty, and potentially having undiagnosed FASD themselves. Lenora Marcellus argues for a feminist ethic perspective for treating women using substances during pregnancy, as they often have health issues, receive limited prenatal care, suffer from food insecurity and are experiencing poverty (731). Patrick Corrigan et al. have identified the high level of public stigma experienced by birth mothers of children with FASD and conclude that substance-using behaviour contributes to women being blamed for the birth outcomes of a child with prenatal alcohol exposure (1167). Public perceptions of mothers are that they are both bad and responsible for the outcome for their child, which places them in the precarious position of facing insurmountable amounts of stigma and being disenfranchised from the support services that they are often criticized for not accessing. It is essential to ask why women do not access these services when they are faced with the potential risk of losing their child to the system.

Framing of Good and Bad Mothers

Although women and mothers occupy a multiplicity of contested spaces, there are few spaces as contested and complex as a mother's womb. This space is both hers and not hers, part of her, but belonging to someone/something else. Katha Pollitt's contestation of individual women as solely responsible for the health and wellbeing of their fetus continues to be relevant today. Contemporary fetal rights discourses are an assault on women through the monitoring of maternal bodies and behaviours, which are deeply situated within gendered expectations of motherhood. Within these discourses, the archetypes of a good mother, and therefore a bad one, become narrow depictions of motherhood, which places women in the precarious position of measuring themselves or other mothers against a standard (Choi et al. 168).

Marcellus highlights the need for a feminist ethic in providing support and treatment to women who are often disenfranchised from healthcare services. Engagement in child protection services is frequently grounded in fear, as it is often involuntary and can be a difficult experience for women, particularly for those who have multiple vulnerabilities. Child removal is a real and terrifying possibility for these women and further contributes to the archetype of a bad mother— an identification that is entrenched in such words as failure, disenfranchisement, and disempowerment. The notion that women who use alcohol during pregnancy should just stop, exercise self-control, and seek treatment is unrealistic and potentially harmful. A harm reduction frame is a more humanizing approach to understanding mothers. Haskell suggests that a trauma lens helps us to recognize that early experiences of child abuse and neglect are "defining life experiences that can shape and even distort core aspects of a person's identity" (qtd. in Poole and Greaves 9). There is a need to reframe and to see women's lives from a holistic, trauma-informed perspective by recognizing that FASD is a signifier of interpersonal challenges that require supportive care rather than judgment and/or further trauma. A trauma-informed lens calls for flexibility on the part of counsellors and supports the view that behaviour can be reframed and recognized as coping strategies and adaptations that women make to survive trauma. Furthermore, the health risks for mothers who give birth to a child with FASD, including premature death, are markedly increased, and they can be attributed to cancer, injuries, and alcohol-related disease (Li et al.1332). Qing Li and colleagues suggest that an FASD diagnosis should be used as a marker to promote and support the health of mothers to reduce the risk of early mortality.

Child Protection

The complex lives of women who use substances during pregnancy become invisible in the child protection system, which tends to dichotomize bad and risky mothers when using substances or good and safe mothers when not. Diana Gustafson refers to this phenomenon as the "good mother/bad mother binary" (25). Studies have demonstrated the effects of being categorized as a risky mother, as mothers with substance use issues often had higher levels of engagement with the child protection system, particularly those between sixteen and nineteen years of age (Broadhurst et al. 2255). Martha Canfield et al. note that mothers who use substances are at high risk of losing their children to care; they suggest there are limited ways in which to break the cycle of repeat child welfare involvement when they give birth to more children (12). Key problems noted in Canfield et al.'s research contributing to child removal were drug and alcohol use during pregnancy, mental health concerns, including a history of adverse childhood experiences, and low socioeconomic status, which contributed to stress on many levels.

From a child protection stance, children are often seen as "innocent victims" (Swift 158), particularly when they are young, and providing help to mothers is about benefiting the child and not always about prioritizing the mother's needs. Mothers who live away from their children are often not doing so by choice, such as the case of child removal, which Gustafson identifies as a process of "unbecoming a mother," where limited social support systems often play a key role (32). In turn, this leads to increased identification as a bad mother, which creates significant barriers to having children returned to their care. Grant notes that mothers involved with the child welfare system who experience child removal often have subsequent births of substance-exposed infants because they lose the motivation for change without their child in their life (16). The PCAP program's intensive case management and recovery coaches support women to have fewer substance-exposed births and keep children in their care. At the core of the PCAP program is the recognition that women do not intend to cause harm by using substances while pregnant; rather, women have unplanned pregnancies, often have traumatic histories, and use substances as a means to cope. In the context of having a child with FASD, child protection is highly unlikely to judge mothers as being good enough to care for their own child (Choate and Engstrom 368). Once a child protection case goes to trial in a family court, mothers will rarely have a child returned to their care. Furthermore, the impact of the mother's FASD on parenting capacity will unlikely be assessed by a professional expert in FASD (Choate et al. 294)

Social discourse that holds maternal factors as solely responsible for the birth outcome requires a paradigm shift, as this is a stigmatizing and unjust notion and is reflective of a paternalistic medical model that requires adaptation. Mothers know their children with FASD already face struggles and are concerned their children's voices may be discounted and their future compromised in a society that may not understand or accept their children's differences or have the capacity to offer required resources.

Humanizing mothers in these circumstances requires moving toward a trauma-informed perspective (Poole and Greaves). Programs such as the PCAP in Alberta offer hopeful interventions through their focus on long-term mentoring for women who give birth to children who are diagnosed with FASD. This program advocates and supports mothers in the child welfare system through mentoring programs, practical support services, and advocacy work. Mothers may end up involved with the family court system, particularly when child apprehension occurs and legal support is often required. Mentors support mothers in connecting with lawyers and provide support in the often contentious legal proceedings related to child removal, whether on a temporary or permanent basis. A key goal of PCAP is prevention and the positive impact for women working with mentors deeply influences future birth outcomes, including non-exposed subsequent births directly contributing to the prevention of FASD (Grant et al. 12).

In addition to the PCAP program, child welfare workers in Alberta are required to take training courses in Indigenous awareness, signs of safety, trauma-informed practice, and FASD. A key component of this training is to ensure that workers have a basic understanding of how trauma unfolds in the lives of people with complex social, health, and emotional histories who become involved with the child welfare system. When trauma is not recognized, client responses to child welfare intervention are often misunderstood and may cause further harm. Although child protection spaces have somewhat acknowledged the often lifelong and irreparable harm done to mothers and their children when separated, the immediate risk associated with substance use can lead to child apprehension or the assumption of care (Marsh et al. el)

The Intersection of Indigeneity, Child Protection, Mothering, and FASD

In both Canada and Australia, the systematic removal of Indigenous children from their families and communities has contributed to a history of harm and violence in the child welfare system (Tilbury 57). The First Nations Caring Society of Canada has found that it is critical to provide holistic community-based FASD training and services, and the Truth and Reconciliation Commission (TRC) of Canada's Call to Action #34 demonstrates a need to collaborate across all levels of government (Stewart and Glowatski, 4). In 2016, the First Nations Caring Society successfully sued the Government of Canada for overt discrimination of Indigenous children/families in child protection systems, but to date, no meaningful action has been taken to address this discrimination—even in the context of the TRC. Instead, high rates of child apprehension of Indigenous children continue. In many families in Canada and Australia, mothering has been extended to grandmothering in order prevent child apprehension and it has been noted that significant "granny burnout" exists for Indigenous grandmothers who navigate maintaining their health and wellbeing as long as possible to provide care for the increasing numbers of children in the community (Hammill 72). Cindy Blackstock et al. indicate that governments in both Canada and Australia continue to discriminate against Indigenous children and their families through underfunding, and this is a major factor contributing to the overrepresentation of Indigenous children in care in both countries. Underfunding contributes to inequitable service and a lack of resources for children and families (Blackstock et al. 3).

The intersection of FASD and Indigeneity is important to acknowledge and deconstruct. Indigenous women are less likely to drink alcohol in general than non-Indigenous women in Canada. However, Indigenous women who do drink heavily often do so to cope with stressors linked back to the ongoing trauma of colonization and challenges in determinants of health (McKenzie et al. 380). The assumption that Indigenous women are at a higher risk for FASD contributes to further colonial stigma, stereotyping, and surveillance of these women at the individual level (Salmon 165; Tait 209). This surveillance becomes another barrier, likely making Indigenous women hesitant to seek support from non-Indigenous community or health organizations; it highlights a need for culturally safe and decolonizing trauma-informed approaches (McLean 9). We embrace a social determinants of health perspective in relation to mothers who use substances. Such a perspective is aligned with a trauma-informed perspective in that it moves beyond the shaming and blaming of individual mothers to recognizing the deep-seeded impacts that gender-based oppression, racism, ableism, colonization, and poverty have on this population. Specifically, in Canada and Australia, the long-term impacts of colonization and intergenerational trauma are implicated in the wellbeing of Indigenous mothers. An essential component of decolonizing trauma-informed care for Indigenous families experiencing intervention is led by Indigenous people themselves. Dian Million suggests that healing trauma is a cautionary process that is not disconnected from historical racism, colonialism, violence, and critical Indigenous responses to trauma include both self-determination and human rights. As noted by Clark, trauma narratives can serve to stigmatize and "further colonize girls' health and their bodies" (e 1), and it is critical to develop safe spaces for girls and young women to share their truths and experiences.

Recently, a "culture as intervention" approach is beginning to receive its rightful, central place in the framework of service delivery (Dell and Acoose e261), and Carina Fiedeldey-Van Dijk et al. identify the need for Native wellness assessments that are culturally sensitive (186). We suggest that a trauma-informed and a social determinants of health perspective calls for a significant shift in care towards culturally safe service provision for Indigenous children and families.

The Voices of Indigenous Mothers

A tension arises as noted above in referring to mothers of children with FASD as "biological" or "bio" mothers versus simply using the term "mother." The implication of the term "biological/biomother" is not generally ascribed to mothers, and thus when mothers of children with

FASD are referred to in this way, they experience this as stigmatizing. As one mother stated in a 2019 community meeting in Vancouver, British Columbia: "We are maternal mothers! We do not need to be called biomothers; it feels like we are being blamed for our children's disabilities." In deconstructing this experience further, Lisa, an Indigenous woman and a mom of children with FASD, has written about these experiences and discusses the stigma she has experienced and highlights that there are few safe spaces for these mothers and their children (Stewart and Glowatski 123). As a community-based para-professional, Lisa works directly in the community and supports women during pregnancy and focuses her work on women feeling safe and experiencing support through relationship. As Lisa writes, "If women do not feel safe, they never come back to us" (Stewart and Glowatski 125). Lisa indicates that during her pregnancy, she drank before she knew she was pregnant and faced multiple judgments and clearly identified "the racism that surrounds the disability-and specifically mothers." She continues: "I knew the stereotype, that they were stereotyping us as Aboriginal women" (qtd. in Stewart and Glowatski 126). Lisa articulates that judgments exist within systems, such as healthcare, within social service systems, and as a professional, she has often heard others at conferences and other venues speak about "those mothers," which immediately contributes to marginalization and othering. Rachel has shared her experience of raising her son with FASD to adulthood. He once asked his mom when his girlfriend became pregnant, "Is my baby going to be smart.... I hope my baby's not going to be dumb like me," which felt like an indictment from the past. Stewart et al. highlight the need to pay attention to the experiences of micro and macro aggressions that Indigenous mothers experience whose children have FASD. Both Lisa and Rachel speak positively about the contributions mothers with this experience can make in relation to prevention and in the sharing and living of their stories in their communities.

Supporting Mothers and Children: Ways Forwards

We recommend that every child protection jurisdiction in Canada and Australia deliver training on FASD and trauma-informed care within their child protection and youth justice systems. It is also critical to hear the voices of marginalized groups, such as women who have lived experience and are willing to share their stories with others. The voices of women are powerful and should be invited into the discourse that focuses on learning about FASD in a respectful and protected way to ensure privacy and dignity.

A singular focus on the individual mother and/or her child can distract healthcare professionals to overlook the social determinants of health. As medical systems are entrenched with increasing demands of efficiency, it is difficult for doctors and healthcare professionals to take the time to contextualize their patients. What is seen is alcoholism rather than how alcohol use is a symptom of several complex aspects of her life. This immediately occludes the possibility of care provided in a supportive and safe way that does not retraumatize women. Specifically, for Indigenous women, care may be provided in a culturally unsafe and ineffective way, which can contribute to further harm. A key component of reducing harm is for providers to provide culturally sound care, particularly within rural, northern, and isolated Canadian contexts. In order to understand women's health issues that are important in FASD prevention work in rural and northern settings, it is critical to understand historical and ongoing oppression and trauma, problematic alcohol use, child welfare involvement, and therefore, the impact on communities. FASD prevention work needs to be grounded in community, and local support is essential to meaningfully address and support connection to the land, traditional culture, and local food to promote health (Badry and Wight Felske e5).

Women and children have suffered deeply in child protection interventions where FASD is a concern. However, it is recognized that the protection and safety of a child is paramount, and where it is essential, children are removed from parental care. The ways in which this work is carried out are highly problematic, contributing to significant loss and grief (Marsh e9), and every effort should be made to engage differently with women through novel approaches to treatment, such as foster care for the family. Mother mentoring programs, such as those offered by PCAP, have emerged as the single most protective factor for prevention of FASD and effective intervention with women. This program has supported countless women in relation to child welfare interventions through support and advocacy and through working over the long term with women from a relational framework.

This program model should be replicated across Canada and internationally.

Summary and Conclusion: Contextualizing Mothering, FASD, and Child Protection

The use of alcohol and other substances offers a challenge across the health and social service sectors, and mothers who have addictions are highly stigmatized and live in constant fear of the child welfare system. It is critical to recognize that women with traumatic histories often use alcohol and other substances as a means to self-medicate and do not intend to harm themselves or the fetus while pregnant. Thus, how do we reframe and humanize the experience for mothers living on the edge? The mother-child connection is often the motivation for change in relation to substance use, and it is critical to raise the voices of mothers, such as Lisa's and Rachel's, as earlier noted. The care that mothers intend to provide for their children, including those with FASD, is often overlooked because of stigmatizing discourses that dominate both service provision and social attitudes. Armstrong asks: "Is the disorder we diagnose ... caused by exposure to alcohol in utero, or is it caused by poverty, social distress, and deeply rooted inequality?" (*Conceiving Risk* 217). This question leaves us much to think about as we work to reframe viewpoints and position mothers who use alcohol during pregnancy as parents with potential.

What becomes clear in this chapter is that trauma-informed caring approaches, such as PCAP or similar programs, are urgently needed to support families impacted by FASD. There is no doubt that mothers who use alcohol and other substances during pregnancy face daunting challenges in the child protection system, in which they face multiple disadvantages. The devastating effects of colonization have contributed to the emergence of FASD as a reflection of intergenerational trauma, which has not been either deeply explored or deconstructed. The time has come to stop harmful narratives suggesting that FASD is completely preventable without structural change. It is time to create new narratives for mothers and to challenge and discuss contested spaces, such as FASD and child protection. One way to support changing the narratives about mothers is through offering FASD-informed care. As much as children who have FASD deserve to have workers who are fully trained and understand their disability, mothers also require workers who are clinically trained and knowledgeable about FASD and about the reasons alcohol use in pregnancy occurs. Such workers must stop blaming women who are in these circumstances. An ethical imperative exists for systems to provide training on FASD to all child protection workers and allied health professionals who have a duty of care for children and families in the child protection sphere. While often dismissed, the voices of mothers often become whispers that are silenced by systems who do not have a clear understanding of the complexity of FASD. Opportunities need to be created to support these voices being heard. This can be one small step in shifting the discourse.

Works Cited

Armstrong, Elizabeth. *Conceiving Risk, Bearing Responsibility: Fetal Alcohol Syndrome and the Diagnosis of Moral Disorder.* Johns Hopkins University Press, 2003.

Armstrong, Elizabeth. "Making Sense of Advice About Drinking During Pregnancy?: Does Evidence Even Matter?" *The Journal of Perinatal Education*, vol. 26, no. 2, 2017, pp. 65-69.

Armstrong, Elizabeth, and Ernest L. Abel. "Fetal Alcohol Syndrome: The Origins of a Moral Panic." *Alcohol and Alcoholism*, vol. 35, no. 3, 2000, pp. 276-82.

Badry, Dorothy, and Aileen Wight Felske. "An Exploratory Study on the Use of Photovoice as a Method for Approaching FASD Prevention in the Northwest Territories." *First Peoples Child & Family Review*, vol. 8, no. 1, 2013, pp. 143-60.

Badry, Dorothy, and Peter Choate. "Fetal Alcohol Spectrum Disorder: A Disability in Need of Social Work Education, Knowledge, and Practice." *Social Work and Social Sciences Review,* vol. 17, no. 3, 2015, pp. 20-32.

Blackstock, Cindy, et al. "Indigenous Ontology, International Law and the Application of the Convention to the Over-representation of Indigenous Children in Out of Home Care in Canada and Australia." *Child Abuse & Neglect,* 2020, p. 104587, doi.org/10.1016/j.chiabu. 2020.104587. Accessed 7 June 2022.

Broadhurst, Karen, et al. "Connecting Events in Time to Identify a

Hidden Population: Birth Mothers and Their Children in Recurrent Care Proceedings in England." *The British Journal of Social Work*, vol. 45, no. 8, 2015, pp. 2241-60.

Brownell, Marni, et al. "Health, Social, Education, and Justice Outcomes of Manitoba First Nations Children Diagnosed with Fetal Alcohol Spectrum Disorder: A Population-Based Cohort Study of Linked Administrative Data." *The Canadian Journal of Psychiatry*, vol. 64, no. 9, 2019, pp. 611-20.

Canfield, Martha, et al. "Maternal Substance Use and Child Protection: A Rapid Evidence Assessment of Factors Associated with Loss of Child Care." *Child Abuse & Neglect*, vol. 70, 2017, pp. 11-27,

Choate, Peter, and Dorothy Badry. "Stigma as a Dominant Discourse in Fetal Alcohol Spectrum Disorder." *Advances in Dual Diagnosis*, vol. 12, no. 1-2, 2019, pp. 36-52.

Choate, Peter, and Sandra Engstrom. "The 'Good Enough' Parent: Implications for Child Protection." *Child Care in Practice*, vol. 20, no. 4, 2014, pp. 368-82.

Choi, P., et al. "Supermum, Superwife, Supereverything: Performing Femininity in the Transition to Motherhood." *Journal of Reproductive and Infant Psychology*, vol. 23, no. 2, 2005, pp. 167-80.

Clark, Natalie. "Shock and Awe: Trauma as the New Colonial Frontier." *Humanities (Basel)*, vol. 5, no. 1, 2016, p. 14.

Clifford, Anton C., et al. "A Systematic Review of Suicide Prevention Interventions Targeting Indigenous Peoples in Australia, United States, Canada, and New Zealand." *BMC Public Health*, vol. 13, no. 1, 2013, p. 463.

Corrigan, Patrick W., et al. "The Public Stigma of Birth Mothers of Children with Fetal Alcohol Spectrum Disorders." *Alcoholism: Clinical and Experimental Research*, vol. 41, no. 6, 2017, pp. 1166-73.

Dell, Colleen A., and Sharon Acoose. "Indigenous Culture as Intervention in Addictions Treatment." *Drug and Alcohol Dependence*, vol. 100, no. 146, 2015, p. e261.

Dowsett Johnston, Ann. *Drink: The Intimate Relationship between Women and Alcohol.* Harper Collins Publishers Ltd., 2013.

Carina, Fiedeldey-Van Dijk, et al. "Honoring Indigenous culture-as-intervention: Development and Validity of the Native Wellness

Assessment.™" *Journal of Ethnicity in Substance Abuse*, vol. 16, no. 2, 2017, pp. 181-218.

Fallon, Barbara, et al. "Placement Decisions and Disparities among Aboriginal Children: Further Analysis of the Canadian Incidence Study of Reported Child Abuse and Neglect Part A: Comparisons of the 1998 and 2003 Surveys." *Child Abuse & Neglect* vol. 37, no. 1, 2013, pp. 47-60.

First Nations Caring Society. "FASD Training Study: Final Report." *First Nations Caring Society of Canada*, 2006, fncaringsociety.com/sites/default/files/docs/FASD_TrainingStudy.pdf. Accessed 7 June 2022.

Goodman, Deborah, et al. "A Profile of Investigations with a Noted Child Functioning Concern of FAS/FAE in Canada in 2008." *Canadian Child Welfare Research Portal,* 2015, pp. 1-5.

Grant, Therese, et al. "Improving Pregnancy Outcomes among High-Risk Mothers Who Abuse Alcohol and Drugs: Factors Associated with Subsequent Exposed Births." *Children and Youth Services Review,* vol. 46, 2014, pp. 11-18,

Gustafson, Diana. *Unbecoming Mothers: The Social Production of Maternal Absence.* Haworth Clinical Practice Press, 2005.

Hammill, Jan. "Granny Rights: Combatting the Granny Burnout Syndrome among Australian Indigenous Communities." *The Society for International Development*, vol. 44, no. 2, 2001, pp. 69-74.

Harding, Kelly, et al. "Policy Action Paper: Toward a Standard Definition of Fetal Alcohol Spectrum Disorder in Canada." *Canada FASD Research Network*, 2019, canfasd.ca/wp-content/uploads/2019/08/Toward-a-Standard-Definition-of-FASD-Final.pdf. Accessed 7 June 2022.

Health Canada. "Canadian Alcohol and Drug Use Monitoring Survey." *Health Canada*, 2012, www.hc-sc.gc.ca/hc-ps/drugs-drogues/stat/_2012/summary-sommaire-eng.php#s7a. Accessed 7 June 2022.

Huggins, Janet E., et al. "Suicide Attempts among Adults with Fetal Alcohol Spectrum Disorders: Clinical Considerations." *Mental Health Aspects of Developmental Disabilities*, vol. 11, 2008, p. 33.

Jones, Kenneth, and David Smith. "Recognition of the Fetal Alcohol

Syndrome in Early Infancy." *The Lancet*, vol. 302, no. 7836, 1973, pp. 999-1001.

Lawson-Te Aho, Keri, and James H. Liu. "Indigenous Suicide and Colonization: The Legacy of Violence and the Necessity of Self-Determination." *International Journal of Conflict and Violence (IJCV)*, vol. 4, no. 1, 2010, pp. 124-33.

Li, Qing, et al. "Fetal Alcohol Spectrum Disorders: A Population Based Study of Premature Mortality Rates in the Mothers." *Maternal and Child Health Journal*, vol. 16, no. 6, 2012, pp. 1332-37.

Marcellus, Lenora. "Feminist Ethics Must Inform Practice: Interventions with Perinatal Substance Users." *Health Care for Women International*, vol. 25, no. 8, 2004, pp. 730-42.

Marsh, Christine A., et al. "Making the Hidden Seen: A Narrative Analysis of the Experiences of Assumption of Care at Birth." *Women and Birth,* vol. 32, no. 1, 2019, pp. e1-e11.

McKenzie, Holly A., et al. "Understanding Addictions among Indigenous People through Social Determinants of Health Frameworks and Strength-Based Approaches: A Review of the Research Literature from 2013 to 2016." *Current Addiction Reports*, vol. 3, 2016, pp. 378-86.

McLean, Sara, and Stewart McDougall. "Fetal Alcohol Spectrum Disorders. Current Issues in Awareness, Prevention, and Intervention." *Australian Institute of Family Studies,* vol. 29, 2014, pp. 1-19.

Million, Dian. *Therapeutic Nations : Healing in an Age of Indigenous Human Rights.* University of Arizona, 2013.

Motz, Mary, et al. *The Breaking the Cycle Compendium Volume 2—Healing Through Relationships.* Mothercraft Press, 2020.

O'Connor, Mary J., et al. "Suicide Risk in Adolescents with Fetal Alcohol Spectrum Disorders." *Birth Defects Research*, vol. 111, no. 12, 2019, pp. 822-28.

Pollitt, Katha. "Fetal Rights: A New Assault on Feminism." *Nation*, vol. 250, no. 12, 1990, pp. 409-18.

Poole, Nancy, and Lorraine Greaves. *Becoming Trauma Informed.* Centre for Addiction and Mental Health, 2012.

Popova, Svetlana, et al. "Global Prevalence of Alcohol Use and Binge Drinking during Pregnancy, and Fetal Alcohol Spectrum Disorder."

Biochemistry and Cell Biology, vol. 96, no. 2, 2018, pp. 237-40.

Popova, Svetlana, and Christina Chambers. "Fetal Alcohol Spectrum Disorders Must Be Recognized Globally as a Large Public Health Problem." *The International Journal of Alcohol and Drug Research,* vol. 3, no. 1, 2014, pp. 1-3.

Public Health Agency of Canada. *Canadian Incidence Study of Reported Child Abuse and Neglect—2008: Major Findings.* Government of Canada, 2010.

Roozen, Sylvia, et al. "Worldwide Prevalence of Fetal Alcohol Spectrum Disorders: A Systematic Literature Review Including Meta Analysis." *Alcoholism: Clinical and Experimental Research,* vol. 40, no. 1, 2016, pp. 18-32.

Salmon, Amy. "Aboriginal Mothering, FASD Prevention and the Contestations of Neoliberal Citizenship." *Critical Public Health,* vol. 21, no. 2, 2011, pp. 165-78.

Singal, Deepa, et al. "The Psychiatric Morbidity of Women Who Give Birth to Children with Fetal Alcohol Spectrum Disorder (FASD): Results of the Manitoba Mothers and FASD Study." *The Canadian Journal of Psychiatry,* vol. 62, no. 8, 2017, pp. 531-42.

Stewart, M., and K. Glowatski. "Truth and Reconciliation Call to Action #34: A Framework for Action." *Canada FASD Research Network,* 2018, canfasd.ca/wp-content/uploads/2018/10/TRC34-A-Framework-for-Action.pdf. Accessed 7 June 2022.

Swift, Karen J. *Manufacturing 'Bad Mothers': A Critical Perspective on Child Neglect.* University of Toronto Press, 1995.

Tait, Caroline. "Disruptions in Nature, Disruptions in Society: Aboriginal Peoples of Canada and the 'Making' of Fetal Alcohol Syndrome." *Healing Traditions: The Mental Health of Aboriginal Peoples in Canada,* edited by L. J. Kirmayer and G. G. Valaskakis, University of British Columbia Press, 2009, pp. 196-218.

Thanh, Nguyen X., and Egon Jonsson. "Life Expectancy of People with Fetal Alcohol Syndrome." *Journal of Population Therapeutics and Clinical Pharmacology,* vol. 23, no. 1, 2016, pp. e53-e59.

The Society of Obstetricians and Gynaecologists of Canada. "Alcohol Use and Pregnancy Consensus Clinical Guidelines." *Journal of Obstetrics and Gynaecology Canada,* vol. 32, no. 8, 2010, pp. 1-33.

Tilbury, Clare. "The Over representation of Indigenous children in the Australian Child Welfare System." *International Journal of Social Welfare,* vol. 18, no. 1, 2009, pp. 57-64.

Chapter 9

Systemic Unmothering: Mothers, Their Children, and Families at the Intersection of the Child Welfare and the Carceral Systems

Lauren Hawthorne and Brooke Richardson

Introduction

Several chapters in this book (Jenney, Ion, and Badry, et al) problematize dominant discourses of the good mother, which leaves little (if any) space for mothers involved with child protection systems. For mothers who bear the title of "criminal," there is even less space to be considered a good mother (Walsh and Crough). Standing "at the margins of socially constructed rubrics of motherhood" (Walsh and Crough 160), the stories and experiences of incarcerated mothers are rarely visible to the public. When they do hit the media, the stories usually rely on sensationalized coverage of controversial cases which incite public fear and/or collective disgust. Headlines including "criminal" and "mother" capture the public's attention because the actions of criminalized women so blatantly contradict the socially accepted mores of motherhood (Comack; Kilty and Frigon).

Mothers who are or have been incarcerated rarely get the opportunity to tell their stories of resistance, resilience, and repair as they try to maintain interrupted relationships with their children, families, and society. This chapter shares the stories of two mothers who, alongside their children and families, survived the carceral process and managed to (re)establish meaningful relations with each other. As their stories illustrate, these women retained human connection despite, rather than because of, these institutions. Though heartbreaking and infuriating at times, their stories ignite optimism and suggest that it is possible to mitigate the interpersonal trauma inflicted by maternal incarceration.

The Canadian Carceral Context

Women are the fastest growing prison population in the world (Walmsley 2). In Canada, the number of women admitted to custody in provincial, territorial, and federal carceral institutions has increased by more than 50 per cent between 2005 and 2015 (Sapers). Although these women are incredibly diverse in a variety of ways, over 70 per cent of federally incarcerated women have something in common: They are mothers to children under the age of eighteen (Sapers). Consequently, the nationwide escalation in female incarceration has produced inevitable yet relatively unacknowledged repercussions for Canadian children and families.

In addition to there being more women incarcerated in Canada than ever before, the category of federally sentenced women presented by national data is also notably racialized. As of 2015, Indigenous women accounted for 35.5 per cent of all women in federal custody across Canada (Sapers) while only representing 4.3 per cent of the total female population in Canada's 2011 census (Milan 14). Likewise, the number of incarcerated Black women increased by 54 per cent between 2002 and 2010 and again by 28 per cent in the following two years (Office of the Correctional Investigator). And, as of the 2011 census, Black women make up only 3 per cent of the female Canadian population (Milan 17). As such, examining the experiences of incarcerated mothers is of particularly importance to Indigenous, Black, and other minority populations who continue to disproportionately bear the brunt of discriminatory child protection and carceral practices. The mothers whose lived experiences inform this chapter did not identify as racialized. However, one family, including the child residing in kinship care and her guardians, identify as Indigenous. Their stores of inter-generational state intervention, child apprehension, and family trauma reflect Canada's history of ongoing discrimination and violence against Indigenous peoples.

Maternal Incarceration as an Adverse Childhood Experience

We cannot speak about incarcerated mothers without also recognizing the inextricably connected experiences of their children. Not surprisingly, the incarceration of a parent is considered an adverse childhood experience (ACE) related to trauma, stress, as well as negative health and quality of life outcomes (Arditti and Savla; Gjelsvik et al). The American Psychiatric Association (APA) defines trauma as "an emotional response to a terrible event like an accident, rape or natural disaster." However, narrowing the origin of trauma to an isolated event—whether natural, accidental, or criminal in nature—is exclusionary. This perspective focuses on a physical threat to life and ignores the potential for psychological or emotional danger to impact an individual in similarly devastating ways. In her work with children affected by the carceral system, Joyce Arditti advocates for "a more expansive definition of child trauma," which "acknowledges not just the threat that parental incarceration holds for psychologically wounding a child but also the complex and sometimes prolonged disruptions to children's relationships and beliefs about the world that stem from the imprisonment of a parent" (182). These experiences are often subtle and happen quietly over time; they chip away at a child's social and emotional world until it is unrecognizable. Such "prolonged disruptions" (Arditti 182) are scarring for children of incarcerated parents. While often viewed as inevitable, collateral damage of a mother's criminal behaviour, this chapter questions to what degree the suffering of children with incarcerated mothers occurs by design.

Intersection of Carceral and Child Protection Systems

The carceral process does not exist in a vacuum. It occurs at the intersection of several institutions and systems, including social assistance, education, healthcare, and, notably, child protection.

Because being incarcerated requires the forced physical separation of mothers from their children, families must navigate both of these systems in tandem. In some cases, a substitute caregiver is not able or available to care for the children. In other circumstances, the criminal conviction of a mother may be enough to warrant the involvement of child protection authorities. Although both child protection and justice systems embrace a rhetoric of "corrections," "rehabilitation," and/or "support," these systems are punitive and dehumanizing. Furthermore, mothers involved with these systems are typically in vulnerable and powerless positions with few (if any) resources to influence decision making. At a systems level, their thoughts, voices, and experiences do not hold weight, given their categorization as amoral criminals and therefore bad mothers.

A critical understanding of the incarcerated maternal experience through systemic academic inquiry lags considerably. As noted by Katarzyna Celinksa and Jane Siegel, "relatively few studies in the field of criminal justice and corrections focus on women offenders' experiences as mothers" (448). In their anthology on incarcerated mothers, Gordana Eljidupovic and Rebecca Bromwich further observe that "Whatever writing there is about incarcerated mothers has only very rarely been taken from a Canadian perspective" (10). This chapter offers a small step towards refocusing scholarship on the human experiences of families at the intersection of Canada's child protection and carceral systems.

Theoretical Orientation

Incarceration as a Relational Process

Existing literature on criminalized women can be crudely divided into two categories: pathways and resilience/outcome-focused research. Pathways research aims to understand how women come to be incarcerated—that is, their pathways to prison. In the 1970s, feminist researchers attempted to fill a gendered gap in the literature by questioning whether "theories developed 'by men, about men' could account for women's experiences" (Daly and Chesney-Lind; Walklate qtd. in Barlow and Weare 87). As a result, the social context of women's lives prior to incarceration became central to understanding gendered pathways to crime. Alternatively, resiliency or outcome-focused research is centred on women's recidivism and perceived success postincarceration—that is, their pathways out of imprisonment. These pathways will often take the form of classic comeback stories: tales of triumph over hardship through personal evolution, self-help, and resilience. Although these stories, and the optimism they inspire, are an important component of program development and improvement, some scholars have problematized these narratives. Such stories are often rooted in individualism, locating the problem and solution within the personal rather than contextual or relational realm. As a result, personal empowerment and determination become the solution to reducing recidivism rather than systemic change (Hannah-Moffat, 510; Comack).

Rather than focusing on pathways into prison or mapping outcomes following incarceration, Brittnie Aiello and Jill McCorkel argue for an alternative approach "that focuses on incarceration as a process" (353). When incarceration is conceptualized as a relational process between the state, a woman, and her family, it is no longer positioned as a neutral, inevitable outcome for lawbreaking women. We do not understand incarceration as a static thing in itself—something that women arrive to or leave from. Rather, we understand incarceration as an ongoing, relational process rooted in embodied subjectivity and action. Incarceration is performed and enforced by actors through choice, design, and measured institutional practices. The widespread inertia to the trauma and violence this process instantiates for mothers and their children has deeply ethical (and political) implications. This chapter brings attention to the ways the carceral system—in combination with the child protection system—actively wields power to punish, exclude, and transform women and children on the margins of society.

In viewing maternal incarceration as a process rather than an outcome, we are able to clearly see the familial dimensions of imprisonment. Ecological theory provides a framework with which we can map multiple levels of influence. Urie Bronfenbrenner's ecological theory acknowledges that our experiences are situated in relations at every level: micro (i.e., personal relationships), meso (i.e., relationships with community organizations/structures, such as schools or places of work), macro (i.e., the local and national sociopolitical and economic context) and exo (i.e., broader global order). In this way,

Bronfenbrenner's theory asserts the carceral experience is, at its core, inherently relational: The experience of women cannot be extricated from their relationships with family, friends, communities, and broader social, economic, and political forces.

Methodology

This chapter emerges from a Social Science and Humanities Research Council of Canada funded Master of Social Work (MSW) project. Approved through the Research Ethics Board at Wilfrid Laurier University, the project took the form of a multicase study involving three families' co-constructed narratives of life before, during, and after a mother's federal incarceration in Southwestern Ontario. Participants were recruited through professional networks and snow-ball sampling. Data were collected using collaborative family interviews (hereby referred to as "interviews") (Akesson). Children, their mothers, and their kinship caregivers were invited to share their thoughts, feelings, and experiences through an in-person, semi-structured interview (with the first author) with the family unit. Data were collected in 2019, prior to the global COVID-19 pandemic, although the findings have important ramifications in the post-pandemic era. The interviews were transcribed verbatim and manually analyzed according to Sharan Merriam and Elizabeth Tisdell's two stage model of within-case analysis and cross-case analysis (234).

In a conscious effort to avoid retraumatizing families, the interviews focused on coping rather than recounting suffering or hardship. In many ways, the interviews were a celebration of the families' abilities to adapt with resilience, flexibility, and care for one another in the context of incarceration. Still, within these co-constructed narratives of survival, state violence and familial deprivation were omnipresent. Painful experiences of child removal, placement, supervision, and/or deprivation are woven into each family's story. The interview data drawn upon for this analysis specifically focus on how the intersection of child welfare and incarceration systems in Ontario contribute to the systematic unmothering of incarcerated mothers.

Case Studies and Analysis: Case Study A: Breanne and the Hart Family

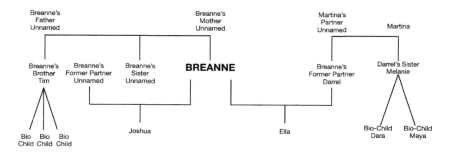

Figure 1: Breanne's Family Diagram

Kinship Arrangement

Breanne's family interview was completed in her Southern Ontario hometown in the summer of 2019. Prior to our meeting, she explained her two children's caregiving arrangements; Joshua was eight, and Ella was five at the time of the interview. Her story was complicated by the fact that her two children had different fathers and were cared for in two separate kinship placements. Joshua had been living with Breanne's older brother, Tim, his wife, and three children for five years. Due to distance and family commitments, Joshua and Tim could not participate in the interview.

Breanne was incarcerated six months after Ella was born. Although it was difficult for Breanne to separate her children, she felt it was important for Ella to stay connected to her paternal Indigenous culture and therefore temporarily placed six-month-old Ella with sister-in-law, Melanie Hart. Ella's father Darrel—with whom Breanne had an on-and-off-again relationship for years—did not live with the family. As Breanne explained, "I knew that if I let Ella go with my family [Tim and family], that they [Melanie and Martina] would never get to see her." At the time, Melanie was single and had no children of her own. However, Melanie became pregnant with her daughter, Dara shortly after Breanne went to jail. Because this period of incarnation was relatively short in duration, it was Breanne's intention to continue to mother Ella upon her release. However, Breanne's interaction with the justice system escalated before it got better. She was sentenced to serve federal time: a duration of over two years. Prior to her prolonged incarceration, Breanne granted Melanie—now a single mother to her daughter Dara—full custody of two-year-old Ella. Breanne agreed to this arrangement to reduce the presence of child protective services in her family's life, as this type of permanency felt preferable to the constant surveillance and intervention of child welfare authorities.

At the time of our interview, Ella was still in Melanie's care but was spending increasing amounts of time with Breanne (full days as opposed to short, supervised visits). Ella, Melanie, Martina, and I gathered at Melanie's house to conduct the interview.

Unmothering

For the Hart Family, the title "mother" was flexible and applied to multiple women within the family network. Melanie acted as Ella's primary caregiver from the time she was six months old. Melanie recalled: "I always referred to myself as auntie, but once she started talking and going to daycare and everything—she sees 'mommy mommy mommy.'" Additionally, Ella and Dara were of a similar age and had grown up together in Melanie's care. Ella referred to Dara as her sister, and Dara called Melanie "mommy." It thus made sense for Ella that Melanie would be her mommy, too. Martina, Ella's paternal grandmother, recalled that she, too, was often called "mommy" by Ella when caring for the girls. Prior to the interview, Breanne explained that Ella may refer to any or all of the women present in the interview as "mommy." She explained that she, Melanie, and Martina did not know whether Ella actually comprehended who among them was her biological mother. Given her age, they had decided against correcting her. Breanne clarified calmly: "I'm okay with that because they're being their mom and dad. Where am I? Not there."

Whereas some families are able to maintain contact with an incarcerated parent, Breanne encountered several systemic obstacles in parenting from prison. As a prisoner, Breanne could make $5.80 per working day. From her wages, 30 per cent was deducted for room and board, and an additional $14.00/month was charged for cable. With what little money she had left, Breanne was responsible for buying a phone card—which she could use towards exorbitantly priced telephone calls—as well as envelopes, stamps, and stationery. Breanne regularly drew pictures for Ella and mailed them to Melanie who then kept them in storage and never wrote her sister-in-law back. (There were ongoing periods of tension between Breanne and Melanie, as Breanne was released and then reoffended.) Although collect calls could be made, they had to be placed to a landline, and the receiving party had to assume the charges. For Melanie, the cost of collect calls was prohibitive.

Moreover, both children's caregivers lived several hours from the prison. If Melanie or Tim were to bring Ella or Joshua for a visit, their actual contact with Breanne would have amounted to only a fraction of the time they spent in the car journeying to the prison. Breanne felt she could not ask this of her young children, Tim, or Melanie (and their other children). Breanne presented the option of seventy-two-hour overnights, which would allow her children to interact with her over a longer period of time, justifying the trek to prison. However, in order to access this program, the prison requires families to have completed four regular visits, lasting two hours each. Breanne explained: "When your other family members are caring for your kid, and then they have their own, like my brother and my sister-in-law. They have to bring their own children, plus my son. Where do they find the time to drive from [redacted location] to the prison, four times?" Even if her family were able to coordinate this and subsequently receive eligibility for the seventy-two-hour overnight visit, her children's kinship caregivers would "have to come into the visit and sleep there for those 3 days so that I can visit with my [children]." Given the fact that both Joshua and Ella's caregivers had children of their own, this simply was not an option.

These logistical and financial barriers were augmented by strife within the family. While imprisoned, Breanne went twenty months without seeing or talking to her daughter. Ella's moms explained:

Breanne: No, Melanie was pretty upset with me.

Melanie: Yeah, like after time and time again of going through, I was like super upset with Breanne. Like cause every time I was like "no this time it's gonna be different, like she's gonna ... you know ... she's gonna take Ella back home."

Melanie referred to the cyclical nature of Breanne and Ella's biodad

Darrel's carceral experiences a number of times, explaining "They're coming. They're going." This created a "routine of seeing kids taken away." Melanie recalled her frustration, remembering how she would ask: "How dare you? How dare you do this again? How dare you do this to her?" Outraged, Melanie completely halted all access to Ella. Breanne reflected on this complete removal and separation from her children—due not only to incarceration but also to strained familial relationships and a lack of systemic supports. She said:" Because I couldn't really see or talk to my kids, I kind of tried to forget about them ... 'cause it was easier to get my time done, pretending that they weren't ... didn't exist, than to think about them every single day.... It's the only way I would have been able to get through that."

Breanne expressed this sentiment with resignation to the system and determination to survive it, exemplifying how the carceral process requires mothers to shed their maternal identity in order to emotionally and psychologically survive imprisonment. Dominant maternal constructs simply cannot account for a mother pushed to this extreme without categorically casting her as a bad mother. After all, no good mother could forget about her children. However, this unmothering was systematically enacted through a lack of institutional supports and/ or structures to keep the mother-child relationship intact. Breanne did not surrender her identity as a mother. It was systematically and purposefully stripped from her by the state.

Remothering Post Incarceration

After nearly two years in federal prison, all without contact with Ella, Breanne was released from custody. However, her relationship with Melanie, and therefore Ella, remained fractured. Prior to her federal sentence, Breanne had awarded Melanie full custody of Ella. At the time, the two had agreed upon a visitation schedule that allowed Breanne to maintain her mother-daughter relationship following incarceration. Yet Breanne did not see or speak to Ella while incarcerated or for months after she was released. Melanie explained that "back when [Breanne] first got out.... It's like 'I don't believe you.'" Unsure of what this transition might bring, she remembered how she "just didn't want, like, [Breanne] coming out and ... demanding to me, feeling superior than me." She explained that "It's like a lot of stress and tension and you just, like, you feel like your life is getting interrupted.... That's how I saw it ... like 'you're interrupting our whole life and routine and because of you ... because of your wants.'"

Ultimately, Melanie said, "I'll go to court if I have to go to court," reintroducing child protective services and family law back into Ella's life. In remembering this time, she clarified: "I wasn't trying to be selfish. I'm just protecting this little person." Melanie explained that she felt a need to protect herself, too. As Melanie had cared for Ella from the time that she was six months old, the prospect of losing Ella to Breanne was frightening. She explained that "I'm close with Ella. Like, I love her, like she's my child." She said that having raised a child from infancy, she had become attached. Melanie became tearful when she wondered aloud whether Ella would forget about her. These fears mounted which led Melanie to become increasingly defensive. Melanie recalled saying to Breanne: "What about me. Look at what I've done for you—look what I've done for our kid!"

Despite their initial conflict, Melanie's trepidations were slowly eased as Breanne remained sober and out of prison, adhering to her parole conditions. As Breanne remembered: "After like I completed rehab and I was at the halfway house.... I think that she...like eventually seen that I was doing well, so then, I just kind of earned the trust back ... and then it just started to get a little bit better." Melanie described the softening of her gatekeeping behaviour: "Now that she's proving herself.... This is the first time she's actually like proving it." At the time of our interview, Breanne and Melanie were discussing plans to have Ella spend a full day with her biological mom. Breanne was still in the process of re-earning the privilege of raising Ella at the time of our interview—a process mediated by Melanie. The Hart family had no intentions of formally clarifying mothering roles or identifying parentage in the immediate future.

Summary Analysis of the Hart Case

This case illustrates the overwhelming complexities incarcerated mothers, their children, and families face. Breanne's experience is a prototypical example of systematic unmothering, whereby a lack of systemic supports led to the deprivation of mothering for Breanne and forced separation for Ella. To survive prison on a daily basis, Breanne tried to forget about her children; mothering from behind bars was not a viable option for her or for her children's caregivers. The extreme strain on her relationship with her children's caregivers—particularly with Melanie—led to Breanne's estrangement from Ella and vice versa. Interestingly, child protection authorities—the force that required Breanne to surrender her mothering role to Melanie—played no role in supporting either Breanne, Melanie, or Martina in fulfilling their caregiving responsibilities.

What is remarkable about the Hart family is how the three women arrived at a place of sharing the mothering role in Ella's life. This cooperation occurred in opposition to both the child protection and carceral processes. At the time of the interview, it had become possible for all three women to actively mother Ella, and each woman appeared to genuinely value the role of the other women. Although rebuilding trust was ongoing, each woman found a way to forge a meaningful and caring relationship with Ella and each other against all odds.

The Harts' experiences of maternal incarceration and kinship care —particularly the decisions that were made about Ella's placement— are inextricably linked to their intergenerational experiences of child removal as Indigenous people. Melanie and her siblings had been removed from Martina's care many years ago and had been placed in foster homes, where they had unsafe, damaging experiences. At one point during our interview, Martina began crying, abruptly stood up and cradled Ella. Melanie explained this marked shift: "Because she's seen it. She understands. It's like ... the thought of Ella going into foster care. It's like 'no, absolutely not.'"

To appreciate the Hart family's resilience and resistance, it is vital to attend to the ways their pain is borne from a history of personal and collective trauma. Their experiences are set against the haunting backdrop of residential schools, the Sixties Scoop, and the current overrepresentation of Indigenous children in care (Blackstock 331; Ontario Human Rights Commission, "Interrupted Childhoods"). The three women's inherent distrust of Children's Aid Societies as agents of government—or church-based child removal and out-of-home/ community incarceration further explains their dedication to remain outside of the system through kinship care.

Case Study B: Kari's Family

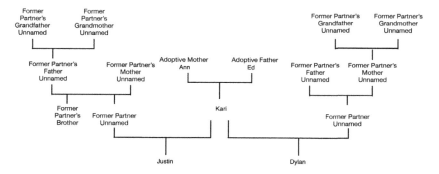

Figure 2: Kari's Family Diagram

Kinship Arrangements

Kari's interview was completed in the summer of 2019 at her adoptive parents' home, along with her two children: Justin, aged nineteen, and Dylan, aged sixteen. As children, both Justin and Dylan were placed with their paternal families in multigenerational homes. Kari's adoptive parents—Ed, aged seventy-eight, and Ann, aged seventy-six—had only occasional access to the boys while they were growing up and Kari was incarcerated. Kari was adopted as an infant by her parents, Ed and Ann, from foster care. At the age of twelve, Kari was charged with her first criminal offence. In response, Ed and Ann transitioned their daughter back into foster care. She lived in a group home eighty-five kilometres away from their home until aging out of the child welfare system.

Kari became pregnant with her eldest son, Justin, at the age of twenty. When Kari and Justin's dad ended their relationship, Justin's paternal grandparents became his primary caregivers. Struggling with addiction and intermittently using sex work to make ends meet, Kari was not able to care for her son on a full-time basis. Justin's father resided in his paternal family home on and off, coming and going over the years. Justin remembered his relationship with his dad as violent and inconsistent, reporting repeated physical and verbal abuse. While Justin remained in contact with his maternal grandparents, his paternal grandparents refused to grant him unsupervised time with them. As such, time spent with Ed and Ann was limited and always supervised by a paternal family member.

Three years after Justin's birth, Kari and her new partner had Dylan. Dylan also lived with his paternal extended family from infancy, separated from his older brother. Dylan's paternal caregivers lived in a multigenerational household, including his great grandmother, great grandfather, grandfather, grandmother, as well as his father and his father's partner. Dylan's great grandmother and grandmother were his primary caregivers; his father had a less active role in parenting within the household. In our interview, Dylan described profound neglect as a child by his paternal family members. He described how he struggled to meet basic developmental milestones. He and his mother also discussed how his clothes were often old and ill fitting, how his belly was empty, and his room was littered with cigarette butts. Like Justin, Dylan's access to his maternal family was limited by his paternal family. However, he was occasionally able to stay with and vacation alongside his maternal grandparents unsupervised.

Throughout the boys' childhoods, Kari was criminally charged thirty times. She served short sentences at the provincial level until she was arrested on a charge that resulted in federal time. Kari was incarcerated in a federal prison for about two years.

At the time of Kari's release from federal prison, she was eager to gain custody of her children, who were now teenagers. Justin elected not to be cared for by his mother. He recalled the strong attachment he felt towards his friends as well as the logistical challenges of moving cities and schools. Dylan, in contrast, was eager to return to his mom's care. Dylan's father was willing to grant Kari custody of their son but required a significant amount of financial compensation in exchange. Mobilizing personal relationships and relying on family support, Kari was able to pay Dylan's father an agreed upon sum. Within five days of her release from prison, Dylan was living with Kari.

Then Kari relapsed. As a result, Dylan was relocated back to his paternal grandparent's home. Kari was able to regain sobriety and once again sought out a relationship with her children. She was concerned about Dylan's health and safety in his paternal family's care. This concern peaked one day when she picked up Dylan and her ex-husband was under the influence of a substance. That day, Kari removed her son from his paternal family's home—packing his things and taking him to her parents' home. The police and child protection services became involved in the custodial dispute, but ultimately withdrew their presence and Dylan remained in Kari's care from then on. Justin, an adult now, lived in the city where he had grown up with his paternal family. He made the trip to his maternal family home to participate in the interview.

Unmothering

After learning of Justin and Dylan's complex caregiving experiences, I (first author) remarked: "[It]sounds like both of you have had tough parenting relationships ... substitute caregivers in your lives." Halfway through this sentence, I changed my vocabulary from "parenting relationships" to "substitute caregivers" based on Dylan's and Justin's visible reaction to the implication that their kinship caregivers acted as parents. Their body language cued me. To follow up I clarified: "Do you feel like you were parented? Is that an appropriate word to use?" They responded:

Dylan: No.

Justin: I mean, I think I parented myself to be completely honest.

First author/me: Right, so neither of you would say that you were parented?

Dylan: No. I mean, you can say you parented yourself. I just don't think I had anything.

Kari's boys were forthcoming about the challenges they experienced as children. Some of their stories of loss and neglect were graphic and difficult to hear. Kari readily acknowledged her role in the family's experiences. She explained: "I feel bad. And all of this is my fault. It is. My actions. You know?" While displaying transparent accountability on multiple occasions during our conversation, Kari simultaneously grappled with issues of criminalization and stigmatization. In particular, she problematized the ways her mothering was demonized as a result of her criminalization. She took issue with the social condemnation of her nonviolent behaviour, given the neglect, cruelty, and abuse Dylan and Justin were exposed to through their kinship caregiving relationships. The children had been placed out of her care for their health and safety, supposedly. For instance, Kari said the following: "I might be a bad mom for my [lawbreaking] actions, but I don't tell my kids they're worthless ...'You're a piece of shit' and 'You're not gonna be anything.'" She said, "I have to undo—to this day—I have to undo things because words hurt."

She then recalled that years after her federal incarceration, the police and child protective services came to her home. She remembered the police using her incarceration against her, 'Oh so you do drugs?' I said 'No, I've been clean [for several years] but yes I was a drug addict, absolutely, and now I'm not'". Kari clearly demonstrated her navigation of two identities: that of a criminalized person and that of a mother. In particular, she problematized the way that these two identities are placed in opposition to each other. She suggested these are not binaries: Women can be both. She can be a former drug addict and a good mother.

Dylan remembered his time with his paternal grandparents as lonely. In describing his home life, he said, "I felt isolated from the whole outside world." Dylan's paternal grandparents limited his socializing, television consumption, and did not allow him to attend extracurricular activities or sports. He reflected on his time in their care: "I was just going to school as this child trapped in a house, without information of the outside world like every other kid did." Dylan felt that his caregivers' motives were to keep him from learning too much and having access to his mother. In order to visit his mom in prison, Dylan relied on his maternal grandparents to secretly take him there: "I don't believe that the whole house had knowledge that that's where I was going.... Because they wouldn't ... allow me to see her."

I inquired whether Dylan thought his paternal grandparents acted this way from a position of love, wanting to protect him from hurt. Dylan corrected me, explaining that his caregivers were "protective, not protecting." I asked what the difference was, and he told me: "They wanted to be protective, and it was more in the sheltering way. It was 'Oh no you can't do this. We're just trying to keep you safe' ... but I was never safe.... It was more just a limiting sort of protection."

Driving this painful reality home, Dylan recalled the day he moved back in with Kari. He remembered thinking: "What are these new things? Uh, how is this? What is this feeling?" Kari interrupted, asking "What was this feeling?" And Dylan calmly stated: "I don't know. It's just like I hadn't understood what like care felt like and like being nurtured and not being alone." I asked him how his life changed when mom was free and healthy, and he told me that he finally became a person. For Dylan, kinship care was dehumanizing and isolating. His mom's freedom is/was his own, too.

Justin's paternal grandparents took a similar stance to Dylan's, prohibiting his contact with Kari during her incarceration. Kari remembered Justin's caregiver promising that they would bring her son to visit her in prison. When she mentioned this, Justin jumped in, exclaiming: "Never. She didn't. Not once." Moreover, Justin's paternal grandparents did not allow him to speak with his mother via telephone unless supervised. They required that mother and son talk only using speakerphone in their presence. Adapting to these restrictions, Kari told me that she wrote her sons letters each day. Dylan received none, whereas Justin "got some of them.... But after they were already open." Through Kari, Justin, and Dylan's stories, the intersection of Canada's carceral and child welfare systems comes into view. The carceral system removed Kari from her children's lives, both physically and relationally. Simultaneously, child protective services failed to secure safe, nurturing environments for them to grow. By exposing the boys to harm within their changing family ecosystem—under the guise of justice and protection—Kari's family was subject to institutional violence.

Kari's parents understood the relationship between these institutions all too well. They struggled to navigate the criminal justice system as well as the child welfare arrangement of two kinship caregiving networks. Their grandsons were placed in different homes, with different families. For Ed and Ann, these ecosystems were complex and wrought with conflict. The boys' maternal grandparents felt they could do little to support or even access their grandchildren.

> Ed: But, basically, we've felt our hands were tied quite often.... Because legally, we had no way that we could just take both boys because.... Because their fathers, ah, they—as they were—had legal...
>
> Me: Rights.
>
> Ed: First rights.

Without guardianship, Ed and Ann had no legal or institutionally coordinated pathway to connect with their grandchildren. It became their responsibility to navigate these changes in the family's ecosystem, negotiating two separate (and often oppositional) kinship caregiving arrangements. In this way, it was not only Kari who was systematically unmothered by the carceral system but also her parents who were denied the opportunity to play a much needed caring role in her boys' lives.

Another Way?

Poignant in this family's narrative was the possibility of doing things differently. In a highly emotive conversation for all interviewees, Kari imagined and articulated the role of someone who could have advocated for her and her children.

> Kari: Somebody needs to be in the middle and advocate for the kids. Not the caregivers.

> Justin: Yeah, there should be a second party.

> Kari: There should be somebody in whatever institution that is that person—so if it's a social worker, a CYW [child and youth worker], whatever—they should be the one coordinating.

She role played what a person in this position might have said: "Okay, so this child, Justin, he's gonna visit his mom." She emphasized, "He is going to. Not might." She embodied this person, passionately proclaiming: "He is going to have a visit with his mother Kari. It's gonna happen on this date. If transportation is needed, we can co-ordinate that. This is not an option; this is what's happening." This idea resonated strongly with Dylan, as he too had clear ideas of how things could have been different. He suggested that an advocate or another agency might enable "phone calls [between incarcerated mother and child] that cannot be avoided.... Letters that will be delivered... Just, something to make sure things happen. Because I'm sure there's other situations similar to ours." This discussion appeared to bring up many painful memories for Dylan, as he clearly felt that, as a child, he had no path to establishing or maintaining a relationship with his mother. Dylan expressed grief and regret that there was never any account-ability to him, the child of an incarcerated mother. He suggested that if planned contacts between children and mothers do not occur, someone should be asking "Why didn't it go through?" Dylan argued there should be checks in place to ensure custodial caregivers not act as gatekeepers keeping children from their mothers.

Dylan wondered if this imagined advocate could have prevented the harmful isolation or neglect he experienced.

Dylan: I really feel like it was just so much trust was put out there, and it was kind of just "Oh well, if they're [letters] not being delivered—that sucks!" "Oh you're not getting phone calls? Too bad!"

Me: Right, so they just trusted the caregivers.

Dylan: Yeah. It's just—you're putting a lot of trust in that, and sometimes that trust is misused.

Justin: "That's how I always felt."

Just as Melanie's and Martina's intergenerational experiences with the carceral realities of the child welfare system informed Breanne's decision to place her daughter in kinship care, so too did Kari's own experience in foster care and group homes. Kari was born with neonatal abstinence syndrome (NAS) and was subsequently placed for adoption through child welfare services. Ed and Ann, Kari's adoptive parents, cared for her from infancy until the age of twelve. Unable (or unwilling) to manage Kari's behaviour and interaction with the justice system at that young age, Kari was absorbed back into the system. Kari moved back and forth between the carceral spaces of child welfare institutions and the justice system. In Kari's experience, the relationship between these institutions is inherently intertwined; their stigmatizing, punishing conditions are nearly interchangeable. Kari's decision to place Justin and Dylan in the kinship care of their paternal families echoes Breanne's, Martina's, and Melanie's distrust of child protective services and reliance on family networks.

Discussion

These case studies, and the preliminary analysis offered above, illustrate the overwhelmingly complex, emotionally wrought situations that incarcerated mothers, their children, and families experience throughout the carceral process. Breanne and Kari clearly expressed a strong need and desire to see, talk to, and spend time with their children but faced insurmountable, institutionally erected (or at least permitted) barriers to maintaining relationships with their children and thus their own maternal identities. Viewed through an ecological lens, it becomes impossible to ignore how the maternal carceral experience is inherently intertwined with children's and family's experiences, while also illustrating how individual human experiences (micro level) are embedded within intentional structures and relations at the community (meso) and state (macro) level.

As Kari's and Breanne's stories illustrate, the ways in which the carceral process interacts with child protection systems systematically strips mothers of their power, efficacy, and agency. Rooted in the assumption that the identity of criminal occludes the possibility of being a good mother, the mother-child relationship transforms into a mother-state-child triad. The state becomes the overwhelming, powerful, and impermeable barrier between them, much like the plexiglass that separates visitor from inmate in no-touch interactions. It is only through scheduled, surveyed, and nearly impossible to co-ordinate visits that the incarcerated woman can maintain any relationships with her children. Indeed, the prevailing assumption appears to be that any relationship is preferable (i.e., safer) to that of one between an incarcerated mother and her children.

Sadly, to survive, Breanne felt her only option was to forget about her children during her time in prison. After her last release from prison, Martina and Melanie managed to pull together to jointly mother Ella, preventing continual, unwanted intrusion into their lives by the child welfare system. All three women expressed fear and shame in relation to the continued presence of the child welfare authorities in their lives. Though in a different context, Kari's children, Dylan and Justin, were also highly critical of child protective services in the carceral system. Kari, along with her parents and children, experienced the systematic unmothering of the carceral process. Her children, meanwhile, bore the brunt of unsafe, neglectful substitute caregiving relationships in full view of child welfare authorities.

Although it is tempting to applaud and glorify families who manage to survive the carceral process and keep relationships intact, to do so can invalidate or occlude the significant pain and suffering of the mothers, their children, and their families. Breanne, Melanie, Ella, and Martina as well as Dylan, Justin, Kari, and Kari's parents survived and reestablished meaningful relationships with each other despite rather than because of the system. All members of the two families interviewed continue to navigate incredible challenges and complexities in their daily lives, many of which can be related back to the carceral process. As a mother quoted by Lucy Baldwin observes: "Any sentence for a mother is a life sentence really" (263).

Recommendations

The main message learned from the heart-wrenching stories of these women and their families was that the system need not operate this way. Incarceration itself does not lead to unmothering. Where child protection and the carceral system intersect lies the opportunity to think and do things differently—to facilitate, enable, and repair relationships rather than to compound existing trauma. Dylan, Justin, and Kari readily provided an alternative vision: a child welfare system that actively facilitates contact between incarcerated mothers and their children. Such a role is entirely consistent with the mandate of the Association of the Childcare Aid Societies of Ontario: "to support ALL children, youth, families, and communities to thrive."

Yet to do this would require a fundamental rethinking of the current surveillance approach of child welfare organizations alongside a critical questioning of the maternal ideals that ontologically occlude criminalized women from being good mothers. It is entirely possible for these institutions to embrace a path that prioritizes the ongoing relationship between incarcerated mothers, their children, and their families. In order to do so, the mothers' and children's voices must hold weight in the carceral and child protection process. It is imperative that we re-center these families from mothering on the edge—from the periphery of our collective gaze (and conscience)—to re-imagine what justice truly means.

Works Cited

Aiello, B. L., and J. A. McCorkel. "'It Will Crush You Like a Bug': Maternal Incarceration, Secondary Prisonization, and Children's Visitation." *Punishment & Society,* vol. 20, no. 3, 2018, pp. 351-74.

Akesson, Bree. *Contradictions in Place: Everyday Geographies of Palestinian Children and Families Living Under Occupation.* PhD dissertation. McGill University, 2014.

Akesson, Bree. "Research with Young Children Affected by Family Violence: Proposing a Robust Research Agenda." *Early Childhood Matters,* vol. 116, 2011, pp. 22-25.

Arditti, Joyce. "Child Trauma Within the Context of Parental Incarceration: A Family Process Perspective." *Journal of Family Theory & Review,* vol. 4, no. 3, 2012, pp. 181-219.

Arditti, Joyce, and Jyoti Savla. "Parental Incarceration and Child Trauma Symptoms in Single Caregiver Homes." *Journal of Child and Family Studies,* vol. 24, no. 3, 2015, pp. 551-561.

American Psychiatric Association. "Trauma." *APA,* www.apa.org/topics/trauma/. Accessed 7 June 2022.

Baldwin, Lucy, editor. *Mothering Justice: Working with Mothers in Criminal and Social Justice Settings.* Waterside Press, 2015.

Barlow, Charlotte, and Siobhan Weare. "Women as Co-offenders: Pathways into Crime and Offending Motivations." *The Howard Journal,* vol 58, no. 1, 2019, pp. 86-103.

Blackstock, Cindy. "First Nations Child and Family Services: Restoring Peace and Harmony in First Nations Communities." *Child Welfare: Connecting Research, Policy, and Practice,* edited by Kathleen Kufeldt and Brad McKenzie, Wilfrid Laurier University Press, 2003, p. 331.

Bronfenbrenner, Urie. "Toward an Experimental Ecology of Human Development." *American Psychologist,* vol. 32, no. 7, 1977, pp. 513-31.

Celinska, K., and J. A. Siegel. "Mothers in Trouble: Coping with Actual or Pending Separation from Children Due to Incarceration." *The Prison Journal,* vol. 90, no. 4, 2010, pp. 447-74.

Comack, Elizabeth. "The Feminist Engagement with Criminology." *Criminalizing Women: Gender and (In)Justice in Neoliberal Times,* edited by Gillian Balfour and Elizabeth Comack, Fernwood Publishing, 2006, pp. 11-43.

Elijdupovic, Gordana, and Rebecca Jaremko Bromwich. "Introduction." *Incarcerated Mothers: Oppression and Resistance*, edited by Gordana Elijdupovic and Rebecca Jaremnko Bromwich, Demeter Press, 2013, pp. 1-25.

Gjelsvik, Annie, et al. "Adverse Childhood Events: Incarceration of Household Members and Health-Related Quality of Life in Adulthood." *Journal of Health Care for the Poor and Underserved*, vol. 25, no. 3, 2014, pp. 1169-82.

Hannah-Moffat, Kelly. "Prisons that Empower: Neo-liberal Governance in Canadian Women's Prisons." *British Journal of Criminology*, vol. 40, no. 3, 2000, pp. 510-31.

Kilty, Jennifer, and Sylvie Frigon. "Karla Homolka—From a Woman in Danger to a Dangerous Woman." Women & Criminal Justice, vol. 17, no. 4, 2006, pp. 37-61.

Milan, Anne. "Female Population. Women in Canada: A Gender-Based Statistical Report." *Statistics Canada*, 2015, www150.statcan.gc.ca/n1/en/pub/89-503-x/2015001/article/14152-eng.pdf?st=9OKrUvfw. Accessed 7 June 2022.

Merriam, Sharan, and Elizabeth Tisdell. *Qualitative Research: A Guide to Design and Implementation.* Josey-Bass, 2015.

Office of the Correctional Investigator. "A Case Study of Diversity in Corrections: The Black Inmate Experience in Federal Penitentiaries." *Government of Canada*, 2014, www.oci-bec.gc.ca/cnt/rpt/oth-aut/oth-aut20131126-eng.aspx. Accessed 7 June 2022.

Ontario Association of Children's Aid Societies. "Mission." *OACAS*, www.oacas.org/who-we-are/mission. Accessed 7 June 2022.

Ontario Human Rights Condition. "Interrupted Childhoods: Over-representation of Indigenous and Black Children in Ontario Child Welfare." *OHRC*, www.ohrc.on.ca/en/interrupted-childhoods#4.1.Indigenous%20children. Accessed 7 June 2022.

Sapers, Howard. "Annual Report of the Office of the Correctional Investigator 2014–2015." *Government of Canada*, 2015, www.oci-bec.gc.ca/cnt/rpt/annrpt/annrpt20142015-eng.aspx#sl0. Accessed 7 June 2022.

Walmsley, Roy. *World Imprisonment List.* Institute for Criminal Policy Research, 2017.

Walsh, Christine, and Meredith Crough. "Mothering Through Adversity: Voices of Incarcerated Women." *Incarcerated Mothers: Oppression and Resistance*, edited by by Gordana Elijdupovic and Rebecca Jaremnko Bromwich, Demeter Press, 2013, pp. 160-72.

Chapter 10

Coda

Brooke Richardson

Since these chapters were first drafted, the COVID-19 pandemic has dramatically shaken all aspects of social, political, and economic life. Scholars, politicians, NGOs and journalists of all stripes have noted the gendered impact of the pandemic, as mothers have experienced overwhelming stress in terms of increased caregiving alongside paid work responsibilities (Alon et al.; Del Boca et al.; Government of Canada; Perelman; Statistics Canada; United Nations). Throughout the pandemic, mothers have been isolated, often without any familial, state, or third sector support. There has been a widespread acknowledgement that the risk of domestic violence and child abuse has increased with the pandemic due to the increased financial stress alongside the constant caregiving of children (Caldwell et al.; Teo and Griffiths). We do not know what the overall impact of this has been or will be. However, it is worth pointing out that in the face of a global pandemic, society did not hesitate to put mothers at the helm, looking to them to provide the bedrock of familial and economic functioning.

As has been the case in many wealthy English-speaking nations, children—and those caring for them—are an afterthought. During the pandemic, childcare and other familial support services were never prioritized as essential: For example publicly funded emergency childcare was available for essential workers in Ontario only during periods of acute emergency (the height of the first and third wave). Child protection workers were not identified as essential in any Canadian province, although they continued to provide services, in some cases remotely (Caldwell et al.). It is possible that for some mothers, not having the added stress of Children's Aid Society authorities surveying and judging their parenting decisions was a relief. For others, a lack of access to child protection services may have proved deleterious or even fatal. For others still, the pandemic caused prolonged investigations, whereby children were unable to visit with their parents due to public health measures (see Leigh for an account of three mothers' stories).

What we do know is that pandemic or not, the way our society currently approaches motherhood and childhood is neither equitable nor sustainable (Cliffton; Peterson). At the very least, the pandemic has shone a light on the urgent necessity of establishing the social infrastructure necessary for mothers, children, families, the economy, and society to be well. Canada's former Governor General Julie Payette's September 23, 2020, speech from the throne clearly embraced a gendered approach to pandemic recovery (coined a "she-covery"), including a commitment to "long-term, sustained funding for a pan-Canadian childcare system." If constructed thoughtfully and in collaboration with mothers, families, and childcare professionals, such a system could go a long way in concretely supporting mothers in their caregiver role and prevent families from becoming involved in state-sanctioned child protection systems in the first place.

Perhaps a silver lining of the pandemic is that there has been an emergence of a "we're in this together" mentality. Although mothers still do the bulk of the care labour, there has been a burgeoning awareness that all citizens bear some responsibility for ensuring every member of society is well cared for and can, in turn, care for themselves and others. The work is now turning this awareness into action at the micro, meso, and macro levels.

Key Takeaways

As mothers (and I insert myself here), we do our best to establish a safe, responsive, and caring relationship with our children in what often feels like an unsafe and uncaring world. But it cannot be solely up to us to do this. That we have historically mothered in oppressive conditions does not justify continuing on this course. Systems, and in turn our societies, are created for and by people. It is my intention to do what I can to work alongside mothers—many of whom face intersection oppressions that I could never understand—to ensure our voices and experiences are seen and heard at the academic, practice, and political levels. As this anthology has illustrated, there is little to no space for mothers to be seen and heard in contemporary, risk-based, and forensically oriented child protection systems. The complexities and intricacies of people's relationships and lives simply cannot be categorized through the standardized risk assessment tools currently used.

To meaningfully move forwards, we need to bring mothers into the child protection conversation through both empirical research and meaningful participation in policy process. This work must begin with genuinely listening to mothers who have been involved in child protection processes. Inspired by the many mothers, researchers, and activists before me, I am hopeful we can move towards the more humane systems of child protection envisioned by Brid Featherstone et al. With mothers, children, and families playing a meaningful role in practice and policy reform, it is possible that humility and care rather than risk and liability will come to define child protection systems.

Works Cited

Alon, Titan et al. "The Impact of Covid-19 on Gender Equality." *Covid Economics*, vol. 4, no. 14, 2020, pp. 62-85.

Caldwell, Johanna et al. "Essential" Services, Risk, and Child Protection in the Time of Covid-19: An Opportunity to Prioritize Chronic Need." *Opinion and Debate*, vol. 2, no. 3, 2020, pp. 20-223.

Cliffton, Linden van der. "The Moms Are Not Alright: How Coronavirus Pandemic Policies Penalize Mothers." *The Conversation*, 3 Sept. 2020, theconversation.com/the-moms-are-not-alright-how-coronavirus-pandemic-policies-penalize-mothers-144713. Accessed 11 June 2022.

Del Boca, Daniela, et al. "Women's Work, Housework and Childcare, before and During Covid-19." *IZA Institution of Labour Economics*, 2020, papers.ssrn.com/sol3/Delivery.cfm/dp13409.pdf?abstract id=3636638&mirid=1. Accessed 11 June 2022.

Featherstone, Brid et al. *Protecting Children: A Social Model.* Policy Press, 2018.

Government of Canada. "Speech from the Throne." *Government of*

Canada, 23 Sept. 2020, www.canada.ca/en/privy-council/campaigns/speech-throne/2020/speech-from-the-throne.html. Accessed 11 June 2022.

Leigh, Jadwiga. "'It Was the Best of Times; It Was the Worst of Times': The Impact of Covid-19 on Families in the Child Protection Process." *Qualitative Social Work*, vol. 19, no. 5-6, 2020, pp. 779-83.

Perelman, Deb. "In the Covid-19 Economy, You Can Have a Kid or a Job. You Can't Have Both." *The New York Times*, 2 July 2022, www.nytimes.com/2020/07/02/business/covid-economy-parents-kids-career-homeschooling.html. Accessed 11 June 2022.

Peterson, Sara. "After the Pandemic, We'll Finally Have to Address the Impossible State of Motherhood." *InStyle*, 2020, www.instyle.com/lifestyle/pandemic-exposing-impossibility-working-motherhood?fbclid=IwAR1Epd67uQqpNnR-zoqnyXqoxsahjQunivz733RbQbqeuQEolxPcPmEgd9I. Accessed 11 June 2022.

Statistics Canada. "Impacts of Covid-19 on Parents and Children." *Governmnet of Canada*, 2020, www150.statcan.gc.ca/n1/en/pub/11-631-x/2020004/pdf/s8-eng.pdf?st=9qlEstEJ. Accessed 11 June 2022.

Teo, Stephen, and Glenys Griffiths. "Child Protection in the Time of Covid-19." *Journal of Paediatrics and Child Health*, vol. 56, no. 6, 2020, pp. 838-40.

United Nations. "The Impact of Covid-19 on Women." *United Nations*, 2020, www.un.org/sites/un2.un.org/files/policy_brief_on_covid impact_on_women_9_april_2020.pdf. Accessed 11 June 2022.

Notes on Contributors

Dorothy Badry is a professor in the Faculty of Social Work at the University of Calgary and worked in the child protection system for sixteen years. Her research focuses on FASD and child welfare issues, disability, women's health/FASD prevention, homelessness, loss and grief, and a current grant is focused on FASD and suicide prevention in Alberta. Dr. Badry is the child welfare research lead for the Canada FASD Research Network and has received multiple research grants from provincial and national funders.

Sarah Bekaert is a senior lecturer in child health at Oxford Brookes University, UK. Her research focuses on teenaged pregnancy and parenthood, relationship abuse, sexual exploitation, and safeguarding. Sarah is a cofounder of CHYPS Plus, a teenage health demonstration site in Hackney, which was commissioned by the Department of Health to provide creative and innovative healthcare for vulnerable young people.

Meredith Berrouard is a PhD student in social work at Wilfrid Laurier University. Meredith's practice and research interests centre around how risk is defined and operationalized within child welfare practice and the impact of this on the lives, experiences, and identities of mothers as well as whether and how the field of child welfare can work towards more genuine and transformative critical, feminist, antioppressive, and anticolonial practice.

Lori Chambers is a professor in the Department of Gender and Women's Studies at Lakehead University, where she teaches courses on feminist theories, gender-based violence, and gender and the law. Her current research explores intimate partner violence and response by police, police responses to sexual assault, and harm reduction approaches in domestic violence shelters. She has a long history of feminist activism, particularly with regards to violence against women.

Peter Choate is a professor of social work and program coordinator at Mount Royal University. His current research focuses on assessing parenting capacity (with specialties in mental health, domestic violence, and child abuse and addictions); child and adolescent mental health, including maltreatment, neglect, and abuse (physical, sexual, and emotional); FASD; and these issues within family systems. He has also appeared on over 150 occasions as an expert witness in child protection matters.

Kelly Harding is a research associate with the Canada FASD Research Network (CanFASD) and a member of CanFASD's Prevention Network Action Team (pNAT). She is also an adjunct professor in the Department of Psychology at Laurentian University. Her current research focuses on FASD prevention with an emphasis on health services in rural and remote communities, the social determinants of health, and the role of alcohol in women's lives.

Lauren Hawthorne works as a clinical therapist for a publicly funded children's mental health service in Ontario, Canada. She holds a Master of Science in Global Health as well as a Master of Social Work, for which she was awarded a SSHRC grant and Wilfrid Laurier's Gold Medal for Academic Excellence. Lauren's practice and research are grounded in the lived experience of families shaped by institutional violence, as well as complex and intergenerational trauma.

Angela Hovey is an associate professor in the School of Social Work at Lakehead University who came to academia after many years of clinical social work practice in federal and provincial prisons, community agencies, and private practice settings. Her current areas of research focus on domestic violence shelters and harm reduction, alternative housing models for women's shelters in response to COVID-19, domestic violence and policing practices, restorative justice, and male survivor treatment.

Bernadette Iahtail is a registered social worker and cofounded Creating Hope Society. Her work has brought her across Canada, South Africa, New Zealand, and Hawaii and on and off reserves in various capacities as a social worker, facilitator, and presenter. Bernadette is an educator, a producer, an advocate, and an ally. She plays a vital role in the welfare of Indigenous and non-Indigenous people and has influenced and brought awareness specifically of the injustices of Canada's history.

Allyson Ion is currently an assistant professor (contractually limited appointment) in the School of Social Work at McMaster University. Allyson has contributed to community development, education, and research in the HIV movement since 2001. Allyson's research and activist contributions are informed by the principles of antioppression, harm reduction, community engagement, and ensuring meaningful partnerships with people on the receiving end of health and social care in research and practice.

Angelique Jenney is an associate professor and the Wood's Homes Research Chair in Children's Mental Health in the Faculty of Social Work, University of Calgary. Her community-based research and practice interests focus on the impact of intimate partner violence (IPV) on children, including family-based interventions for childhood trauma, child protection responses to IPV cases, and the use of reflective, simulation-based learning approaches to training both social work students and practitioners in the field.

Erin Leveque holds a Bachelor of Social Work and a Bachelor of Arts from the University of Calgary. She is currently a research assistant in the Faculty of Social Work at the University of Calgary and with the CanFASD Research Network. Erin is particularly interested in sharing narratives and perspectives from lived experiences to inform system, practice, and social change, especially in the areas of mental health and disability.

Gabrielle Lindstrom (née Weasel Head) is a member of the Kainaiwa Nation, which is a part of the Blackfoot Confederacy. As an educational development consultant for Indigenous ways of knowing, Gabrielle works closely with the TI and vice-provosts of teaching and learning and Indigenous engagement to advance Indigenous ways of knowing in campus teaching and learning communities, cultures, and practices. Her teaching background includes instructing in topics around First Nation, Métis, and Inuit history and current issues, Indigenous Studies (Canadian and International perspectives), Indigenous cross-cultural approaches, and Indigenous research methods and ethics.

Brooke Richardson is an instructor and adjunct faculty in the Department of Sociology at Brock University in Ontario, Canada, and teaches undergraduate and graduate courses in early childhood studies, education, sociology, and child and youth studies at several universities in Ontario. Her research and scholarly work focuses on the privatization of childcare in Canada, political representations of the childcare policy problem, reconceptualizing and reasserting care in early childhood education, and reimaging child protection systems through an ethics of care perspective.

Susan Scott is an associate professor in the School of Social Work at Lakehead University who brings extensive practice experience in community work, social policy, and program design, implementation, and evaluation. She teaches courses on community work, organizations, and social policy. Susan's current research deals with domestic violence and policing, alternative housing models for women's shelters in response to COVID-19 restrictions, and harm reduction in domestic violence shelters.

Robyn Williams is a Nyoongar woman, with expertise in fetal alcohol spectrum disorder (FASD), community development, advocacy, and building capacity within our community. In 2019, her dissertation received a chancellor's commendation for excellence. Robyn is recognized as a FASD trainer both nationally and internationally and is mentored by leading international FASD experts. Her other qualifications include a Master of Arts and a Bachelor of Art in sociology and anthropology, respectively.

Deepest appreciation to
Demeter's monthly Donors

DEMETER

Daughters
Rebecca Bromwich
Summer Cunningham
Tatjana Takseva
Debbie Byrd
Fiona Green
Tanya Cassidy
Vicki Noble
Naomi McPherson
Myrel Chernick

Sisters
Amber Kinser
Nicole Willey
Christine Peets